Visual Litigation

Visual Communication Strategies and Today's Technology

Ronald H. Clark
Distinguished Practitioner in Residence
Seattle University School of Law

Patrick M. Muscat
Assistant Prosecuting Attorney
Deputy Chief/Special Prosecutions Division
Wayne County Prosecutor's Office (Detroit, MI)

Thomas M. O'Toole
President, Sound Jury Consulting

D1571706

The cover of this book features studies by Spanish printmaker and painter Jusepe de Ribera. A follower of Caravaggio in seventeenth century Naples, de Ribera is primarily remembered for his austere treatment of classical and religious subjects. The image is provided courtesy of Rijksmuseum under a CC0 1.0 Universal Public Domain Dedication.

A Full Court Press, Fastcase, Inc., Publication.

Printed and bound in the United States of America.

10 9 8 7 6 5 4 3 2 1

ISBN (print): 978-1-949884-35-7
ISBN (online): 978-1-949884-36-4

This book is (and we are) dedicated to our families.

To Nancy, Brady, Soojin, Malachi, Riley,
Clancy, Kara, Beatrice, Samuel,
Colby, and Darren—my family.
Ronald H. Clark

To Alyse, Ashlyn, Mom (the teacher), and Dad (the police officer)
My family and motivation for all I do.
Patrick M. Muscat

To my wife, mother and father, sister and brothers,
and Harry Hood, and in memory of
Thomas Griffin and Robert Sargent.
Thomas M. O'Toole

Summary of Contents

Contents

Acknowledgments

Although the cover names three authors, the contributions of many others are shown throughout the book. We not only thank them but also share credit with them for this book. We are grateful to those individuals and organizations who are listed in the credits at the end of the book for granting us permission to display their visuals here. We are thankful to many individuals who provided insights and support: Laurie Sleeper Wells, administrative assistant; Mahmoud Awadallah, Assistant Prosecuting Attorney, Cuyahoga County, Ohio; and the Velvet Hammer—Karen Koehler, attorney at law. Our acknowledgment and appreciation to Joe O'Toole, who designed many of the trial graphics shown in this book. His artwork inspired many of the discussion points raised in this book. A special thank you to Marilyn J. Berger and John B. Mitchell, Seattle University Professors Emeriti, for their friendship, guidance, and scholarship.

Many thanks for the support and assistance provided through Seattle University School of Law: Dean Annette C. Clark, Vice Dean Paul Holland, Associate Dean for Academic Affairs and Professor of Law Andrew Siegel and Dean for Finance and Administration Richard Bird.

Finally, thanks to our friends and professional colleagues at Fastcase/Full Court Press: Morgan Morrissette Wright, Publisher/Product Manager; Steve Errick, Chief Operating Officer; Sharon D. Ray, Production Editor; and a very special thanks to Susan Raleigh Jenkins, our editor, who pored over the manuscript and made it markedly better.

About the Authors

Ronald H. Clark is a Distinguished Practitioner in Residence at Seattle University Law School, where he teaches Pretrial Advocacy, Visual Litigation and Today's Technology, Trial Advocacy, and Essential Lawyering Skills. He is a nationally known lecturer and author. His previous books include *Jury Selection Handbook: The Nuts and Bolts of Effective Jury Selection*; *Pretrial Advocacy*; *Trial Advocacy*; *Opening Statement and Closing Argument*; *Evidence: Skills and Strategies*; and *Cross-Examination Handbook*. Mr. Clark has lectured for numerous bar and other associations across the country, as well as for the Department of Justice in Bosnia, Croatia, and Kosovo. Mr. Clark served in the King County Prosecutor's office in Seattle, Washington, as a senior deputy prosecutor, head of the trial teams, and, for ten years, as the Chief Deputy of the Criminal Division. Subsequently, Mr. Clark was the Senior Training Counsel at the National Advocacy Center in South Carolina.

Patrick Muscat is an Assistant Prosecuting Attorney in Detroit. During twenty-six years of service to Wayne County, he has tried over 100 homicide jury trials using courtroom technology. APA Muscat currently serves as the Deputy Chief of the Special Prosecutions Division overseeing the Homicide Unit, the Major Drug Unit, the Community Prosecution Unit, the Grand Jury Unit, and the Crime Lab Liaison Unit. Since 2003, Pat has taught courses on a wide range of topics, including the Visual Trial, Digital Authentication, and other trial advocacy courses for the American Bar Association, the National District Attorneys Association, the Prosecuting Attorneys Association of Michigan (PAAM), and for many other groups, associations, or firms nationwide. In February 2017, Pat was awarded PAAM's Distinguished Faculty Award. Pat has taught Litigation Technology at the University of Detroit Mercy School of Law since 2008.

Thomas O'Toole, Ph.D., has practiced across the nation for fifteen years in nearly every litigation type. He has consulted on matters as small as low-exposure medical malpractice and as large as "bet-the company" MDL class actions and billion-dollar environmental claims. His cases have been featured in the *New York Times*, *Wall Street Journal*, and *Washington Post*, and have been the subject of feature films and documentaries. He co-authored the book *Jury Selection Handbook*, published by Carolina Academic Press, and is the host of the popular podcast, *The Sniper Defense*. Tom received his Ph.D. in litigation psychology and communication at the University of Kansas.

Chapter 1

Introduction to Book and Online Supplement

"Be sure of it; give me the ocular proof."

William Shakespeare (1564-1616),
Othello, act 3 scene 3

A. Visual Litigation—Ocular Proof

We live in a visual culture. Since the dawn of humanity, we have been making judgments with our eyes. The earliest incarnations of humans made simply visual decisions about the safety and security of their surroundings. Logic, rationality, and all of our other thoughts processes evolved long after our sense of visual judgment. From this evolutionary standpoint, our eyes have always been the predominant force in our decision-making. While we have evolved from our caveman days, research has consistently shown the influence of visual communication. Consider a study on information recall, which showed that people remember only 10 percent of what they hear three days after hearing it, compared to remembering 50 percent of what they saw and heard three days after seeing it.[1] Technology, social media, and the emergence of the millennials and Gen Zers have only compounded this reality.

---

1. Dale, Edgar, *Audio-Visual Methods in Teaching*, 3rd ed., Holt, Rinehart & Winston, New York, 1969, p. 108.

1

This has important implications for trial attorneys. Successful litigators rely on visuals to persuade during both pretrial and trial. Today's jurors receive information over the television and the Internet. The millennial generation that makes up over 40 percent of the jury pool nationally grew up with information being delivered to them visually through pictures and videos on their phones, tablets, and laptops. Members of the Z Generation, who have begun to enter jury pools across the country, have been raised on visuals at least equally if not more than millennials. Consequently, jurors are not only visual learners but also are receptive to information being delivered to them visually, and they expect that trial lawyers will communicate information to them visually with the aid of modern technology. To be a successful litigator you need to know: how to communicate visually; how to create visuals; what software and hardware can produce the desired results; and what visuals are persuasive. In fact, research has shown that visual communication increases retention, comprehension, and overall persuasiveness.

A Cornell Law Review article entitled "What Jurors Really Think" describes the importance of technology in today's trial work based upon a study of 500 jurors in federal district court trials in Chicago, Illinois, from 2011 to 2017:

> Just as technology has become a mainstay in almost every area of modern American life, it has also become a mainstay in the courtroom. Jurors expect attorneys to use technology to aid their trial presentation. This is no surprise, given the ever-increasing prevalence of technology as a learning tool both in classrooms and in the workplace. Many jurors are accustomed to learning through technology, and technologically enhanced presentations present an ideal platform to summarize and connect the dots between the evidence presented at trial and the applicable law in a way that is especially useful for visual learners.[2]

In fact, the value of visual communication in the courtroom is not limited to jurors. Judges are also influenced by visual communication, which has led many of the nation's top litigators to incorporate visuals, such as photographs, graphics (such as timelines of events), and visual tutorials on complex subjects, into pleadings and briefs.

Modern technology enables a lawyer to create and display electronic and conventional visuals faster and in ways that were only dreamed about a few years ago. *Visual Litigation: Visual Communication Strategies and Today's Technology* examines the potentials for today's visual advocacy and technology. The book's instructions for operating the software programs, such as PowerPoint, Sanction, and TrialPad, and the necessary hardware are written so that even if you do not have a background in working with technology, you can easily understand them.

---

2. *Honorable Amy J. St. Eve & Gretchen Scavo, What Jurors Really Think*, 103 Cornell Law Review, 149, 169 (2018).

This book is not confined to just the creation and displaying of electronic visuals; it examines four other essential and related subjects. First, it discusses how in today's digital world, lawyers can use technology, such as Sanction and TrialPad, to bring the full case file (exhibits, witness statements, depositions, visuals, and so on) to court with only a tablet or laptop. Gone are the days when it was necessary to cart loads of three-ringed binders to a mediation or to court. Second, it explores all types of visuals that a lawyer can call upon to prove a case, including: animations; simulations; courtroom demonstrations; video depositions; diagrams; summary charts; and more. Third, the book explains how lawyers use visuals during alternative dispute resolution (settlement negotiation, mediation, and arbitration). Fourth, *Visual Litigation* discusses other types of technology that a lawyer can rely upon to assist in pretrial and trial advocacy.

B. Book Overview

Because effective pretrial and trial advocacy depends upon the use of visuals and accompanying technology, today's litigators must have a working knowledge of them. With this knowledge, a lawyer can create visuals and effectively operate the needed technology and do so at a minimal cost. Even if the lawyer is working a large case with a substantial budget that allows for the employment of a litigation consulting company to create and display the visuals in an alternative dispute resolution (ADR) setting and/or in trial, the lawyer is still ultimately responsible for the what visuals are to be developed and how they are displayed. This means that the lawyer should know the critical information that this book provides.

This book is designed for litigators from beginners to veterans, as well as law students. It is also a resource for technicians who could be either a paralegal, associate, professional technician, or any other person who is responsible for operating the technology or creating the visuals. Unquestionably, every litigator and law student who is inclined to become a litigator should learn about litigation technology and visual communication because they are integral parts of modern litigation practice.

This book can be utilized for professional development continuing legal education (CLE) seminars and law school litigation technology, pretrial advocacy, and trial advocacy courses as well as clinics. With this book, any lawyer, law student, or technician can learn the fundamentals of the technology needed for visual advocacy. Even veteran litigators can revisit this book for new ideas for litigation visuals and technology as they prepare the next case.

The best way to create and display persuasive visuals is to learn from successful trial lawyers and by observing the visuals that have worked well for them. *Visual Litigation: Visual Communication Strategies and Today's Technology* draws on the work of other trial lawyers, providing examples of their visuals and explaining how they were used in ADR and trial. You will be able to apply their strategies and techniques for preparing and using visuals in your cases. And, you can modify the types of visuals they used so that they apply to your case. Great trial lawyers are those who take from other great trial lawyers.

Some of the examples of trial visuals are from famous trials, such as the Dr. Conrad Murray's Michael Jackson manslaughter trial, the Paul Manafort tax and bank fraud trial, and the Michael Peterson murder trial (featured in the documentary movie *The Staircase*). Other examples of visuals are either from carefully selected civil and criminal cases or are hypothetical illustrations created by the authors. Credits for the visuals shown in the text are listed at the end of the book. Our choices of visuals for this book are motivated by a desire to offer you the best in litigation visuals.

Visual Litigation begins with Chapter 2 that explains what visuals can offer to persuasively communicate your case theory. It provides an orientation to currently available software that can be used to create and display electronic visuals. Also, the chapter describes the hardware that will be needed in a pretrial venue or in the courtroom to retrieve and display visuals.

The next four chapters are devoted to discussions and illustrations of effective electronic and conventional visuals for stages of trial as follows: Chapter 3, "Opening Statement Visuals"; Chapter 4, "Closing Argument Visuals"; Chapter 5, "Direct Examination Visuals"; and Chapter 6, "Cross-Examination Visuals." Chapter 7 explores how visuals can play an important role pretrial, particularly in your pleadings and ADR.

In order to introduce any visual into evidence, the trial lawyer must lay an evidentiary foundation. Chapter 8 both explains how to lay evidentiary predicate and offers case examples of those evidentiary foundations.

Chapter 9 explores software that can be used to create demonstrative and illustrative exhibits. While a litigation consultant can prepare demonstrative and illustrative exhibits, doing so can be expensive, and the case budget may not allow it. When the budget does not permit a vendor to be hired, that does not mean that the party cannot have persuasive litigation visuals. Either counsel or a member of the litigation team can create visuals with ease and without artistic talent. PowerPoint is a dynamic platform that allows attorneys to go beyond bullet-points and template backgrounds to create sophisticated animations and graphics. Programs such as SmartDraw software and others like it are relatively inexpensive. SmartDraw can be used to produce graphics including floor plans, landscapes, crime scene diagrams, as well as timelines. Also, in Chapter 9, we explore software that can be used to record, edit, and create video evidence.

Chapter 10 is devoted to ethical and legal challenges to the use and display of visuals as well as discovery and preservation issues.

Chapter 11 concentrates on how to get the most out of the services that a litigation communication expert can provide to a trial lawyer, such as creating trial visuals and sitting in during trial to operate the courtroom technology that will retrieve and display the visuals.

The next two chapters discuss presentation software programs. In Chapter 12 we discuss today's nonlinear software programs, including Sanction TrialDirector, ExhibitView, and OnCue that can be utilized to create, store, retrieve, and/or display visuals. Also, this chapter explores how these software programs facilitate pretrial preparation. Chapter 13 explains how to make the most out of linear software programs, such as PowerPoint and Keynote.

Chapter 14 examines how to use a tablet and applications in litigation. For example, TrialPad is an application made for an iPad. Visuals, documents, and other exhibits can be stored in its database. With this relatively inexpensive application on your tablet, an Apple TV, and a wireless courtroom, you can deliver an effective presentation.

Chapter 15 covers what you need to know about hardware and the six prerequisites that must be fulfilled in order to display visuals in a courtroom.

Chapter 16 offers exercises in working with litigation visuals and technology. These exercises provide experiential learning for professional training CLE workshops and law school classes and clinics. The chapter provides summaries of both a civil and a criminal case followed by assignments for assignments that will give the participants experience in creating demonstrative exhibits and in working with litigation visuals, linear and nonlinear software, and technology. The participants can draw on case files for the civil and criminal cases to perform the assignments. The case files contain legal documents, visuals, witness statements, jury instructions, and so on.

A Teacher's Manual is provided to instructors of professional development workshops and law professors. Also, instructors will receive an Actors' Guide that contains instructions for the actors who will play the roles of witnesses for the assignments.

While the book focuses on using visuals as a means of communicating with jurors, obviously visuals come into play during a bench trial. For a bench trial you should gauge how many visuals and the type of visuals you will offer based upon your assessment of how receptive your judge will be to them. For example, you could decide that you do not need to offer a summary chart of the contents of bank records to the judge although the chart would be critical to proving your case in a jury trial.

Finally, throughout the book, we use the Federal Rules of Evidence and the American Bar Association's Model Rules of Professional Conduct because most states have adopted them or adopted versions of them.

C. Visual Litigation Online Supplement

Visual Litigation comes with a robust companion website http://www.fast case.com/visuallitigation. A supplement that is periodically updated is particularly important to the subject of technology because of how rapidly technology changes. The website supplement also contains the case files for both the criminal and civil cases. As previously mentioned, these online case files provide the information needed to perform the assignment exercises. Also, most of the visuals in this book are featured on the website in color.

Chapter 2

Overview: Visuals and Today's Technology

A. Visuals
   1. Persuasion
   2. Purposes Served
      a. Narrative Visuals
      b. Argument Visuals
      c. Educational Visuals
      d. Concession Visuals
   3. Design Criteria for Demonstrative Evidence
   4. Designer
B. Comfort Zone
C. Competency
D. Preparation
E. Redundancy
F. Advantages of Technology
G. Computer Software
   1. Linear Software
   2. Nonlinear Software
   3. TrialPad
H. Conventional Visuals
I. Hardware
   1. Antiquated Courtroom
   2. Up-to-Date Courtroom

"Make sure that you always have the right tools for the job. It's no use trying to eat a steak with a teaspoon, and a straw."

Anthony T. Hincks, author

A. Visuals

I. Persuasion

Why is it imperative that litigators utilize visuals to persuade? At least five reasons exist. First, your audience—judge, jury, arbitrator, mediator, or your opponent—is accustomed to receiving information through visual media—Internet, videos, and broadcasts. They are attached to cell phones, laptops, and tablets. They expect to have information delivered with images. They are immersed in visual communication. Second, a major segment of the population is composed of visual learners as opposed to auditory and kinesthetic learners. Third, we retain more of the information if we receive it visually. Fourth, visual communication, such as seeing a picture of an injury, can be much more powerful than mere words describing it. Visuals can dynamically present a story and an argument. Fifth, visuals help an audience reach a consensus. For example, if a trial lawyer in an automobile tort case merely told the jury that a collision took place at an intersection, each juror will have a different mental picture of the intersection based on his or her own life experience. However, if the lawyer shows the jury a picture of the intersection in question, all of the jurors will be on the same page, seeing the same image of the intersection. Visual communication of a message is successful persuasion.

Visuals can be employed in all phases of litigation. They can be used in pretrial briefings and in alternative dispute resolution settings, as we describe in Chapter 7, or in any phase of trial from opening statement through closing argument, as we discuss in Chapters 3-6.

2. Purposes Served

Visuals can serve at least four purposes. First, narrative visuals relate the factual theory of the case; they are storytelling images. Second, argument visuals present the proponent's arguments for a favorable settlement or verdict. Third, educational visuals teach, explaining complicated information in a way that can be understood by the jurors. Fourth, concession visuals are designed to extract admissions from the opposing party or adverse witness during cross-examination or to discredit the witness who denies what is apparent in the concession visual.

a. Narrative Visuals

The popular saying is that an image is worth a thousand words. This has become a cliché because of how true it turns out to be. Images tell stories. Narrative visuals can bring the story of the case alive and make it clear for the audience.

A narrative visual is ideal for opening statement, which is the golden opportunity for counsel to be a storyteller. A narrative visual helps the jury understand the facts. For example, with the aid of an anatomical drawing, plaintiff's counsel in a personal injury case can relate a human story about the plaintiff's injuries that are at the core of the case. The images of the injuries and the plaintiff's recovery from those injuries can tell a profoundly sympathetic story that motivates jurors to want to compensate the plaintiff. Furthermore, counsel can effectively communicate the events that took place with the aid of a timeline that will help the jury understand and retain the chronology of those events. Another example of a narrative visual that can help the jury understand and retain information is a relationship visual, which is a diagram with pictures of players in the case with arrows between them along with short labels showing how they are connected with one another. Finally, the defense might rely on a decision-tree graphic that shows a pattern of poor decision making by the plaintiff that led to the unfortunate outcome. We discuss many more narrative visuals in Chapter 3 on opening statements.

b. Argument Visuals

An argument visual is a visual aid that counsel can use to communicate the attorney's argument during summation. As opposed to narrative visuals that convincingly relay facts during opening statement, argument visuals explain why the jury should decide in the party's favor. Argument visuals ideally are simple, easy to understand, and persuasively communicate the lawyer's argument. There are an infinite number of argument visuals because there are a vast number of arguments that counsel can make in closing. For example, defense counsel may use the visual below to highlight jurors' temptations to overlook key hurdles for the prosecution in a criminal case or the plaintiff in a civil case.

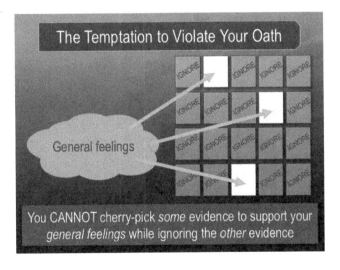

Argument visuals also can be used to undercut the other side's case. For instance, counsel can utilize a chart contrasting the superior qualifications of the party's expert with the opposing party's expert's qualifications when arguing that the jury should rely on their expert. Consider the following example that was used in a legal malpractice case.

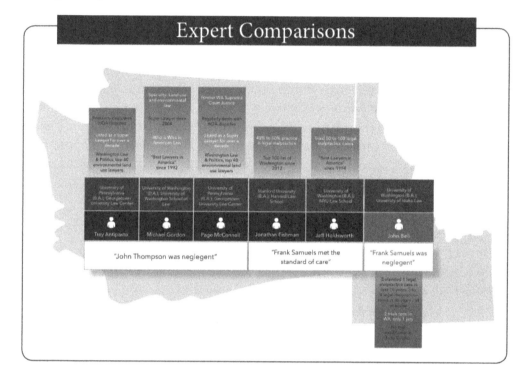

In the foregoing example, the defense used this graphic to argue that its experts are local, reputable Washington attorneys, while the plaintiff's expert was an out-of-state Idaho attorney with limited experience and expertise. The defense experts' qualifications are described in the five boxes on the left with summaries of their qualifications. The plaintiff's expert is depicted on the right below the line with a text box that states:

> Defended 1 legal malpractice case in the last 10 years:
> 3 to 4 legal malpractice in 36 years—all in Idaho.
> 2 trials total in WA only 1 jury
> No trial experience in WA

Another example of an argument visual is a chart contrasting the portions of the testimony of the other side's key witness with conflicting credible evidence, such as in the following example.

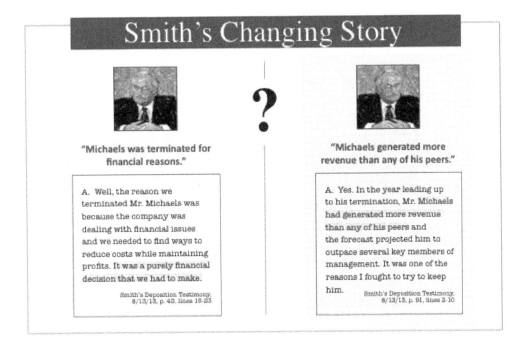

In Chapter 4 on closing arguments, we discuss several other powerful argument visuals.

c.　*Educational Visuals*

Educational visuals can be employed to help the audience understand the evidence. When the evidence is complex, educational visuals can be particularly helpful. Evidence can be complex when it is technical, and it can also be complex when it is voluminous. Indeed, Federal Rule of Evidence 1006 codifies this principle that a visual may be useful in communicating information by authorizing the use of a summary chart "to prove the content of voluminous writings...."

Educational visual aids are a staple for an expert witness's direct examination, enabling the expert to employ a visual to explain and simplify the complex. For example, a physician can employ a medical illustration to explain her findings and conclusions, such as in the following example where a medical expert was educating jurors about the sacroiliac joint.

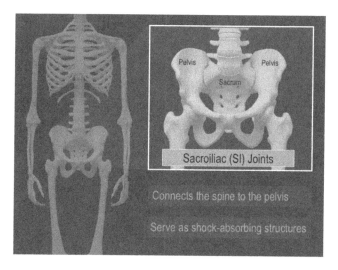

Alternatively, a vehicular accident reconstructionist may use a forensic video animation of a collision,[1] such as the one below, to help the jury understand the expert's findings and opinions. We provide several of the education visuals in Chapter 5 on direct examination.

d.   Concession Visuals

Concession visuals are those that do one or more of the following: force a witness to make a concession favorable to a cross-examiner; impeach the witness; or highlight a key concession in closing argument. There are some things a witness either must admit or in denying them, label the answer a lie, mistaken, or ludicrous.

---

1. https://highimpact.com/.

A concession visual can destroy a witness's credibility. A concession visual is one that reveals the irrefutable truth, which can be proven by direct or circumstantial evidence or by plain common sense. In Chapter 6 on cross-examination we provide several examples of concession visuals that impeached the witnesses who were confronted with them. An example of a concession visual is a witness's prior inconsistent statement in a video deposition. When the witness is shown the prior inconsistent statement, the witness must concede that he made the statement or stamp his denial as false.

3. Design Criteria for Demonstrative Evidence

For a piece of demonstrative evidence (hereafter also referred to as "a demonstrative") to produce a favorable impression, it must satisfy certain design criteria. The design of these demonstratives (here we are referring to graphics, such as a diagram, timeline, drawing, or animation) must be credible, interesting, and easily understood by the audience.

First, the demonstrative evidence must be credible. Edward Tufte, American renowned statistician, artist, and author, stated:

> Making an evidence presentation is a moral act as well as an intellectual activity. To maintain standards of quality, relevance, and integrity for evidence, consumers of presentations should insist that presenters be held intellectually and ethically responsible for what they show and tell. Thus, *consuming* a presentation is also an intellectual and moral activity.[2]

An audience will only be swayed and/or educated by what they see as believable. Therefore, the designer of the demonstrative evidence should make sure that the visual portrays the indisputable. An image is credible when it states the law, such as an argument visual that tracks the wording of a jury instruction. A visual that shows what is irrefutable or overwhelming evidence is credible. A visual that makes common sense is believable. A visual that shows what is accepted as common knowledge is credible.

Second, to be effective the visual should be interesting. It should engage the jurors. When a visual is creative, it can be interesting. When the visual presents the unexpected, it is likely to capture the jurors' attention. This is important because keeping jurors' attention is critical at trial, though it is becoming more and more difficult. Research on social media and technology suggests that one consequence of the technology revolution is diminished attention spans. Visual communication can help overcome this hurdle by engaging jurors and capturing their attention.

---

2. Edward Tufte, *Beautiful Evidence*, 9, Graphics Press LLC (2006).

Third, the demonstrative should be easily understood by the audience. In 1968, American educator Malcomb S. Knowles developed an adult learning theory that included the concept that adults have experiences to draw upon and that instructors of adults can capitalize on that experience to get adults to grasp new ideas. Knowles states that an instructor should move from what the adults know to the new concepts. Thus, if possible, the demonstrative should integrate the known and lead to an understanding of the new information.

When creating a demonstrative, the designer should simplify the information. The value of visual communication is in its ability to enhance the message by simplifying it. This may seem obvious, but it is easy to lose sight of this point in the design process. It is commonplace for litigation timelines to have way too many entries, making it difficult for the trier-of-fact to follow along.

A graphic that is overloaded with information can lead to what one might call a visual migraine. If it is stressful to look at and extraordinarily difficult to understand, it is an ineffective graphic. Instead, such a graphic might create the impression that the audience has not a chance at understanding what they need to understand, which could undermine their motivation to work hard to understand it. This can have devastating consequences in jury deliberations.

That is not to say that the demonstrative should not communicate complicated information. Tufte put it this way, "What is to be sought in designs for the display of information is the clear portrayal of complexity. Not the complication of the simple; rather the task of the designer is to give visual access to the subtle and the difficult—that is, the revelation of the complex."[3] To simplify the visual, remove extraneous information. If the visual involves text, limit the number of words.

4.   Designer

In the next section, we discuss the competency of the technician who will operate the software and hardware that can be used to create and display litigation visuals. Here, we want to focus on the question of who should design the litigation visuals. Should you design them? In Chapter 9, we examine SmartDraw, which is a software program that will empower almost anyone to create basic visuals. However, if you are not a graphics designer, you are not likely to produce the quality of graphics, even with SmartDraw, that a professional graphics designer could. Therefore, if you have a budget that allows you to employ a graphic designer, it would be advisable to consider hiring one. If you lack any artistic talent and do not have the budget to hire a professional, you may have someone in your office or an acquaintance who can design the visuals.

---

3. https://www.standardco.de/what-i-learned-from-edward-tufte-s-one-day-lecture-on-presenting-data.

B. Comfort Zone

If you have any trepidations about presenting with today's technology, this section and the following ones discuss how you can become comfortable with it. Here we offer ways in which you can develop confidence by becoming competent with technology, being prepared, and having a backup plan. This chapter also contains an orientation to the hardware and software that are currently available for creating and displaying electronic visuals. Specifically, the chapter discusses and introduces you to software, including PowerPoint, Keynote, Sanction, TrialDirector, and TrialPad. Also, it provides a broad view of the hardware that will be needed in the courtroom and a pretrial venue to retrieve and display visuals. We do not want to leave you with the impression that all the necessary technology is discussed here because in this digital era something new comes along practically every day. We will endeavor to update information about the software and hardware discussed in this book as well as new products in the book's online supplement at http://www.fastcase.com/visuallitigation.

You want to be comfortable with any technology that you use to present your case in an alternative dispute resolution venue or a courtroom. And, you want to be able to present your case without avoidable distractions and concerns. Perhaps one of your concerns is whether you will be able to operate the hardware and software that would enhance your presentation of the case. The first step toward being in a comfort zone when working with technology is to think about the hardware and software as powerful tools that will enable you to persuasively present your case. You want to have all the tools of persuasion at your disposal.

Being comfortable working with technology will come to you as a result of competency, preparation, and redundancy, which we will cover in the following sections.

C. Competency

It is axiomatic that to effectively present your electronic evidence with technology you will need to be competent in operating it. Ineptitude in working with technology can result in a disruption in the presentation of a case and can even cause disastrous results. For example, if a document containing the witness's prior inconsistent statement does not come up on the screen when you need it during cross-examination, you will be forced to stumble around searching through your files to find it while the jury waits. This can create a negative impression with jurors that you are disorganized or do not know what you are doing. Or worse, if you are unfamiliar with the court's equipment, and cannot produce the electronic evidence when you need to, the court could order you to move on without it, which essentially messages to the jurors that the judge thinks you are incompetent.

Generally, courts do not tolerate incompetency when it comes to being able to present with technology. Incompetency is very likely to damage your credibility with the court. Normally, counsel will be told to just move on without it. Indeed, because of the failures of lawyers to efficiently use technology in prior cases, the trial judge may disfavor the use of today's technology in your case and not allow it.

Federal courts and many state and local courts with modern technology have established standards of competency for the use of the court's equipment. For instance, the United States District Court for the Eastern District of California has published online its "Electronic Evidence Submission/Presentation" standing directives that contains a description of the equipment that the court has available for use by the parties as well as its standards. The court's directives make it clear that the parties must become competent to present evidence electronically if they wish to use the court's equipment. The "Evidence Presentation Obligations" section states:

- Parties who intend to present evidence electronically via the Court's electronic evidence presentation systems must be familiar with the systems prior to the hearing/trial. No court/jury time will be provided during court proceedings to allow the parties to troubleshoot issues with the parties' equipment or the equipment in the courtroom. If a party is unfamiliar with the Court's systems, they are strongly encouraged to attend an orientation with the Court's IT representative prior to the hearing/trial (see procedures below). The Court will not tolerate any delays during any proceedings caused by a party's unfamiliarity with the Court's systems or by the failure of a party's equipment. The parties will be required to present their cases without the aid of the electronic evidence presentation systems in the event that the systems are unavailable due to the party's unfamiliarity, due to equipment failure or due to any other "technology" delays.
- In addition to familiarizing themselves with the Court's electronic evidence presentation systems in advance of the hearing/trial, the parties must familiarize themselves with their own equipment and how to connect their own equipment with the Court's systems prior to the hearing/trial. Specifically, the parties should be familiar with:
  o Adjusting the refresh rate on their computer (to 60 Hz)
  o Adjusting the resolution on their computer (to 1024x768)
  o In Fresno: Switching the display on their computer to send video to the Court's A/V system (the Court uses the Extron DSC 301 HD compliant scaler and XTP R (& T) HDMI systems at the

attorney tables and the Extron DVS 605 compliant scaler and XTP R (&T) HDMI systems at the lectern).

o   In Sacramento: Switching the display on their computer to send video to the Court's A/V system (the Court uses the Extron RGB580 xi interface at both attorney tables and lectern location.

Making the physical connections between the electronic evidence presentation systems and their equipment. The parties are responsible for providing any cable adapters required to connect to their equipment to the Court's systems. For example, to display content from an iPad to the Court's systems, the parties must provide their own iPad-to-VGA or iPad-to-HDMI adapter. **Please note that the Court's staff cannot work on and/or provide support for any non-court equipment.**[4]

The court's admonition bears repeating: "The Court will not tolerate any delays during any proceedings caused by a party's unfamiliarity with the Court's systems or by the failure of a party's equipment."[5]

Courts with technology available for use by the parties commonly offer training on how to operate the court's equipment. For example, the United States District Court for the Eastern District of California makes such an offer online:

Electronic Evidence Presentation Systems Orientation

Any party wishing to familiarize themselves with the Court's electronic evidence presentation systems *are strongly encouraged* to set up an orientation session with the Court's IT staff.

To do so, please contact the courtroom deputy *at least three (3) weeks before your trial or hearing*. The courtroom deputy will coordinate with the Court's IT representative to schedule a convenient time to conduct the orientation.

Parties who attend an electronic evidence presentation systems orientation should bring the equipment they will use to connect to the systems as well as samples of the content they intend to present at the trial/hearing through the systems.[6]

Technology that is built into the courtroom is becoming more and more common. Newer courthouses typically have better technology for case presentation.

---

4. http://www.caed.uscourts.gov/caednew/index.cfm/attorney-info/electronic-evidence -presentation/.

5. *Ibid.*

6. *Ibid.*

For example, the courtrooms in the Seattle division of the Western District of Washington have flat-screen monitors in the jury box for each of the jurors to see. Attorneys can show their PowerPoint presentations on these screens or use Trial-Director to show exhibits and highlight key portions. At the end of this chapter, we show you the inside of that courtroom and its technology.

The instructions provided in this text are designed to be easily understood by any non-tech-savvy person, and they should make it possible for you to master the skills you need to work with the technology. These instructions will need to be combined with hands-on practice in order to fully master the software and hardware. In this book, we also provide you with access to other resources that allow you to become competent with software and hardware. The resources include links to downloadable manuals and tutorial videos for software products that are discussed here. Again, if you appear in federal courts and in some state and local courts that have modern, fully equipped courtrooms, you will need, and may be required, to engage in pretrial training on how to use the court's equipment.

It will take some time for you to acquire the knowledge and skills to be competent to make presentations with technology and to feel comfortable with it. But you can do it. You may decide to begin with linear software, such as Power-Point or Keynote, which are simple to operate and provide effective linear presentations for opening statement, closing argument, or to accompany testimony of an expert witness explaining the field of expertise, findings, and expert opinions. You may opt for nonlinear presentation software, such as Prezi.

Naturally, if you have not achieved the level of competency to effectively present with technology, you should either find a technician in your law firm or, if you can afford it, hire a technology consultant from a vendor to handle the technology. In the absence of a technician, it would be better to do without technology than derail your presentation.

D. Preparation

As with every other aspect of trial work, the key to success in making effective presentations with technology is preparation. Only when you are well prepared can you feel confident—comfortable with your use of technology to present electronic evidence. First and foremost, you must prepare yourself by acquiring the knowledge and skills to do the job of operating the software and hardware.

Second, preparation entails having the right and up-to-date software and hardware. You will need to scout the pretrial venue or courtroom to determine what, if any, technology is in place and whether it is compatible with your presentation. Even if you will be in a modern courtroom, you will still need to determine whether it has all that you require to properly present. If not, you will need to augment that equipment (with the court's permission, of course).

It is also important to talk with the courtroom staff about your intended use of technology. Judges sometimes have strong preferences for how technology is set up in a courtroom. For example, a judge might have strong preferences about where a projection screen needs to be located, which may be different from what you had planned. The judge's preferred location may limit the size of the projection screen you can use, or whether it is realistic to use one at all.

Also, you will want to determine how you can back up your technology, for example, either with a switcher and another computer or a document camera. Is your presentation designed for the courtroom monitor's resolution? Note that the United States District Court Eastern District of California directive that parties should be familiar with "[a]djusting the resolution on their computer (to 1024x768)," which is a low resolution and unlikely to clearly display a visual created in a higher resolution.

Similarly, as you design your PowerPoint presentation, you should consider how it will be displayed. If it is displayed on a projection screen, you probably want to use the default slide dimensions. However, if the PowerPoint presentation is going to be shown on wide-screen monitors, you may want to adjust the size of your slides to fit this widescreen format, which creates more space for your timelines or other graphics. You may want to adjust to the widescreen monitors simply to avoid the appearance of being outdated via the black bars on each side of the slide that will appear on a widescreen monitor with a PowerPoint that is designed in the additional 4:3 format.

Third, you need to prepare your case. This involves gathering all the visuals—documents, photographs, videos, depositions, everything visual. Rudyard Kipling's poem[7] is a helpful guide for the image-collecting process:

> I keep six honest serving-men
> (They taught me all I knew);
> Their names are What and Why and When
> And How and Where and Who.

Like journalists and narrators who have turned to these six helpers to frame report writing, litigators can rely upon them during the trial preparation process to come up with impactful visuals. For example, plaintiff's counsel could enlist the six for a vehicular tort case, and they could produce the following: *What* (images of the crushed vehicles in the aftermath of the collision); *Why* (a chart showing the defendant's high breathalyzer reading contrasted with the legal limit); *When* (a timeline showing the projected time it will take for the defendant's partial recovery

---

7. Rudyard Kipling, "I Keep Six Honest Serving-Men."

from the spinal cord injury); *How* (a video animation of the defendant's vehicle crossing over into the lane in which the plaintiff was driving); *Where* (a diagram of the highway); and *Who* (a picture of the hospitalized plaintiff in traction).

The visuals and other materials that you gather can be stored and organized in a software program, such as PowerPoint, Sanction, TrialDirector, TrialPad, OnCue, ExhibitView, or the like. We will explore this phase of preparation in more depth in Chapter 12 on nonlinear software, Chapter 13 on linear software, and Chapter 14 on tablets and litigation applications. Often, how you organize and label exhibits will be guided by the court's instructions. Once you have organized and stored the electronic evidence, you need to prepare how you will present it at an ADR venue or in a courtroom. This means you need to practice quickly locating and displaying the visuals on a monitor or screen. If you plan to show electronic evidence during direct examination of your witnesses and you want to do so in a persuasive manner, you must show the evidence to the witness and practice the testimony. Never show a witness an exhibit, electronic or otherwise, for the first time on the witness stand. It is not a nice experience to have your witness say that they haven't a clue what you have just shown them when you thought they would surely recognize it. But, practicing with your equipment and your witnesses is not enough.

Fourth, to fully prepare, you must practice with the hardware in place in the courtroom and then retest it on the day of trial before the jury comes out or, if it is a bench trial, before the judge takes the bench. Some courts, such as the United States District Court Eastern District of California encourage the parties to contact the court about technology well in advance of trial for an orientation to the court's technology.[8] Even if all went well when you tested the equipment prior to the day of trial, always arrange to get to the courtroom when it opens in the morning every day of trial to test the equipment and make any necessary adjustments. You never know what could have happened to the technology during the time between when you first tested it prior to trial and the first day of trial. And, the same goes for the time between the end of the court day and when court opens the following day. We will discuss this phase of your preparation in greater detail in Chapter 15 "Hardware and Effective Courtroom Presentations."

E. Redundancy

Expect the unexpected. You are feeling pretty comfortable about your electronic presentations. You have the requisite knowledge about how to operate the

---

8. http://www.caed.uscourts.gov/caednew/index.cfm/attorney-info/electronic-evidence -presentation/ "contact the courtroom deputy at least three (3) weeks before your trial or hearing. The courtroom deputy will coordinate with the Court's IT representative to schedule a convenient time to conduct the orientation."

technology. You have practiced with the technology. You have acquainted your witnesses with the technology and the electronic exhibits. You have tested the equipment. All is good, right? Wrong. Remember Murphy's law. The projector's bulb burns out. The computer crashes. The Wi-Fi does not work. Your technology consultant is in the hospital following a car accident that just happened as she was driving to the courthouse. Expect the unexpected. What now?

You are calm, collected, and confident because of redundancy. Here we do not mean "redundancy" in the sense of no longer being needed or useful as you would be if you had not planned for the unexpected. Instead, we mean "redundancy" in the engineering sense—"the inclusion of extra components which are not strictly necessary to functioning, in case of failure in other components." You are ready because you have a backup in case of any failure of technology.

You should definitely have a backup laptop computer. You can have a backup computer connected with a switcher to the computer you are actively using. If the computer fails for any reason, you can seamlessly switch to the backup.

If your software fails, the simplest and tried-and-true backup is a document camera, which is discussed further at pages 323-24. If the courtroom is not equipped with a document camera, you can supply one. A document camera is not very expensive. You place a document, photograph, or other visual on the bed of the document camera, and it is projected onto the monitor or screen. If you were going to show a PowerPoint presentation, bring printouts of the slides that you can display with the document camera.

If the unexpected does occur and you have a technological failure or other snafu, you probably will not be calm and collected as you move to your backup plan. But, as with all other trial work, never let them see you sweat.

F. Advantages of Technology

In the first chapter, we discussed the advantages to the parties of using technology, and we will explore the advantages in greater depth in later chapters on each phase of trial from opening statement through closing argument. Electronic visuals are persuasive.

Here, we focus on the main advantages of technology to the court—efficiency and the resultant conservation of the court's valuable time and expense. Understandably, the court may be reluctant to have the parties use technology if they lack the skills or preparedness to do so efficiently. However, when the parties are competent and prepared, court time can be saved. Rather than fumbling around for a documentary exhibit and then passing it among the jurors, counsel with today's technology can not only pull up the visual for the jurors to view but also annotate it with the computer's annotation tools. During opening statement and closing argument, counsel with linear software can readily project visuals on a screen rather than having to use boards or a flip chart. By modernizing the federal courts with today's technology, the federal courts tacitly acknowledged that technology makes the court process more efficient, provided that the parties are trained to use it.

Another instance where a court saved time and money by transitioning to today's technology occurred in San Diego. The San Diego County Superior Court banned the use of boards except for murder cases because of the cost of storing them. As a consequence, the San Diego District Attorney's Office turned to TrialPad, an application that allows prosecutors to display electronic exhibits on a monitor.[9]

G. Computer Software

I. Linear Software

The two most commonly used presentation software programs are Microsoft's PowerPoint[10] and Apple's Keynote.[11] PowerPoint is also available for Apple products. Yet another bold alternative to PowerPoint and Keynote software is Prezi, which is also a linear software.[12] With these presentation software programs, you can create slides and design a slideshow for trial. Utilizing a computer, projector, and a screen or a monitor, a trial lawyer or assistant can show those slides in the courtroom with a remote (preferred) or a mouse. Manuals and other resources on how to design slides for PowerPoint, Keynote, and other types of computer presentation software are readily available.

Slideshows developed with these types of presentation software programs are usually linear in nature, showing one slide after another in sequence, rather than like the trial software described in the next section that enables the technician to retrieve documents and media from a case file during trial in any desired order. The linear presentation can include a wide variety of media because the software enables the developer to insert those visuals that are on the computer into slides. Thus, images can include documents, videos, screenshots, text, diagrams, symbols, and so on. However, PowerPoint and Prezi have nonlinear options that allow more sophisticated graphic designers to incorporate hyperlinks into slides that permit attorneys to jump around as needed rather that follow the standard slide progression.

---

9. https://www.youtube.com/watch?v=k2oo4vHImBM.

10. https://www.microsoft.com/en-us/p/powerpoint/cfq7ttc0k7c6?activetab=pivot %3aoverviewtab.

11. https://apps.apple.com/us/app/keynote/id409183694?mt=12.

12. https://prezi.com/.

Today, a lecture without an accompanying PowerPoint slideshow is a rarity. Likewise, in trial, when the lawyer is addressing the jury during opening statement or closing argument, both of which are linear in nature, a PowerPoint presentation is ideal for communicating the message visually. Another occasion during trial when a PowerPoint slideshow works well is when an expert witness is explaining the witness's field of expertise, findings and opinions to a jury. See pages 94-98 for examples of how visuals can be shown during an expert's testimony.

2. Nonlinear Software

In trial, counsel must be able to promptly retrieve and show the desired visual or exhibit. The low- or no-tech means of accomplishing this is to have a well-organized system. A better approach begins by loading the exhibits and trial visuals into a computer database with the necessary software. Some popular trial software programs are TrialDirector 360 by iPro Tech, LLC;[13] OnCue by Core Legal Concepts LLC;[14] TrialGraphix Inc.;[15] ExhibitView by ExhibitView Solutions LLC;[16] and Sanction by LexisNexis.[17] These programs are nonlinear in nature and enable the trial lawyer or trial support person to perform a wide variety of tasks that organize and deliver visuals to the fact finder. Therefore, these trial software programs are ideal for direct examination and cross-examination, which can be nonlinear, allowing counsel to produce the evidence whenever it might be needed. PowerPoint can be utilized in this way to pull up visuals, but it is not as easy. Slides in PowerPoint can be retrieved and shown by typing in the number of the slide. PowerPoint can also be incorporated into TrialDirector, creating a best-of-both-worlds scenario.

TrialDirector, Sanction, and the like provide systems that enable you to pretrial organize and store exhibits and visuals so that they can be readily retrieved in trial. You can load your documents, photographs, transcripts, video depositions, PowerPoint presentations, and other files into the software program. Once loaded, the files can be sorted and, if you wish, printed out. A workbook feature allows you to organize exhibits. In trial, you can locate and retrieve the files by exhibit number. In presentation mode, you can see the document or media to be displayed before it is shown to the jury. When the exhibit is shown, TrialDirector, ExhibitView, and Sanction have annotation tools allowing you to call out and annotate the visual as it is being shown.

---

13. https://iprotech.com/software/trial-director/.

14. http://www.oncuetech.com/.

15. https://www.trialgraphix.com/.

16. http://www.exhibitview.net/.

17. https://www.lexisnexis.com/en-us/products/sanction.page.

TrialDirector's "transcript manager" permits the transcript to be shown alone or synchronized with the video deposition so that the jurors can see both the transcript and the video on the screen at the same time. Sanction also does this. You just need a synchronized video and transcript database file called an .mdb. TimeCoder Pro is a stand-alone product made by inData that allows you to create an .mdb file from a video and transcript that either you can manually synchronize or pay someone to synchronize. Once the transcript and video have been synchronized, it then can be loaded into Sanction or TrialDirector.

Trial software programs, such as Sanction, OnCue, ExhibitView, and TrialDirector, are particularly valuable tools for rapidly producing and showing transcripts and videos, such as video depositions, as discussed at pages 236-37. For example, during pretrial preparation, counsel can select segments from the transcript and video that counsel expects to use to impeach a witness with at trial.

3.   TrialPad

TrialPad by LIT Software, LLC is unique because it is an application made specifically for an iPad and it is relatively inexpensive when compared to other nonlinear software programs.[18] TrialPad has most of the features that are available in Sanction and TrialDirector. And, with just a tablet in the palm of your hand, you can move around a courtroom with everything you need to try the case. TrialPad is nonlinear, and counsel can readily retrieve and show videos, documents, and other visual exhibits that are stored in its database.

H. Conventional Visuals

Although we devote much of this book to electronic visuals, that is not to suggest that we have abandoned conventional visuals. Parading a single eight-by-eleven-inch photograph of an injured person in front of the jury, looking each juror in the eyes as you go and watching them emotionally absorb the impact of the image, can be the most dynamic way of communicating the harm done. A board with a timeline on it can be an excellent visual aid for an opening statement when counsel guides the jury through the chronology of events in the case. An X-ray placed on a document camera and thereby projected onto a screen can be an impactful visual aid for a physician who is explaining what she found during her examination of the patient.

---

18. https://www.litsoftware.com/trialpad/.

Not only are these and other conventional visuals excellent media for communicating with the receivers but also they can serve as a change of pace from electronic visuals. By altering the media, counsel can better hold the jury's attention. Rather than always projecting an image on the monitor and having the witness discuss it while seated in the witness chair, counsel can have the witness step down from the witness box and walk over to the document camera and annotate the document on the bed of the document camera. Or, counsel can have a photographic exhibit published to the jury by passing it hand-to-hand among the jurors.

Technology has made the creation of conventional visuals easy. Chapter 9 "Creating Demonstrative and Video Evidence" discusses how SmartDraw software can be used to design timelines, crime scenes, landscapes, intersections, and so on. After the software has been used to create the visual, that visual can be enlarged and adhered to a board.

I.   Hardware

1.   Antiquated Courtroom

The hardware that you will be required to bring to court to show your computer presentation depends upon what equipment is already in the courtroom. If you are trying your case in federal court or in a modern courtroom, it may have all you will need, or you may need to augment it with some of your own hardware.

However, you may be assigned to an antiquated courtroom devoid of the necessary equipment for a modern courtroom. This is what happened to Larry Johnson. In the mid-1990s, Johnson, who had been a civil litigator, was on a Steering Committee on Electronic Court Records that envisioned paperless courtrooms in the King County courthouse in Seattle, Washington. Mr. Johnson described the contrast between that vision and his recent experience in King County Superior Court's courtrooms as follows:

> In 1994, I had to switch to full-time e-discovery consulting and serving as an expert witness. I followed my bliss. My work was chiefly in federal courts around the country. Thus, only a few months ago did I find myself once again in a King County Superior Court courtroom reluctantly appearing pro bono as counsel for a relative.
>
> Was that a surprise. I felt I had entered a time warp. I didn't realize that every exhibit intended for use at trial still had to be printed out and put in tabbed binders, with duplicates to the other side and to the judge.
>
> Yes, even though the clerk got the PDF electronic versions via the online ECR (Electronic Court Records) system, as did the judge, paper was still king—and even though it was indeed almost exclusively the

electronic PDF exhibits the judge viewed on his big monitor during the course of the trial.[19]

Larry Johnson's experience is not unique. Many state and local courtrooms around the country are in splendid historic buildings but are technologically outmoded. Do not assume that just because we are in the twenty-first century that your courtroom has caught up with the times. It is not unusual for litigators to end up in courtrooms, especially in smaller counties, that do not accommodate technology. In fact, some rural courthouses may not even have accessible power outlets for attorneys to plug their laptops and projectors into. Then again, the courtroom may fall somewhere in the middle between modern and archaic, having some equipment but not enough.

When the courtroom is ill-equipped to display visuals with today's technology, the litigants must supply the hardware if they wish to utilize it. In Chapter 15, we discuss not only the hardware you will need to take to court for displaying trial visuals but also logistics and how to assemble and operate the hardware. Suffice it to say, you can use a projector and a screen and/or a monitor, and you will need a backup. It bears repeating that in case of a technological glitch, a document camera, which is shown in the picture on the next page, provides a good backup. And, again, if you are planning a PowerPoint slideshow, you can print out your slides, and, if need be, you can place the printout of a slide on the document camera and project it onto the screen.

2. Up-to-Date Courtroom

What follows is a description of the equipment in the U.S. District Court, Western District of Washington, along with the court's online explanations of the equipment, being quoted.[20]

---

19. Larry Johnson, "Why Is Paper Still King in King County," King County Bar Bulletin (January 2019), https://www.kcba.org/For-Lawyers/Bar-Bulletin/PostId/658/why-is-paper -still-king-in-king-county.

20. http://www.wawd.uscourts.gov/attorneys/trial-support/courtroom-basics.

Podium

"This podium has a touch panel monitor, which is located at the podium and witness stand in all courtrooms. You can use your finger to tap or write on the monitor, and the result will be displayed on all monitors in the courtroom. Multiple options for lines and colors are available in the menu for each monitor.

"There are input wells (shown below) at each attorney table as well as at the podium. These input panels can be used to integrate your laptop computer into the courtroom technology so you can display your laptop output on all courtroom monitors. The attorney table wells are labeled with the appropriate PC number corresponding to the remote control. Each well contains VGA cable, 3.5mm audio cable, HDMI cable, network connection, power, and USB charging slots."

Input well

Document camera at the podium

"The document camera is used to display documents as well as other small items on the monitors in the courtroom. Most of the controls you will need to use can be found on the top portion of the device (see below). In addition to zoom and focusing tools, each camera can also capture freeze frames, allowing an image to remain statically on the courtroom monitors even though it may no longer be in use."

Document camera controls

Witness stand

"The witness stand contains a touch panel monitor and microphone. Touch panel monitors are located at the podium and witness stand in all courtrooms. You can use your finger to tap or write on the monitor, and the result will be displayed on all monitors in the courtroom. Multiple options for lines and colors are available in the menu for each monitor." Because witnesses can accidentally touch the screen and create unintended annotations, you should know how to remove those annotations.

Attorney tables

"You will find monitors as well as input connections at the attorney tables. Depending on the courtroom, each well contains a connection for a laptop."

Jury box

"The jury box contains monitors to allow jurors easy viewing of displayed items."

In addition to website descriptions of the equipment and explanations of how to operate it, the U.S. District Court, Western Washington Division offers training sessions.[21]

Checklist—Overview:
Visuals and Today's Technology

Five Reasons to Use Electronic Visuals

1. Your audience (judge, jury, mediator, arbitrator) is accustomed to it and expects electronic visuals;
2. Audience members will be composed of many visual learners;
3. Your audience will retain more information if you present it visually;
4. Visuals can be more powerful than words; and
5. A visual can cause your audience to reach a consensus, rather than each member having an individual mental picture.

Four Purposes Served by Visuals

1. **Narrative** visuals can bring your case story alive;
2. **Argument** visuals can help the jury understand your arguments and be persuaded by them;

---

21. http://www.wawd.uscourts.gov/attorneys/trial-support/courtroom-technology-training.

3. **Educational** visuals can help the jury comprehend complicated and technical testimony; and
4. **Concession** visuals can be used by a cross-examiner to gain concessions or impeach a witness.

Designing Demonstrative Evidence

❑ Ask yourself: "Is the demonstrative evidence **credible?**"
❑ Ask yourself: "Is the demonstrative evidence **interesting?** Will it engage the viewer?"
❑ Ask yourself: "Does the demonstrative evidence make the information **easily understood** by the audience?"
❑ Ask yourself: "Does the demonstrative evidence **simplify the information,** which may be complex or voluminous in nature?"
❑ Ask yourself: "Do I have the necessary **competence** to create this demonstrative evidence or should it be developed by someone else—a professional graphics designer?"

Preparation

❑ Know how to operate the hardware and software and practice using it.
❑ Have the, proper, up-to-date hardware and software for the courtroom or pretrial venue.
❑ Become proficient with linear software, such as PowerPoint, that is ideal for opening statement, closing argument and presentations.
❑ Become proficient with nonlinear software, such as Sanction, that is effective for direct and cross-examination.
❑ Gather the case visuals and store and organize them in a software program, such as Sanction or TrialDirector.
❑ Scout the courtroom to determine what hardware, if any, will be needed and plan accordingly.
❑ Practice with the hardware in the courtroom and retest it daily before the trial day begins.
❑ Plan for the unexpected and have a backup plan, such as using a document camera.

Chapter 3

Opening Statement Visuals

A. Storytelling
   1. Compelling Story
   2. Storytelling Techniques
      a. Structure of the Opening Statement
      b. Storytelling Strategies and Techniques
      c. Illustrations of Storytelling with Visuals
B. Permission to Show Visuals in Opening
C. Computer Software
D. Catalog of Effective Visuals for Opening
   1. Timeline
   2. Scene Diagram
   3. Photographs
   4. Aerial Photographs
   5. Map
   6. Drawing
   7. Documents
E. Displaying Visuals During Opening Statement

"Visual storytelling of one kind or another has been around since cavemen were carving on walls."

Frank Darabont, film director,
Shawshank Redemption

A. Storytelling

Opening statement is a trial lawyer's first and best opportunity to communicate the theme and narrative of the case to the jury. The best way to bring the story alive and persuasively convey it is through visuals. In this chapter, we examine: the proper software for developing a computer slideshow for opening statement; what to include in the slideshow; types of visuals that can persuasively convey the story of your case; and how to deliver a persuasive opening using those trial visuals. Practical and ethical issues, such as whether disclosure of your slideshow to the opposing party is required, are examined. Additionally, this chapter explores the use of effective traditional visuals in opening statement, such as a timeline on a board.

Before we get into what software and visuals work best for opening statement, it is essential we examine what makes a winning opening statement. Like a screenwriter, you want to craft a compelling story. Opening statement motivates jurors to adopt strong views of what most likely happen in the case, which then serves as a filter for the evidence and testimony they hear over the course of the trial. First impressions are very important because jurors form initial beliefs about the case, and research shows that these kind of beliefs fuel confirmation bias, which occurs when jurors focus on evidence and testimony that supports what they believe about the case while discounting, rejecting, or simply ignoring evidence and testimony that runs contrary to what they believe. Therefore, let's begin by describing what makes a compelling story and how to effectively deliver that story.

I.   Compelling Story

A compelling story is made up of at least three elements. The first element of a compelling story is that it is about a human being. Jurors, like all of us, care about people. The Enron trial involving the prosecution of Kenneth Lay, former Enron chairman and CEO, and Jeffrey Skilling, the company's former CEO and COO, for securities and wire fraud serves as a good example of how to construct a compelling story about people. The prosecutors could have presented a case about only corporate corruption and accounting fraud. But the prosecutors focused on the harm done to the shareholders. In her four-hour closing argument, Enron Task Force prosecutor Kathryn Ruemmler stated her theme: "There's nothing wrong with getting rich. But what you can't do is you can't get rich by deceiving. You can't get rich by cheating."[1] She argued that the victims of the deceits of defendants Lay and Skilling were the Enron shareholders—real people "deprived of the truth." Even if the party is a corporation, a human story can be told.

In this respect, a compelling story is really about an antagonist. The headline verdicts are more often the result of anger and frustration with the defendant than sympathy for the plaintiff. Consequently, a compelling plaintiff story is about a defendant that needs to be sent a message.

Conversely, a compelling defense narrative often casts the plaintiff as an antagonist. For example, the plaintiff is someone who refuses to accept accountability for

---

1. Flood, Mary "Lay, Skilling 'cheated,' Enron prosecutor says," Houston Chronicle, May 15, 2006.

his or her own decisions and instead has filed a lawsuit in an effort shift the blame to someone else.

The second element of a persuasive story is that it reflects the values that the jurors share with the values revealed in the story. Fundamentally, we all make decisions that we can feel good about because they endorse something in which we believe. Therefore, it is important for any case theory to represent a value that jurors can endorse. In other words, litigators should ask themselves what value jurors are endorsing if they find in favor of their client.

Human values are those that American psychologist Abraham Maslow identified in what is now referred to as "Maslow's pyramid of values," including these needs: psychological, safety, belonging, esteem, and self-actualization. Every good trial story is about deprivation or the threat of deprivation of one or more of these needs, and the story told in opening should highlight the deprivation of those needs.

For example, in a criminal assault case, the prosecution's story is about either a deprivation of or a threat to personal safety, and if the defense were self-defense, the defense story could likewise be about deprivation of or threat to personal safety. In essence, most trial stories are about good versus evil. The evil either deprived or threatened to deprive the good of something of value. However, you want to avoid referring to your opposing party as evil because that is likely to entitle you to retry the case when a mistrial is granted, or your favorable verdict is overturned on appeal.

Third, a persuasive story needs a theme that encapsulates what the case is about and runs like a thread through the story, holding it all together. An ideal theme expresses a core idea, preferably a moral imperative. It should be a word or short phrase or a line of poetry that is memorable and familiar to the jurors. Samples of themes are: "Trust and betrayal of trust," "Having a scapegoat," "Power and control," "Broken promises," or "Ignoring the consequences."

With an awareness of the elements of a compelling story in mind, during pretrial preparation you can gather and create visuals that will breathe life into your case narrative. For example, visuals showing how your client was deprived of one or more of the crucial human needs are what you want.

As an illustration of how visuals can be used to tell a human story involving human values, consider the visuals shown during opening statements in the trial of Michael Peterson, in Durham, North Carolina. The trial was made famous when it became the subject of a documentary movie series (eight episodes of 45 minutes each) entitled *The Staircase*.[2] Michael Peterson was charged with having murdered his wife, Kathleen Peterson, and the prosecution's case theory was that he

---

2. https://www.netflix.com/title/80233441.

bludgeoned her to death in a staircase. The defense case theory was that Kathleen fell down the stairs and that Michael Peterson was wrongfully accused.

The protagonist in prosecutor James Hardin's opening statement story was Kathleen Peterson, and the prosecutor introduced her to the jury by parading a photograph of her in front of the jury as he said, "This is how she would have looked prior to December 9th of 2001 if you had seen her at home or possibly at work. You can see from this photograph—you can feel from this photograph—that she is a genteel, warm person."[3]

The prosecutor then showed the jury two more photographs of Kathleen that were in sharp contrast to the first. As he displayed a photograph of her laying in a puddle of blood, he said, "Now on December 9th of 2001 at 2:48 when the EMS personnel first arrived they see her in a completely different way, lying at the bottom of her steps just as you see her in this photograph." And he showed another photograph of her, saying, "Later that day, after her body is removed from the home to the medical examiner's office this is one of the first photographs of her lying on a steel gurney in the medical examiner office after they've shaved her head so they can determine where the wounds are."

The District Attorney, in a no-tech way, with only photographs, told a story that humanized Kathleen Peterson and showed how she was deprived of a human need that the jurors' share—her personal safety—her life.

In his opening statement, defense counsel David Rudolf described the death of Kathleen Peterson as a "tragic accident." Rudolf said that it was an accident that "left Michael Peterson a wealthy man but a poor man in a manner very important to him. It left him without a soul mate. Kathleen and Michael connected in a way that few people who are really, really lucky in life have a chance to connect. And they built a family—the two of them built a family out of the strands of their prior families." At this juncture, defense counsel pointed to a screen that showed Michael and Kathleen Peterson with their children, whom Rudolf named one after another. At the conclusion of his opening statement, he had a picture projected on the screen of Kathleen sitting on Michael Peterson's lap, which he asserted was not posed. Rudolf said, "What you see there is the happiness that she felt with him and that he felt with her. Everyone who really knew that relationship—everyone who knew them, knew that they loved each other. Everyone who knew them knows that Michael Peterson had nothing to do with the death of Kathleen Peterson."

Defense counsel, with the family photograph and the photograph of Michael and Kathleen Peterson, told a human story about the couple and one about Michael Peterson's loss—being deprived of the psychological need for love and a relationship, a loss to which the jurors could relate.

---

3. *Ibid.*

Regarding the third element of a compelling story—a theme for the story—both lawyers articulated one in their opening statements. The prosecutor began his opening statement by telling the jury that the case was about "pretense and appearances," referring to the appearance that Kathleen fell down the stairs, when the prosecution's theory was that she was beaten to death, and, as the evidence showed, while it appeared that the couple had a monogamous relationship, Michael Peterson had gay liaisons during the marriage. Defense counsel's themes were that it was a "tragic accident" and that Michael and Kathleen Peterson were "soul mates."

Similarly, consider the example of a civil case against a railroad company involving a plaintiff who was struck by a train. This is a difficult case for the defense because the fact is that the train struck the plaintiff and caused him significant injuries. However, the defense may adopt a simple theme of poor decision-making by the plaintiff and argue that the plaintiff made a series of poor decisions that resulted in this outcome. This defense theory might be effective because patterns are powerful. Patterns of conduct tell us about the conduct of an individual. Therefore, the defense might develop a graphic such as the following:

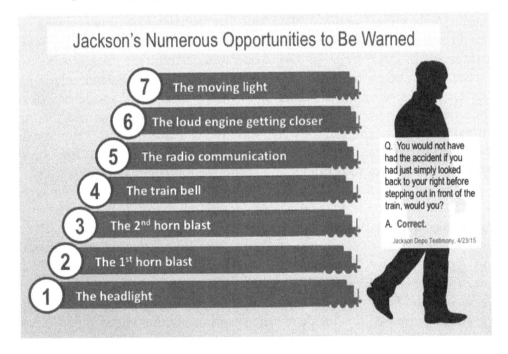

This graphic visually reinforces the pattern of poor decision-making and shows that the plaintiff had numerous opportunities piling up and warning him to avoid the unfortunate outcome that he eventually suffered.

In sum, a five-star opening statement is like a good movie; it has a theme and tells a story about shared values and a human being who has been or is threatened to be harmed by an antagonist.

2.   Storytelling Techniques

a.   Structure of the Opening Statement

A compelling opening statement, again as in a good movie, grabs the jurors' attention and holds it during the body of the opening with a story about a human being—the protagonist who has been or is threatened to be deprived of something important. In essence the body is a description of events embodied in a good-versus-evil story. Finally, once the story has been told, it is followed by a commanding conclusion. Yes, a beginning, middle, and an end. At each stage in the opening, visuals play a critical role.

An introduction to the opening that seizes the jury's attention can be a clear statement of the case theme. Another effective attention-getter is to start with a description of a dramatic scene from your story that will leave a stunning image in the minds of the jurors. If that scene can be shown with a picture that tells the story, all the better.

For example, in 2018, in Seattle, Washington, dozens of plaintiffs went to trial against a local tourism company called Ride The Ducks, which provides duck boat tours throughout the city. The Ride The Ducks case[4] involved an incident where the front axle of Duck #6 broke during operation, causing the duck boat to cross over the centerline on the Aurora bridge into oncoming traffic and collide with a bus carrying international students. Four people were killed and several dozen were seriously injured. The plaintiffs sued the duck boat operators and the duck boat manufacturers. The plaintiffs also sued the city and the state, arguing that they should have placed a barrier between the north and southbound lanes on the highway, which they argued would have prevented this collision.

There was obviously a significant dispute over whether the barriers would have prevented the incident. There was competing expert testimony, but the visuals were powerful. These duck boats were redesigned boats from World War II with front hulls designed to jump over reefs or other barriers that might exist as the boats approached shore. This was obvious from simply looking at the duck boats. Thus, from the defense perspective, a powerful image in opening statement is one that showed the front of the duck boat next to the barrier that plaintiffs alleged would have prevented this incident. Anyone who saw this image would quickly conclude that the barrier would not have stopped the duck boat. The wheels on the duck boat were taller than the barrier. In fact, the imagery suggests the duck boat would have simply jumped over the barrier. The experts disagreed on this subject, but the imagery was powerful.

---

4. *Dinh v. Ride The Ducks Int'l*, No. 16-2-19995-0 SEA. The Ride The Ducks case is the basis for the performance assignments in Chapter 16.

It is important to avoid upstaging your storytelling with preamble, such as: "Your Honor (nodding toward the judge), counsel (turning and bowing your head toward opposing counsel), good morning ladies and gentlemen, in a moment I will address you in what we call an opening statement. As her Honor the Judge has told you 'Counsel's statements are not evidence.' What I'm about to say to you is not evidence...." The jurors have been through jury selection, and therefore, they know who you are, and they have heard from the judge that what you say in opening is not evidence. With these rambling initial remarks all you would be doing is undercutting your presentation. You are not starting with an attention-getter that immediately draws them in and tells them you have something interesting to say. Instead, you are starting with something that probably bores the jurors and reinforces their beliefs that this trial is going to be a painful few days or weeks.

After at most a brief "Good morning" or "Good afternoon" greeting, get on with your grabber. The old learning adage regarding primacy and recency applies. Jurors will remember the first thing you say and the last thing you say in an opening statement. Build an attention step into your opening. A statement of the case theme can be powerful grabber. Alternatively, a quote or a visual that is part of the evidence that will be presented at trial can seize the jurors' attention.

The body of your opening statement introduces the players and tells your compelling story. A chronological narrative is easiest to follow. Another effective approach is to use a flashback: begin with a vivid scene that precedes the main story. Avoid the witness-by-witness approach ("Mr. Weak will testify that... Then, Ms. Little will testify that...") because it does not lend itself to a smooth flowing narrative that is easy for the jury to follow. In a civil case, you will want to discuss damages.

Your conclusion, above all, should be an emphatic statement. In it, you can replay your theme and state the verdict that you, as plaintiff's counsel, will ask the jury to render at the conclusion of the case.

b.   Storytelling Strategies and Techniques

One important visual the jurors will observe during your opening statement is you. It is critical that you project sincerity—an authentic belief in your cause. Prominent trial lawyer David Boies expressed the significance of sincerity in this way:

> And what a jury is looking for is authenticity, someone who is real. A jury is like 12 people who you lock in a boat in a storm and they have no idea how to get out. And then two people come along and one says I know the way, and the other says no, I know the way. If you understand

your job is to be the one that the 12 jurors follow, then you can win your case.[5]

Projecting sincerity begins and ends with your sincere belief in your case and yourself. Studies have shown that a speaker only communicates a small percentage of the message with words; 55 percent of the message comes from body language, particularly movements of small muscles around the eyes that show emotion; 38 percent comes from tone of voice; and only 7 percent is conveyed by the words.[6] In fact, anyone in any kind of relationship knows that *how* you say something is so much more important than what you actually say. If you lack sincerity, your body behavior will betray you, and research has shown that receivers will tend not to believe what you say.[7] Your physical appearance is also a trial visual, and if you wear something distracting (such as ostentatious apparel, jewelry, and the like) or if there is something distracting about your appearance (tattoos, piercings, facial hair, and so on), the jurors may consider it and talk about it. They have been cautioned to not talk about the case until they enter into deliberations, leaving your appearance fair game.

A critical storytelling technique is to tell it from a particular viewpoint because this will make the story engaging. Visuals are valuable trial aids in presenting the opening from a certain viewpoint. Your opening statement could be told from the viewpoint with attending visuals. For example, Karen Koehler, the plaintiff's lawyer in the Ride The Ducks case,[8] adopted the role of the driver of Duck #6 at one point during her opening statement. The driver of Duck #6 wore a yacht captain's hat and served as tour guide, pointing out and bantering about sites along the route. Koehler donned the captain's hat and duck whistle and described what happened from the driver's perspective.

Another way to tell the case story is from the viewpoint of an onlooker, like a Greek chorus. In Greek plays, the chorus was a group of performers who spoke in a collective voice describing the dramatic action. When counsel delivers the opening from this vantage point and shifts tense from the past to present tense, it can have the effect of putting the jury in the moment, watching and hearing the story unfold.

---

5. David Boies, *Lawdragon*, 198 (2012).

6. Albert Mehrabian, UCLA Professor of Psychology; visit his website for more information: http://www.kaaj.com/psych/.

7. Allen and Barbara Pease, *The Definitive Book of Body Language* 27 (Bantam 2004).

8. *Dinh v. Ride The Ducks Int'l*, No. 16-2-19995-0 SEA.

c. *Illustrations of Storytelling with Visuals*

Prosecutor David Walgren's opening statement in the trial of *California v. Conrad Robert Murray* for committing manslaughter by causing the death of Michael Jackson illustrates how to begin an opening statement with an attention-getter and then tell a human story with visuals. Walgren started with his case theme, and then he told a human story about Michael Jackson and how Dr. Murray took his life.[9]

Walgren began his opening as follows:

> Good morning. Ladies and gentlemen, the evidence in this case will show that Michael Jackson literally put his life in the hands of Conrad Murray. The evidence in this case will show that Michael Jackson trusted his life to the medical skills of Conrad Murray. The evidence will further show that misplaced trust had far too high a price to pay. That misplaced trust in the hands of Conrad Murray cost Michael Jackson his life.
>
> On June 25, 2009, Michael Jackson was pronounced dead.

At this juncture, the prosecutor asked that the courtroom lights be dimmed so that he could start his computer slideshow. Appearing on the screen was a picture of Michael Jackson lying on his bed. It was time to talk about the protagonist and who he was. Walgren presented the story from the viewpoint of an onlooker, letting the jury see Jackson as he was when he died. And, Walgren continued:

> He was just 50 years old. He died alone in his bed, on the second floor of his Holmby Hills mansion. In the house at the time were the defendant Conrad Murray and Michael's three young children and some of the staff that help run the home.

Next, the prosecutor turned to the cause of Michael Jackson's death and in order to tell this story he shifted to the viewpoint of the coroner's office. The next slide that the jury saw is one showing the toxicological findings.

Walgren continued his opening statement as follows:

> Because there was no immediate obvious cause of death, the coroner's office took a very active role in the investigation. Not only performing the autopsy but doing detailed toxicology analysis to determine what caused the death of Michael Jackson at 50 years of age.
>
> And what we learn through the investigation is that Propofol, Lidocaine, Diazepam, a metabolite of Diazepam called Nordiazepam, Lorazepam, and Midazolam all testing positive in the heart blood, all administered by Conrad Murray on June 25, 2009.

---

9. Visit this website for the full opening statement transcript including the computer slides: http://muzikfactorytwo.blogspot.com/2011/10/prosecutor-opening-statement-full.html.

Further investigation by the Coroner's office, through statements, through interviews, through the autopsy, through the toxicology findings led to the conclusion that the levels of Propofol found in Mr. Jackson's body were at levels similar to general anesthesia when someone is put under for a surgical procedure....

Following these findings, the Coroner's office concluded that this was in fact a homicide, that Michael Jackson's death was a homicide and more specifically the Coroner's office concluded that the cause of death was acute Propofol intoxication coupled with the contributory factor of additional benzodiazepines in his system.

At this point, the same slide showing Michael Jackson on a gurney appears on the screen for the jury to see but this time a caption with the coroner's finding that it was a homicide is on the picture.[10]

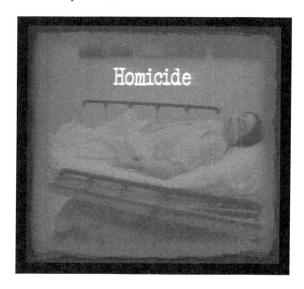

This image is so impactful because the jurors were seeing one of the most famous people of their generation dead on a gurney. It's a jarring image that naturally leads one to believe this should not have happened.

The opening statement went on for some length after this beginning as the prosecutor told the full story of Conrad Murray's grossly negligent treatment of Michael Jackson with the accompanying computer slideshow, and then the prosecutor concluded the good-versus-evil story as follows:

Conrad Murray's actions, Conrad Murray's omissions to act directly caused the death of Michael Jackson. And at the close of this case, after

---

10. *Ibid.*

you observed all the facts in this case, the People will ask you, in no uncertain terms to return with a verdict of guilty for the crime charged involuntary manslaughter, premised on the gross negligence of Conrad Murray.

B. Permission to Show Visuals in Opening

During opening statement, you are entitled to inform the jury of what you intend to prove during the trial. If you have a good faith belief that the evidence will come into evidence at trial, you can show it in opening statement. This proposition is true for visuals contained in a computer slideshow. For example, in *Arizona v. Sucharew*, the Arizona Court of Appeals affirmed the trial court's ruling that permitted the showing of a PowerPoint presentation during opening statement. The court held:

> Prior to trial, the prosecutor informed the court and defense counsel that he intended to use a "PowerPoint" presentation during his opening statement. The presentation consisted of a series of thirty slides including: 1) a title page; 2) photographs of the vehicles and accident scene with superimposed descriptions and headings; 3) a map; 4) a listing of defendant's blood alcohol content and physical symptoms; and 5) a list of the elements of the two charged offenses. Defendant objected on the grounds that he had not received advance notice of the presentation, that Rule 19 of the Rules of Criminal Procedure is silent on the use of such material, and that the presentation referenced evidence that might not be introduced at trial. After reviewing the proposed presentation, the trial court overruled the objection noting that the presentation was not prejudicial or inflammatory and that it did not include anything that was not likely to be admitted at trial.[11]

People v. Green[12] is another appellate decision providing legal authority supporting the use of visuals in opening statement. In *Green*, the California Supreme Court held that the trial court had the discretion to allow the display of photographs and the showing of a movie in opening statement when those visuals would later be admitted in evidence.

While you may be within your rights to display a visual in opening and to have the court rule in your favor if the visual is challenged, nevertheless, you do not want your opening statement interrupted by opposing counsel's objection and a

---

11. *Arizona v. Sucharew*, 66 P.3d 59, 63 (Ariz. 2003).

12. *People v. Green*, 302 P.2d 307 (Cal. 1956).

potential hearing on the use of a visual in opening. Therefore, it is good practice to settle any disputes about whether you can display your visuals before commencing your opening. You need not provide opposing counsel with your full computer slideshow, but rather just tell opposing counsel what exhibits and visuals you intend to show in opening. On the other hand, you could provide either printouts or a USB flash drive containing the computer slideshow.

After you have disclosed the visuals and exhibits that you intend to show, you can seek a stipulation from opposing counsel that you may use them in your opening. Then, if counsel agrees, inform the court of the stipulation and gain the court's imprimatur. If opposing counsel refuses to stipulate, make a motion in limine to pre-admit the challenged exhibit or visual. You may need to call witnesses at a hearing outside the jury's presence to establish the foundation for the admission of the exhibit or visual. If the court rules adversely, you can remove your visual from the slideshow or not display the exhibit during your opening.

Some judges require the parties to exchange any demonstratives or exhibits that they intend to use in opening in advance, whether that be the evening before or a few days before. It is important to check with your judge to see if the court has such requirements. Some judges might not allow any visuals if they have not been exchanged with the other side. In some instances, judges will not allow any visuals if the two sides cannot agree on what will be allowed in opening. Therefore, it is important to have a Plan B in case the judge does not allow you to use the visuals that you planned on using.

In the off chance that your judge is disinclined to permit visuals being shown in opening statement because that "just isn't done," you will need to persuade the court to permit their display by providing the ample legal authority supporting the use of trial visuals in opening.[13]

C. Computer Software

We recommend that you utilize linear software such as PowerPoint or Keynote for opening statement and closing argument because the slideshows can be relatively easily created, practiced, and presented. These are also easy to exchange with the other side if the court requires it, such as with opening statement as previously noted. See Chapter 2 for a discussion of the differences between linear and nonlinear software such as TrialDirector, Sanction, OnCue, and ExhibitView.

---

13. *State v. Smith*, 130 P.3d 554 (Haw. 2006) (PowerPoint in opening and closing); *State v. Caenen*, 19 P.3d 142 (Kan. 2001); Paul Zwier & Thomas C. Galligan, *Technology and Opening Statements: A Guide to the Virtual Trial of the Twenty-First Century*, 67 Tenn. L. Rev. 523 (2000).

D. Catalog of Effective Visuals for Opening Statement

In this section, we discuss and provide examples of common trial visuals that are particularly suited to opening statement. Clearly, we do not cover all types of the potential visuals for opening statement because they are limited only by counsel's imagination and the evidence in the case. The common denominator for these visuals is that they are narrative visuals, which are particularly effective in aiding counsel in tell the story of the case.

1. Timeline

A timeline is a beneficial visual aid for opening statement because it assists the jury in following the chronology of your narrative while it simultaneously highlights the significant events in the story. When the case involves numerous events, a timeline can be indispensable. TimeMap by LexisNexis[14] is a software tool that enables you to easily create a professionally designed timeline by entering the facts of your case into the software. Below is an example of such a timeline created with TimeMap.

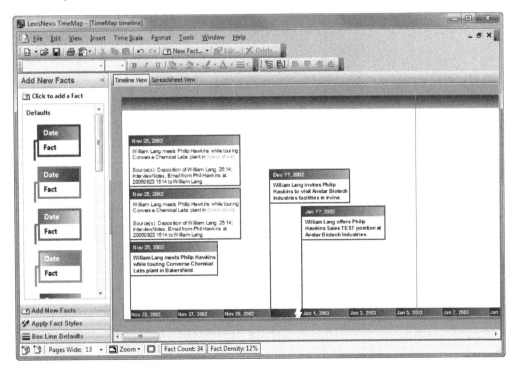

---

14. http://www.lexisnexis.com/.

However, you may choose instead to build your timeline in PowerPoint or Adobe Illustrator, which provide color and other thematic design elements. For example, the timeline below created by Sound Jury Consulting[15] uses color (from left to right—yellow, orange, and red blocks in the center) to emphasize the evolving nature of the individual's questionable conduct. The first yellow block states, "Minor negotiates Magnolia contract." The second block, which is orange, reads: "Minor refers Wilson customers to Magnolia." And the last red block has text stating, "Minor solicits, accepts and services Wilson's customers." The color slide is found in the Appendix, which is on this book's website http://www.fastcase.com/visuallitigation. The slide is animated so that it can be gradually unfolded for the viewer. If that were not the case, the slide would contain too much information for the viewer to adsorb and would be a distraction rather than an enhancement of the storytelling. Always beware of information overflow with timelines and, for that matter, with any visual.

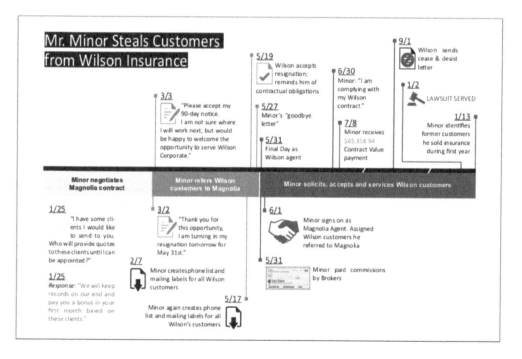

2. Scene Diagram

A trial lawyer can use a diagram of the scene where the main event in the case took place to show and explain that event for the fact finder. A scene diagram may portray the interior of a building, house, room, or a vehicle. Or the diagram could

---

15. http://www.soundjuryconsulting.com.

be an exterior diagram of a building or it could be a diagram of a street, an intersection, and so on. An opening statement without a scene diagram is likely to result in the jurors conjuring up what they think the lawyer is describing, and that mental picture may be inaccurate.

The diagram can be drawn to scale in CAD, a computer-aided software that can be used to design scale diagrams, but this software is expensive. Microsoft's Visio is another software program for diagramming, and it is less expensive. In Chapter 9, we extensively discuss SmartDraw, which is a software program for designing scene diagrams.

On the other hand, a professional designer, such as SKE Forensic Consultants Inc. that created the following illustration of a collision, could be employed to design it.

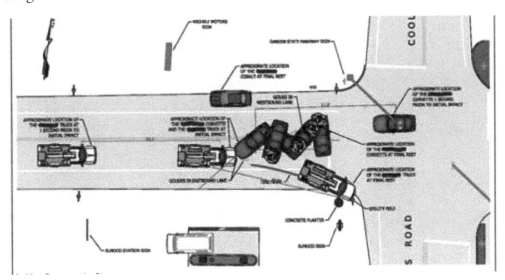

3. Photographs

As the prosecution and defense opening statements in the Michael Peterson trial (pages 35-37) illustrate, photographs of the protagonist in the lawyer's opening can be crucial visuals for opening statement. They can show the jurors the people who are central to the story, thereby causing the jurors to relate to them as human beings.

Typical other photographs that are displayed in opening include those depicting: the scene of the event; injuries; an autopsy; aerial views of the scene; and a product that is the focus of the litigation.

Each photograph, diagram, video, and so on may be displayed individually or they may be grouped together. For example, you could combine a map, shape, and video within one PowerPoint slide to create a dramatic effect. In the following example, the opening statement is told with the aid of a PowerPoint slide. A map has been pasted onto a PowerPoint slide. According to a witness, the shape on the map designates the approximate area taken in by a surveillance camera. Finally, the video from the surveillance camera is superimposed on the map. Consequently, the jury can watch the video in the context of the scene of the crime.

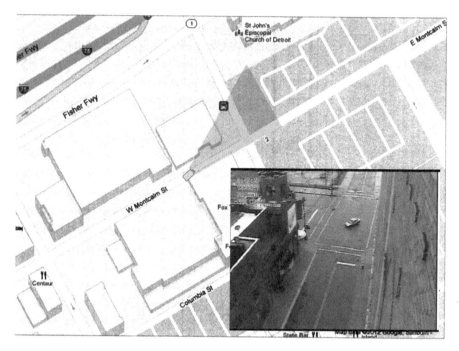

4.   Aerial Photographs

Aerial photographs can help the jurors understand the scene of the event that is at the core of the case. In criminal cases, law enforcement agencies can take the photographs from their aircraft. For example, the New Jersey State Police took the following aerial photograph that was later displayed in a murder trial. A witness at that trial drew the following sketch to show where guns stolen from a murder scene in Michigan were dumped near Atlantic City, New Jersey.

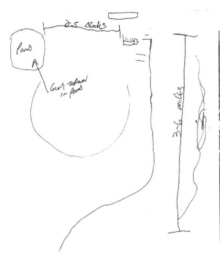

Vendors[16] are available to take original aerial photographs and/or provide stock aerial photographs. An example of a company that can be employed to produce aerial photos and videos is Sky Solutions NW.[17] Further, both law enforcement and civil litigators are using drones to get aerial photographs and video footage.

Alternatively, you might consider Google Earth, which allows you to obtain actual images of the intersection or scene, such as this Google Earth aerial view of the Seattle, Washington, Space Needle:

---

16. https://www.sky-pix.com/index.

17. https://www.skysolutionsnw.com.

5.   Map

The case may call for you to explain a route of travel in opening statement, and you could do so with a map, such as the one below produced by Google Maps.[18] Because Google Maps and Google Earth change over time, it is important that the witness who authenticates it can testify that the map is a fair and accurate map of how it looked on the day in question.

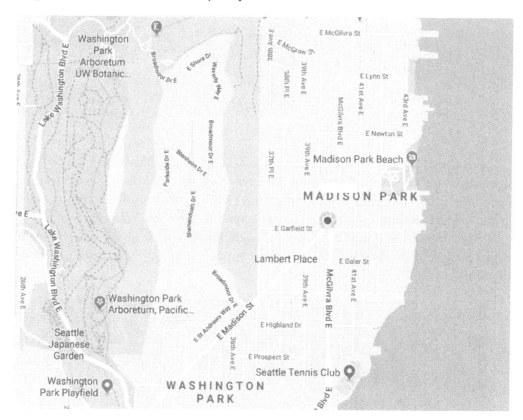

6.   Drawing

A drawing can help the jurors understand difficult information. For example, in a personal injury case, an anatomical drawing can be employed to explain an

---

18. https://www.google.com/maps.

injury to a plaintiff. The drawing below was a visual introduced by the plaintiffs in the Ride The Ducks case.[19]

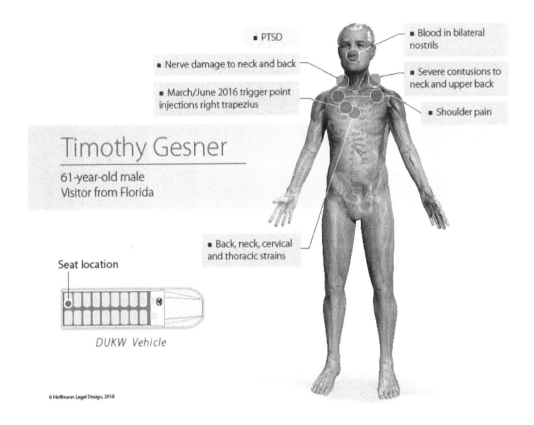

7. Documents

Documents can be the focus of the lawsuit. They could be bank records, phone records, a contract, a transcript, and so on. With PowerPoint tools, or similar software, sections of the document can be highlighted and graphics such as arrows can be used to direct the jurors' attention to a particular place in the document.

---

19. *Dinh et al. v. Ride The Duck Int'l et al.*, No. 16-2-19995-0 SEA.

The example below from the Ride The Ducks case[20] is a Service Bulletin document coupled together with a graphic showing the wheels and axle.

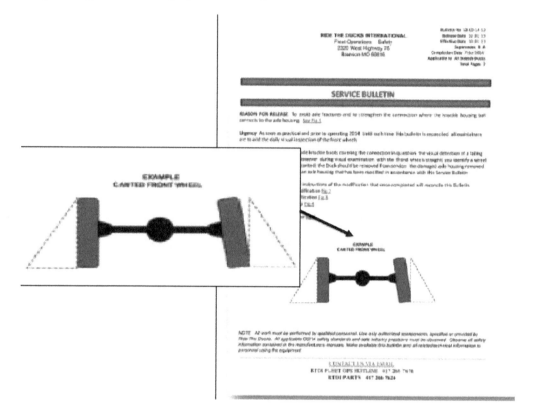

E.　Displaying Visuals During Opening Statement

You may decide to display the trial visuals in a high-tech, low-tech, or no-tech fashion. It's up to you how to present visuals unless you are in a federal or another court that requires that you only present electronic evidence. The prosecutor in his opening in the Michael Peterson case decided it would be most effective to show photographs of Kathleen Peterson in a no-tech way, parading them in front of the jury. On the other hand, defense counsel in the Peterson case and the prosecutor in his opening statement in the trial of Dr. Conrad Murray chose the high-tech method, projecting photographs on a screen with a computer slideshow. To accomplish this, all that was needed was to copy the photographs into the slideshow.

What are alternatives ways of displaying visuals that could have been selected? Counsel could place a visual on a document camera, and thus have the image projected on a screen. Another way to display a visual, such as a photograph, scene

---

20. *Ibid.*

diagram, and so on, is have it enlarged and adhered to a board and, at trial, place the enlargement on an easel for the jury to see. An advantage of an enlarged image on an easel is that it can be placed in a prominent position in front of the jury.

Checklist—Opening Statement Visuals

Storytelling

❏ Opening statement in a jury trial should be designed to persuasively tell the story of the case.

❏ A compelling opening-statement story has at least these three elements:
1. The story is about a human being.
2. The story reflects the values shared by the jurors.
3. The story is summarized in a case theme—a core idea, preferably a brief statement of a moral imperative.

Storytelling Techniques

❏ Counsel should use visuals to bring the narrative of the case alive.

❏ An effective structure for an opening statement follows this pattern:
✓ It begins with an attention-getting statement.
✓ The body of the opening statement tells a compelling story in narrative form.
✓ The opening concludes with an emphatic statement, such as a reprise of the theme.

❏ Counsel should not only be sincere during the storytelling but also visually and orally project that sincerity.

❏ Counsel's appearance should be suitable to the courtroom setting; counsel should avoid wearing something that will distract the jurors' attention from the story.

Permission to Show Visuals

❏ During opening statement, you should only display visuals that you have a good-faith belief will be introduced into evidence during the trial.

❏ If there is a likely dispute over whether you can display a visual during opening, settle the matter pretrial in order to avoid having your opening interrupted by an objection to the visual.

Catalog of Visuals for Opening Statement

❑ Consider employing these visuals, among others, to enhance the opening statement:

- ✓ A chart showing the elements to be proved
- ✓ A timeline
- ✓ A scene diagram
- ✓ Photographs
- ✓ Aerial photographs
- ✓ Map
- ✓ Photographs
- ✓ A drawing
- ✓ Documents

Chapter 4

Closing Argument Visuals

"Don't tell me the moon is shining; show me the glint of light on broken glass."

> Anton Checkhov, Russian playwright and
> short story writer

A. Argument Visuals

In closing argument, counsel is given great leeway in terms of the visuals that can be shown because at this stage counsel is allowed to employ the tools of argument, such as analogies, that can be transformed into an image that can be shown to the jurors. For instance, counsel could show the jurors a picture of a scales of justice slightly tilted more to one side than another as an explanation of the meaning of "preponderance of evidence" (provided the law as expressed in the court's instructions supported such an argument). If argument visuals were offered at earlier stages of trial, they would be inadmissible because they are indeed argumentative.

Closing argument is your opportunity to persuade the jurors that when they apply the law as expressed in the judge's jury instructions to the evidence, they should render a verdict in your client's favor. Therefore, the closing should be consist of these components: (1) an identification of the issue or issues that the jury need to decide; (2) a clear explanation of the law; (3) a summary of the evidence; (4) a description of how the jurors should apply the law to that evidence; and (5) a refutation of the other side's arguments. Argument visuals can assist counsel in tackling each of these components of a successful summation. Additionally, argument visuals can help jurors show how they should deliberate on the issues in the case, which can fundamentally shape the outcome of the case. After all, a verdict is a product of what the jurors choose to talk about when in deliberation. Later in this chapter, we will explore types of visuals that can be persuasive for each of these five elements.

The visuals that can play a role in this final stage of trial are comprised of the exhibits that have been admitted into evidence along with electronic and conventional argument visuals.

B. The Value of Argument Visuals

Visuals can be the source of a powerful argument. Return now to the Michael Peterson trial, which we discussed in Chapter 3. In his summation prosecutor James Hardin sought to drive home his theory that the number of blows to Kathleen's head could not have come from an accidental fall and that Michael Peterson had bludgeoned his wife to death. In his closing argument, he showed the jurors an individual autopsy photograph of Ms. Peterson and other photos mounted on a board on an easel. By displaying the same photographs in his summation that he had used in opening statement, Hardin provided symmetry to the state's presentation of the case.

First, holding a single photograph for the jury to see, Harden argued:

Ladies and gentlemen, this is the first photograph of Kathleen Peterson on the autopsy table. It shows the graphic brutal nature of this killing. Ladies and gentlemen, a picture is truly worth a thousand words. This photograph at least speaks a thousand words. (Gesturing toward another photograph of her on the board) This picture speaks a thousand words.

Look at all of these photographs that show that this woman was beaten. I was thinking if a picture is worth a thousand words and if we only knew what Kathleen Peterson knew at the time of her death. And I started looking around the scene and that stairwell and asked myself, "What if those walls could talk? What would they say?" Ladies and gentlemen, these walls are talking. Kathleen Peterson is talking to us through the blood on these walls. She is screaming at us for truth and for justice. It's all in these photographs. Ladies and gentlemen, they have said that Kathleen Peterson died of an accident. We say she died of murder. And we ask that you return that verdict.

Visuals can also be used to emphasize key points in your case during closing argument. You may recall the opening-statement visual in Chapter 3 (see page 37) that showed a series of poor decisions made by the plaintiff who was suing the railroad company. That visual could also be used in closing argument because it emphasizes the number of opportunities the plaintiff had to be warned of the oncoming train. By organizing them into a single graphic, it helps jurors appreciate just how careless the plaintiff was at the time of the incident. It might be too easy for jurors to lose sight of just how many opportunities he had to be warned if they were just going by memory of the testimony and listening to counsel list them off in closing argument. However, seeing them is different, especially when seeing them stacked as they were in that graphic. Visually, it creates a sense of his negligent acts stacking up. The goal of that visual was to cause jurors to conclude that any additional warning would not have changed plaintiff's conduct because so many warnings had previously failed to do so.

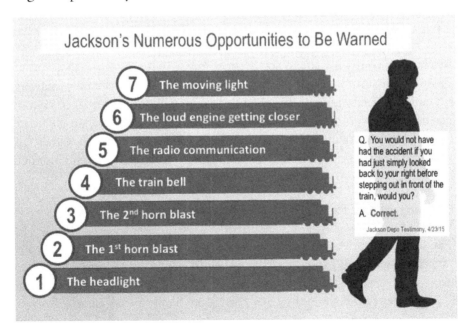

C. Computer Software

When you address the jury either in opening statement or closing argument, we recommend that you use either PowerPoint or Keynote, which we previously discussed at pages 22-23. These are our preferred software programs because they are linear in nature, and, therefore, they lend themselves to situations where you are addressing the jury in what is like a lecture. If you are like some attorneys who do not like the linear nature of PowerPoint or Keynote, meaning that the user must move from slide 1 to slide 2, and then to slide 3, you can avail yourself of software that allows the user to pull up visuals in a nonlinear way. This software is discussed in Chapter 12. Also, in Chapter 12 we discuss how to use PowerPoint's hyperlink feature to permit a nonlinear progression while using PowerPoint (see pages 268-70).

D. Catalog of Persuasive Visuals for Closing Argument

Visuals that are well suited to closing argument will help counsel communicate his or her argument during summation. Although we cannot possibly examine all potential visuals, this section provides many that can be either modified to fit your case or serve as springboards to assist you in creating appropriate visuals. One thing all these visuals have in common is that they are designed to persuade the jurors to apply the law expressed in the jury instructions to the evidence in a way that will compel them to return a verdict in your client's favor.

1. The Law

As counsel, you will want to select those key jury instructions that you intend to discuss in your summation. You want to explain the law to the jury in a way that they can easily understand, and this means that you will oftentimes need to translate jury instructions which often seem designed more to obfuscate than elucidate. To accomplish your goal of clearly explaining the law, you can develop visuals worded in plain English or that offer visual explanations of the language in the instructions.

a. Callouts of Key Portions of Jury Instructions

The law can be overwhelming for jurors. Even the simple cases may involve the judge reading a half-hour's worth of jury instructions at the end of the case. The jurors receive a copy of the jury instructions for their deliberations, but there is no guarantee they will refer to them, or even more likely, appreciate the importance of key language in jury instructions. This is why it is so helpful to use callouts of the jury instructions in closing argument with highlights of key language that you want the jurors to give extra attention to, as in the example below.

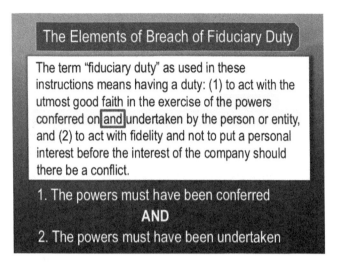

As with the preceding example, in addition to the callout of the jury instruction and the highlighting of key language, the visual may also include an explanation of what these elements mean.

b.   Elements Chart

It is normal for the court's jury instructions, which are mostly drawn from pattern jury instructions drafted by judges and lawyers, to include an instruction that lays out the elements of a crime in a criminal case, the elements of a cause of action in a civil case, or the elements of a defense in both criminal and civil cases.

For example, in a civil case, a pattern jury instruction involving a cause of action alleging that the city or county violated the plaintiff's civil rights by failing to train or supervise reads as follows:

> On [his] [her] claim for failure to [train] [supervise] [instruct], (name of plaintiff) has the burden of proving each of the following propositions:
>
> 1.   That the [city] [county] did not adequately [train] [supervise] [instruct] its [officers] [employees] to properly handle the usual and recurring situations with which they must deal;
> 2.   That in failing to adequately [train] [supervise] [instruct], the [city] [county] was deliberately indifferent to the risk that an [untrained]

[inadequately trained] [officer] [employee] would cause a deprivation of a right protected by the Constitution or laws of the United States;

3. That the failure to provide proper [training] [supervision] [instruction] directly [subjected (name of plaintiff)] [caused (name of plaintiff) to be subjected] to the deprivation of rights protected by the Constitution or laws of the United States; and

4. That (name of defendant's) [actions] [failure to act] [proximately] caused injury or damage to (name of plaintiff).

If you find from your consideration of all the evidence that each of these propositions has been proved, your verdict should be for (name of plaintiff) [on this claim]. On the other hand, if any of these propositions has not been proved, your verdict should be for (name of defendant) [on this claim].[1]

A typical jury instruction on the elements of first-degree murder provides:

To convict the defendant of the crime of murder in the first degree, each of the following elements of the crime must be proved beyond a reasonable doubt:

1. That on or about (date), the defendant acted with intent to cause the death of (name of person);
2. That the intent to cause the death was premeditated;
3. That (name of decedent) died as a result of the defendant's acts; and
4. That any of these acts occurred in the State of Washington.

If you find from the evidence that each of these elements has been proved beyond a reasonable doubt, then it will be your duty to return a verdict of guilty.

On the other hand, if after weighing all of the evidence you have a reasonable doubt as to any one of these elements, then it will be your duty to return a verdict of not guilty.[2]

The wording of these instruction is too cumbersome to include in a visual aid that can accompany counsel's explanation of what the jury must find to establish guilt in the criminal case or liability in the civil case. Therefore, the elements should be shortened to a list of words or phrases. As long as counsel does not misstate the law, the visual can paraphrase or abbreviate.

---

1. Wash. Pattern Jury Instr. Civ. WPI 341.02 (6th ed.).

2. 11 Wash. Prac., Pattern Jury Instr. Crim. WPIC 26.02 (4th ed).

Element charts come in various forms. It could show a checklist of elements or bullets. The following is an example of a chart listing and summarizing the elements of first-degree murder:

```
┌──────────────────────────────────────────────┐
│         Murder in the First Degree             │
│                                                │
│  1.  On or about August 20, 20XX, Steven Lord  │
│      acted with intent to cause the death of   │
│      Nancy Squires                             │
│  2.  Intent was premeditated                   │
│  3.  Died as a result of Lord's acts           │
│  4.  Any act in Casper County                  │
└──────────────────────────────────────────────┘
```

With this elements chart, the prosecutor or defense counsel in the first-degree murder trial could discuss what the state must prove to convict the defendant of first-degree murder and what the state must prove to establish beyond a reasonable doubt that the defendant premeditated the killing.

c. *Explain Legal Concepts*

Visuals can be utilized to explain legal concepts. For instance, in a first-degree murder case, the prosecutor could explain the jury instruction on premeditation in terms that the jury can understand. The jury instruction defining premeditation states:

> Premeditated means thought over beforehand. When a person, after any deliberation, forms an intent to take human life, the killing may follow immediately after the formation of the settled purpose and it will still be premeditated. Premeditation must involve more than a moment in point of time. The law requires some time, however long or short, in which a design to kill is deliberately formed.[3]

Assume that first-degree murder also required that the defendant's act be "willful" and "deliberate," and the instructions state that "willful," as used in this instruction, means intentional and the word "deliberate" means formed or arrived at or determined upon as a result of careful thought and weighing of considerations for and against the proposed course of action.

---

3. 11 Wash. Prac., Pattern Jury Instr. Crim. WPIC 26.01.01 (4th ed.).

With the following visual, the terms "deliberation" and "premeditation" are explained in everyday terms that a jury can clearly understand.

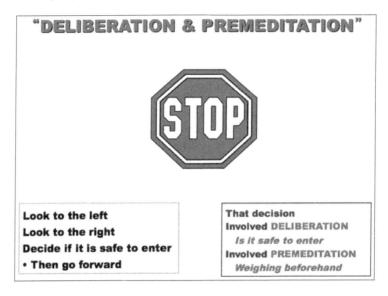

d.   Burden of Proof

At some point during closing arguments, attorneys on both sides will discuss the plaintiff's burden of proof: a preponderance of evidence in a civil case or beyond a reasonable doubt in a criminal case. To make sure the jury understands the burden counsel may enlist an argument visual to explain the burden. However, as was previously mentioned, while it is permissible to paraphrase, abbreviate, and illustrate the law, counsel cannot misstate the law. Courts are particularly sensitive to this when it comes to a visual to characterizing the meaning of a burden as stated in the jury instructions. For example, the California Appellate Court in *People v. Katzenberger* reviewed the prosecutor's closing argument when she used a PowerPoint slideshow of the Statute of Liberty cut into puzzle pieces to argue what a reasonable doubt meant. In the slideshow, six pieces came serially onto the screen and at the end two pieces were missing. The appellate court held:

> The prosecutor's use of an easily recognizable iconic image along with the suggestion of a quantitative measure of reasonable doubt combined to convey an impression of a lesser standard of proof than the constitutionally required standard of proof beyond a reasonable doubt. The prosecutor committed misconduct.[4]

---

4. *People v. Katzenberger*, 178 Cal. App. 4th 1260, 1268 (2009).

The appellate court decided that although the prosecutor committed misconduct, the conduct was not so prejudicial that it required reversal.

You may also want to use visuals to emphasize that the party has the burden of proving each element of a civil cause of action. For example, one common concern for defendants in civil cases is that, if jurors conclude the defendant was negligent, they will simply assume that negligence was the cause of the harm to the plaintiff. Such an assumption is erroneous because the plaintiff has the burden to prove each element independently. Visuals, such as the one below, can help remind jurors that each element of a cause of action (visually represented here by the steps with barricades) must be proven by a preponderance of evidence.

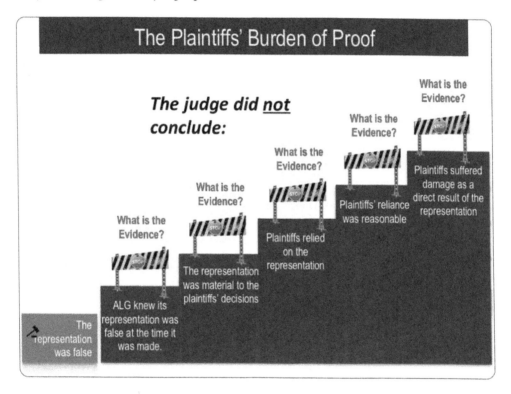

2.   The Evidence

a.   List-of-Evidence Chart

A list-of-evidence chart is exactly that—it lists the evidence that the proponent of the chart claims was proved at trial. A list-of-evidence chart can be persuasive, particularly if the evidence is presented in a creative way on the chart. With a Power-Point presentation, the items on the evidence list can be revealed and checked off by a click of the remote. As the evidence item is revealed, counsel can discuss it.

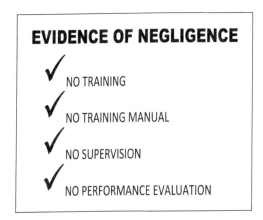

Alternatively, you may use visuals to emphasize the evidence that was not presented at trial. For example, a common graphic used by attorneys focuses on what one would expect to see if the claims were true, and highlights that those things are not present in the case at hand. Consider the following example:

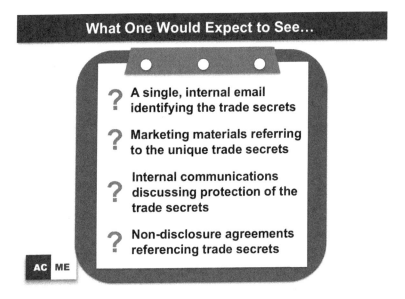

The foregoing example is from a trade secret theft case. The defendant in that case, who was accused of stealing trade secrets, argued that what the plaintiff was focused on was not an actual trade secret. Over the course of the trial, the defendant made numerous efforts to show that the plaintiff never treated it as a trade secret. In closing, the defendant used this simple chart to make the point to the jurors that the plaintiff did not do any of the things that one would expect someone with trade secrets to do.

b.   *Summary-of-Evidence Chart*

State v. Lord,[5] a Washington Supreme Court decision, involved the use of an 8-by-4-foot chart that summarized the state's trace evidence in a death penalty case. Across the top of the chart was a list of evidence that could be connected to the defendant, such as a blue U-Haul blanket, and down the right side was a list of trace evidence items found at the crime scene and on the victim's body. When the trace evidence matched that of evidence connected to the defendant that match was represented by a dot on the chart. Thus, the prosecutor could point to the number of trace evidence items linked to the defendant.

---

5. *State v. Lord*, 822 P.2d 177 (1992).

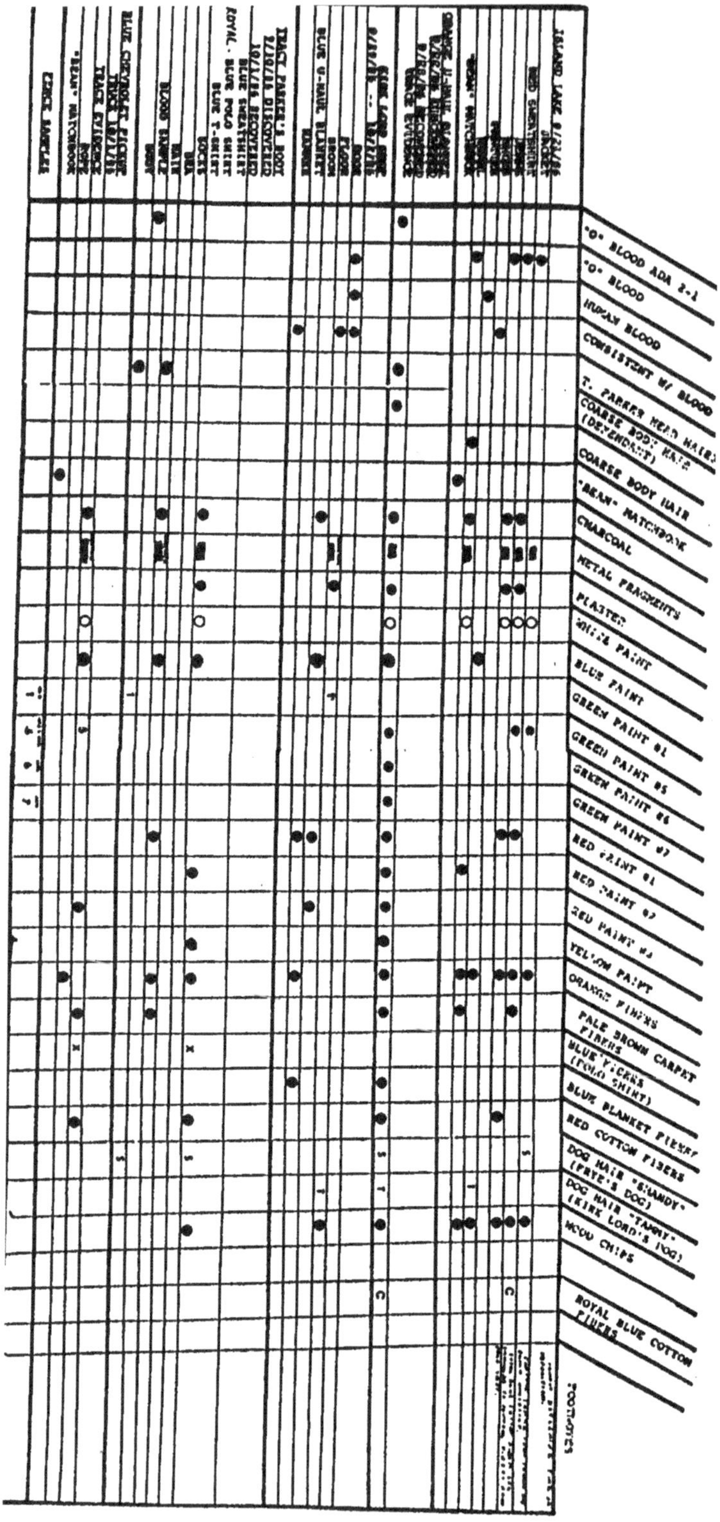
"O" BLOOD ADA 2-1
"O" BLOOD
HUMAN BLOOD
CONSISTENT W/ BLOOD
COARSE BODY HAIR
"BEAN" MATCHBOOK
CHARCOAL
METAL FRAGMENTS
BLUE PAINT
GREEN PAINT #1
GREEN PAINT #5
GREEN PAINT #6
GREEN PAINT #7
RED PAINT #1
YELLOW PAINT
PALE BROWN CARPET FIBERS
BLUE BLANKET FIBERS
RED COTTON FIBERS
WOOD CHIPS
ROYAL BLUE COTTON FIBERS
BLUE U-HAUL BLANKET
BLUE T-SHIRT
SOCKS
FOOTNOTES

The court discussed summary-of-evidence charts at length in *Lord*, including not only its admissibility but also whether it should be sent to the jury room. The court held:

> The use of demonstrative or illustrative evidence is to be favored and the trial court is given wide latitude in determining whether or not to admit demonstrative evidence.... Illustrative evidence is appropriate to aid the trier of fact in understanding other evidence, where the trier of fact is aware of the limits on the accuracy of the evidence.... A summary "can help the jury organize and evaluate evidence which is factually complex and fragmentally revealed in the testimony of a multitude of witnesses throughout the trial."...
>
> Because a summary chart submitted by the prosecution can be a very persuasive and powerful tool, the court must make certain that the summary is based upon, and fairly represents, competent evidence already before the jury.... This does not mean, however, that there can be no controversy as to the evidence presented. Rather, the chart must be a substantially accurate summary of evidence properly admitted. The jury is then free to judge the worth and weight of the evidence summarized in the chart.... (citations omitted)[6]

The *Lord* case also provides a useful discussion of the distinction between an exhibit admitted for illustrative purposes and one offered as substantive evidence as follows:

> When a summary or chart is used for illustrative purposes only and the jurors are instructed that the summary is not evidence, the summary should not go to the jury room. It should be utilized only during the initial presentation of testimony and/or in final argument by counsel. However, if the chart is sent with the jury, reversal is required only if, upon a review of the entire record, the court determines that the defendant was prejudiced. (citations omitted)[7]

The court in *Lord* went on to point out in the footnote that the trace evidence charts offered for illustrative purposes were in contrast to "a summary of complicated or voluminous writings, recordings or photographs admitted pursuant to FRE 1006 is substantive evidence that does go to the jury room...." (citation omitted)[8]

---

6. *Id.* at 193.

7. *Id.* at 194.

8. *Id.* at 242.

c.   *Credibility-of-Witness Chart*

Invariably, in closing argument, you will discuss the credibility of your witnesses and your opponent's witnesses. The jury instructions provide the criteria against which the jury is to evaluate a witness's believability. An effective chart that can serve as a visual aid as you discuss the credibility of witnesses should include a list of the criteria from the jury instructions on the right side of the chart. On the left side, you should list your witnesses and the other side's witnesses. Using this chart, you can discuss each witness one at a time and argue that your witnesses were credible under the jury instruction guidelines and your opponent's witnesses were not believable.

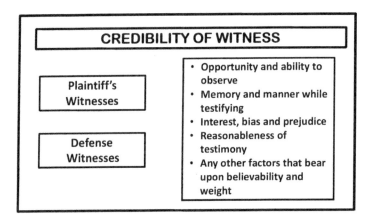

d.   *Comparison and Contrast Charts*

In closing, one party in a lending case may want to highlight how its service compares to others in the industry, perhaps to show it goes above and beyond the standard of care in the industry. The following example is a simple comparison chart focused on the information disclosed by different lenders in the industry.

Mortgage Industry Disclosure Patterns

	Dedicated page on borrowing responsibility	Terms of loan and rates clearly disclosed	Pre-pay penalties clearly outlined	Resale notifications provided to customers	Debt management education
NMPG	✓	✓	✓	✓	✓
HSBC	✗	✗	✗	✗	✗
PNC	✗	✗	✗	✗	✓
SunTrust	✗	✓	✗	✗	✗
Capital One	✗	✗	✗	✗	✓
US bank	✗	✓	✗	✗	✓
Wells Fargo	✗	✗	✗	✗	✗
Bank of America	✗	✓	✗	✗	✗

The top row identifies the party in the case and shows that it discloses information on each of these five key categories. This graphic also uses colors to emphasize good and bad practices. Green, which is typically seen as a positive color, is used for the check marks to indicate positive steps taken by the lenders. Red, which is a negative color, is used for the "X's" to indicate a failure on the part of that lender.

Visuals might also be used in closing to contrast evidence in a case. For example, the following is a simple visual used to contrast the testimony to the facts in the case.

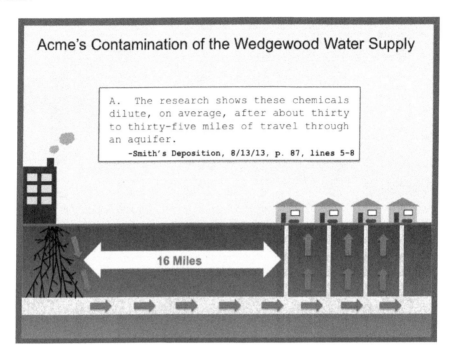

In this visual, the testimony is contrasted to the distance to the plaintiff's home to show that they are clearly within the range of hazardous contamination.

e.   Distractions

You may also use visuals to emphasize evidence that the opposing party relies upon in argument to distract from the actual legal claims in the case. This may be general, as in the example below, or more specific to the actual evidence in question in the case.

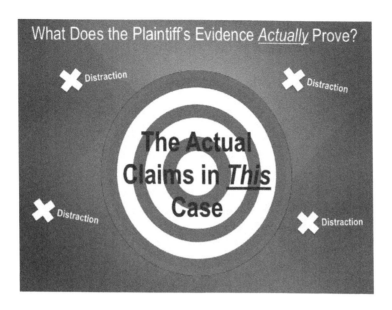

f.   Timelines

As is true for opening statement, you may use a timeline in closing argument to organize key dates and even make arguments via the organization of those key dates. For example, the following timeline was used in a case involving a child who ran out of a playground and was struck by a car. This timeline shows all the warnings that the nanny had that the child might try to run away. This was important because the nanny had testified that it was totally unexpected that the child would run out of the park and into the street. This graphic helps demonstrate that the child had already established a pattern of running out of the park, and the nanny should have known that she needed to watch the child more closely.

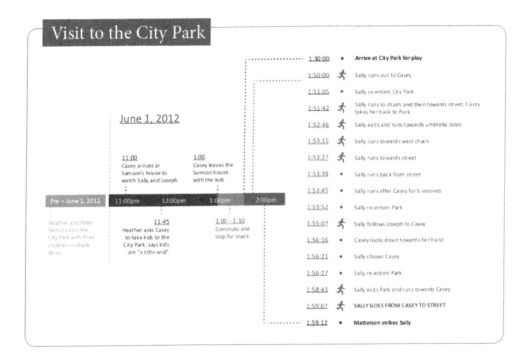

Timelines do not even have to be time specific. For example, they might only show the chronological progression of key stages. Following is an example of an argument visual of one of these stages-timelines.

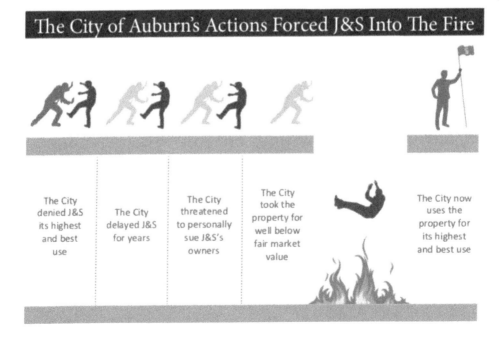

g. *Damages Chart*

You may use a visual to explain damages in a manner that a jury can understand. There are endless ways in which damages visuals can be designed, and here is one example:

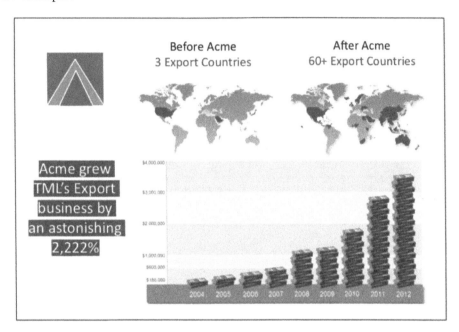

In this case, Acme, the plaintiff, used a visual to show how much it had helped the defendant grow its business in order to establish how much it was owed in compensation.

A defendant might use visuals to argue that the plaintiff is asking for too much in damages, as in the example below. In the example below, the defendant argued that the plaintiff had already received a financial benefit from the defendant's challenged conduct, at hand and, consequently, if the jury were to award the amount requested by the plaintiff, it would essentially mean that the plaintiff was double-dipping.

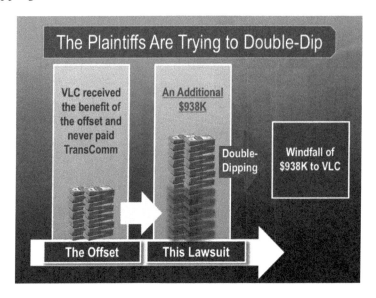

h.   The Exhibits

We saved for last the last-but-most-certainly-not-the-least-important visuals: the exhibits admitted at trial. They are critical to an effective closing argument. The Brenton Butler murder trial illustrates how important exhibits can be as argument visuals. An Oscar-winning documentary *Murder on a Sunday Morning* was made about the Butler trial by the same director, Jean-Xavier de Lestrade, who directed *The Staircase.*[9]

In the Brenton Butler murder trial, one photograph of the 15-year-old defendant was a key piece of evidence for the defense. Defense counsel Patrick McGuinness argued that the detectives had coerced Butler into confessing, as the defendant had testified to during the trial. To support his argument that the police had beaten his client, McGuinness held up a photograph of Butler taken right after he had been taken into police custody. The photograph showed Butler's swollen cheek where counsel argued the detective had hit him with his fist.

---

9. http://www.criminaldefenseattorneyjacksonville.com/news/the-brenton-butler-case-wrongfully-accused.

Butler was acquitted.

E.   Displaying Visuals During Closing Argument

As we stress in Chapter 3 on using visuals during opening statement, you have a variety of ways to display a visual when you address the jury in closing argument. You can put it in a computer slideshow. Place the visual on the document camera so it will be shown on a screen in the courtroom. Parade the exhibit before the jury. Place the visual, such as a chart, diagram, or enlarged photograph, on an easel in front of the jurors. It is up to you to decide what the most effective method for showing it will be.

Checklist—Closing Argument Visuals

Argument Visuals

❑ Ask yourself, "How can I transform my argument, such as an analogy or a statement of the law, into a powerful visual?"
❑ Argument visuals can help counsel:
    1. Clearly explain the law;
    2. Summarize the evidence supporting the argument;
    3. Explain how the jurors should apply the law to the facts;
    4. Identify the central issue for the jury to decide; and
    5. Refute the opponents' arguments.
❑ Argument visuals can help jurors show how they should deliberate on the issues in the case.

❑ Don't overload the jury with too much information on an argument visual. If you think it may be too much, make it into two or more slides.

Catalog of Visuals for Summation

❑ Consider these visuals, among others, to communicate your arguments:
- ✓ Callouts of key portions of jury instructions
- ✓ An elements chart
- ✓ A visual to explain a legal concept
- ✓ A burden of proof visual
- ✓ A visual highlighting irrelevant evidence
- ✓ A credibility-of-witness chart
- ✓ Compare and contrast chart
- ✓ Timeline
- ✓ Damages chart
- ✓ The exhibits

Chapter 5

Direct Examination Visuals

A. The Value of Visuals for Direct Examination
B. Pretrial Preparation
   1. Preparing the Visuals
      a. Gathering the Visuals
      b. Creating the Visuals
   2. Preparing Yourself
      a. Visit the Scene
      b. Know Each Visual
      c. Prepare the Direct Examination
      d. Marshal Your Exhibits
   3. Preparing the Witness
C. Conclusive Proof
D. Displaying the Visual
   1. Controlling the Jury's Focus
   2. Tell, Show, and Tell Again
      a. Tell
      b. Show and Tell Again
      c. Example of Tell, Show, and Tell
   3. Marking the Visual
E. Expert Witness
   1. The Teacher
   2. The Visual Aids
      a. Computer Slideshow
      b. Animation
      c. Medical Illustration
      d. 3D Laser Scanner Images
F. Catalog of Videos for the Case in Chief
   1. Day-in-the-Life Video
   2. Courtroom Demonstration
   3. The Courtroom

"Turn your life-care planner's testimony into a show-and-tell. That keeps her testimony interesting and makes each of the care needs more concrete to the jury. Have her bring things to court—the leg braces, the special dinnerware, the Velcro fasteners for clothing, the urinary catheter, etc. Pass these things around the jury. Rub them with alcohol pads beforehand so that jurors will be comfortable handling them and the room will smell like a clinic.

"Have your life-care planner teach the jury what these things are for—especially how they are used. Have her show videos of the kinds of therapy in her plan. Show a video tour of the rehabilitation center."

David Ball, *David Ball on Damages* 3, 190 (2013)

A. The Value of Visuals for Direct Examination

Visuals serve at least seven purposes when they are utilized during direct examination of a witness. First, visuals, such as photographs of the plaintiff's injuries in a personal injury case, can bring direct examinations alive for the jury. Second, visuals, for instance, those photographs of the plaintiff's injuries, constitute proof of the claim that the plaintiff was injured. Third, because generally jurors have short attention spans, visuals can be generously interspersed throughout a witness's testimony to gain and maintain the jurors' attention. Fourth, visuals, such as a summary chart in a case involving a mass of documents, can simplify the information, helping jurors understand the complex case. Fifth, if the jurors only heard testimony, they would retain only a small portion of what was said; visuals help the jurors retain the testimony elicited on direct examination. Sixth, with visuals counsel can repeat the substance of portions of the witness's direct testimony. For example, the lawyer can first have the witness describe how the collision occurred at the intersection, and, then, with the aid of a diagram of the intersection, have the witness reiterate what happened while showing the jury what happened. Seventh, the visuals can help the witness educate jurors about complex subjects, particularly when displayed during an expert witness's testimony.

In addition to discussing how visuals serve these seven goals, this chapter describes both a pretrial process for gathering visuals and how to prepare a witness for the employment of exhibits during direct examination. Specific visuals that enhance witness testimony are discussed in this chapter, including photographs, scene diagrams, video depositions, courtroom demonstrations, summary charts, animations, and simulations. Finally, trial techniques for getting the most out of these visuals are also provided.

B. Pretrial Preparation

I. Preparing the Visuals

a. Gathering the Visuals

Pretrial preparation entails not only gathering those potential visuals for trial that already exist but also creating new visuals. When you enter the case, certain visuals will already exist, and you will have ready access to them. There is the real evidence, which is the actual evidence in the case. For instance, in a criminal case, the police will investigate and take items, such as a weapon, into evidence, take pictures, collect documents, and generate other real evidence, such as fingerprints from the suspect that can be compared to latent prints collected at the crime scene. If you were a prosecutor, and the case were presented to your office, much of the visual evidence will have already been collected and placed in the police evidence room or in the police department's file. Defense counsel's investigator in a criminal case may perform much the same functions that law enforcement did in gathering and creating real evidence visuals.

In a civil case, the clients may have real evidence visuals that they can provide to their attorneys, and the lawyers' investigators can also gather and create evidence. In a civil case, the lawyer also may need to advise the client to preserve evidence, such as electronically stored information, and may need to notify the opposing party to preserve evidence, thereby preventing spoliation.

Demonstrative evidence can be developed to demonstrate or illustrate a fact or condition that is to be proved in the case. Demonstrative evidence is a visual aid that a witness can use to help the jury understand the case. Demonstrative evidence includes summary charts, animations, anatomical drawings, computer slideshows, scene diagrams, and timelines.

Usually in criminal cases, law enforcement agencies and/or crime laboratories will prepare the demonstrative evidence for the prosecution. That task for criminal defense or for the plaintiff or defense in civil cases will be done by either an attorney or an attorney-employed communication litigation organization.

What are you looking for in visuals? A good trial visual serves one or more of the seven purposes of a visual. You are looking for a visual that will help prove your case; it should support one or more elements of your legal theory. For example, in a breach of contract case, plaintiff's counsel would want a visual that shows the jury the clause in the contract that was breached.

b.   Creating the Visuals

In addition to proving your case, you are looking for a way to display the visual in a way that it grabs the jurors' attention and helps them retain the information, two other purposes of an effective visual. To accomplish this in the breach of contract case, plaintiff's counsel could have the contract provision enlarged and displayed on a board that could be placed on an easel in front of the jury. Or, using Sanction software, counsel could project the contract page onto a screen and then highlight the pertinent clause.

Counsel is not confined to the visuals that exist when counsel accepts the case; counsel can and should create visuals. The only restrictions are counsel's imagination and the rules of evidence. For instance, in an automobile tort case, counsel could have a diagram of the intersection prepared, and a witness to the car crash could use that diagram to explain how it occurred. Or, in a bank fraud case, counsel could have a summary chart prepared that shows the banking transactions, and at trial counsel could have an expert utilize the chart when explaining what took place to the jury.

2.   Preparing Yourself

a.   Visit the Scene

Go to the scene. You will never fully understand your case if you fail to go to the place where the incident took place. You may have looked at photographs of the scene, but you need to see it in three dimensions. For example, in a homicide case involving a shooting in an apartment, only by going to the apartment could the prosecutor and defense counsel get a clear understanding of the layout of the apartment and the exact location of the defendant and the victim at the time of the shooting. Counsel also can observe the distances between places in the apartment and look at significant places and items in the apartment from the vantage points of witnesses.

In sum, a scene visit gives counsel a clear understanding of the scene that counsel can rely upon in conducting a direct examination that recreates the scene so that the jurors also will have a clear picture of the place, the people in it, and what took place.

Four guidelines exist for when and how to visit the scene. First, go to the scene as soon as you can because the scene can change. For example, in the apartment homicide case, the furniture might be moved. Second, it is preferable to go to a scene at the same time of day that the event took place because lighting and sounds can be different at different times of day, and those factors can affect a witness's perception of what took place. Third, if possible, have someone familiar with the location and what happened accompany you to the scene. That person can explain what happened, where it happened, and what the sound and lighting conditions were at the time of the incident. Fourth, take a camera because you may see something that you want to photograph or video.

When you visit the scene, consider whether you might want to move for a jury-scene visit. For example, in the Michael Peterson murder trial (see pages 35-37), the jury visited the Peterson mansion and viewed the staircase where the prosecution alleged Kathleen Peterson was beaten to death but where the defense claimed she fell down the stairs. Did the plush surroundings of the Peterson's mansion affect the jurors?

b.   Know Each Visual

Counsel is responsible for every exhibit and visual offered at trial. While counsel may have a visual prepared by a communication's consulting firm, counsel is still responsible for every aspect of it. Inspect each exhibit and visual closely. Notable and sometimes embarrassing things have resulted when counsel did not carefully inspect an exhibit. For instance, in a convenience store robbery case, the defendant's clothing at the time of the arrest was admitted into evidence without defense counsel's objection, and the jury, during deliberation, found a receipt from the store that was robbed in the pocket of the defendant's jeans despite his denial at trial that he had ever been in the store before. Counsel should also be sure to proof any graphics that are created for trial for simple issues, such as misspellings. It can be easy to miss spelling errors, and that can be embarrassing at trial.

c.   Prepare the Direct Examination

We recommend that you write out the predicate questions that you will ask at trial to lay the evidentiary foundations for exhibits you plan to introduce that might draw an objection. In Chapter 8 "Evidentiary Predicates," we provide templates of predicate questions for exhibits and visuals, and you may be able to modify those predicate questions for your situation.

In preparation for trial, decide how you can best present your visuals to the jury. Will you do it in a computer slideshow? An enlarged image on a board sitting on an easel before the jury? Parade it in front of the jury? Put the exhibit, such as a photograph, on the document camera and have the witness stand by the document camera and point at and discuss and annotate the image projected on the screen? Or, just have the witness hold the exhibit up so the jury can see it? Ask yourself: What method is most effective given the nature of the exhibit?

d. Marshal Your Exhibits

Once you have identified all the exhibits and visuals that you intend to use during your direct examinations, it is time to marshal them so that they are ready for trial. You will want to create an exhibits list of the visuals and other exhibits that you will use with each witness you intend to call at trial.

Trial judges generally have preferences as to how they want the exhibits labeled and presented. The trial judge is likely to want a list of the exhibits that counsel intend to offer in trial. The following is a trial judge's directives to counsel concerning how she wishes the exhibits marked, exchanged, and presented at trial. These directives were posted on the judge's website. If your court does not prescribe the way it wants exhibits listed, marked, and handled, you might consider adopting part of this judge's model approach.

Trial Exhibits

Pursuant to Local Rule 16 (5) the Joint Statement of Evidence is to be filed, not later then 5 court days before the scheduled trial date. As a courtesy to the court clerk please deliver the Trial Exhibits (notebooks) to the Judge's Mailroom (see mailing address above) 2-3 days prior to the trial date along with two copies of the Joint Statement of Evidence. Exhibit List Template.

Counsel will present two sets of exhibits. The first (original set) will be marked by the clerk and used at trial. The second (copy) set is a courtesy copy for the judge. Do not mark directly on any exhibits as this will be done by the clerk

Exhibits should be submitted in three ring binders using numbered tabs to separate each exhibit. Notebooks should be large enough so that the exhibits are not overcrowded. Plaintiff's or petitioner's trial exhibits shall begin with the Number 1, and shall be numbered consecutively up to the last proposed exhibit. Defendant's or respondent's trial exhibits shall begin with the number which follows plaintiff's or petitioner's last proposed trial exhibit.

Depositions are not to be marked as an exhibit since they are part of the court file. Exhibits to the deposition may be marked as exhibits in evidence. Otherwise, all unattached exhibits in a deposition should be stapled or secured inside the back cover of the deposition.

Additional Exhibits presented during trial will be marked and designated by the clerk. Please provide an original for the clerk and a courtesy copy for the judge.

Once an exhibit has been marked by the clerk, it is officially in her or his custody. To withdraw an exhibit prior to the completion of trial, an attorney will need to make a motion to withdraw the exhibit (on the record) in open court.

Please contact Judge Craighead's courtroom regarding the pre-marking of all trial exhibits or any further questions.[1]

3. Preparing the Witness

The extent that you need to prepare a witness for working with visuals on direct examination obviously depends upon whether the witness has testified before, how often the witness has testified, and if the person is an experienced witness. A person who has never testified before will need extensive preparation while a veteran expert witness may not.

If the witness has not testified before, counsel should explain: the roles and functions of the players in the courtroom; the layout of the courtroom; what questions will be asked; and the exhibits and visuals about which the witness will be asked. Only by familiarizing the witness with what to expect will the witness be prepared and confident. Counsel should also consider practicing parts of the testimony in advance with the witness. Not every idea for a visual translates well to the actual execution at trial with witnesses, so practicing in advance can help counsel determine whether the visual is accomplishing the desired goal.

Never ask a witness about an exhibit or visual at trial that you have not shown and discussed with the witness prior to trial. Have the witness review every one of the witness's prior statements (deposition, declaration, and so on). Emphasize that your sole instruction to them about what to testify to is that they are to tell the truth. If the truth hurts, all the more reason to tell the truth. Once you have done that, then explain that they are to review each of their prior statements for accuracy. Tell the witness that she is not wedded to anything in the prior statement that was given, and that if the witness detects something inaccurate, you need to know what it is because only then can you deal with it at trial.

Tell the witness what you will cover in direct examination. Explain the function of evidentiary-foundation questions and run through the foundation and other questions that you will ask at trial. You should advise the witness that she does not need to memorize anything and that you may ask a question that you have not gone over in pretrial preparation, but that that will not present a problem because the witness just needs to remember to tell the truth.

Explain to the witness how you want to display the visual to the jury and what role, if any, the witness will have in doing that. If you intend to have the witness step down from the witness box, step over to the document camera, place a photograph on it, and then explain what the photograph shows and mark the exhibit, go over the process step-by-step with the witness. To accomplish this, you could sketch the courtroom and use the drawing to explain logistics. Better yet, take the

---

1. https://www.kingcounty.gov/courts/superior-court/directory/judges/craighead.aspx.

witness to a courtroom and walk the witness through what you intend to do at trial. If you intend to have the witness draw something on a flip chart in front of the jury, have the witness draw it for you while you are in your office. You don't want to discover that the witness can't draw when you are in front of the jury.

The same commandment—"Never ask a witness to identify and work with an exhibit at trial that you have not done the same with prior to trial"—applies equally to courtroom demonstrations. If you are ever tempted to extemporize with a visual, remember the defense high point in the O.J. Simpson murder trial when prosecutor Christopher Darden got the court's permission to have Simpson put on the XL gloves seized at Simpson's Rockingham house. The jury watched the demonstration as Simpson struggled to pull on the Aris Light glove over the latex glove he was wearing.[2] His counsel, Johnnie Cochran, in closing would not let the jury forget seeing it did not fit.

Did the glove from the murder scene belong to O.J. Simpson? It was an extra-large glove sold exclusively at Bloomingdales, and a credit card receipt from Bloomingdales showed that it was the type glove (one of only 300) that had been purchased by the murder victim, Nichole Brown, O.J. Simpson's ex-wife. When Simpson went to put on the glove, he was wearing latex gloves. The latex glove plus the shrinkage of the glove that had been soaked with blood explain the misfit, but the jurors did acquit.

C. Conclusive Proof

The use of visuals as conclusive proof is ageless. William Shakespeare declared the value of visuals as convincing proof. In *Othello* he wrote, "Be sure of it; give me the ocular proof."[3] In his play *Julius Caesar*, Mark Anthony enrages the crowd

---

2. https://www.youtube.com/watch?v=__reD_phfbg.

3. William Shakespeare, *Othello*, 3.3 (Othello addressing Iago).

against the conspirators who have assassinated Caesar by displaying Caesar's robe and ripping at those who betrayed him:

> If you have tears, prepare to shed them now.
> You all do know this mantle: I remember
> The first time ever Caesar put it on;
> 'Twas on a summer's evening, in his tent,
> That day he overcame the Nervii:
> Look, in this place ran Cassius' dagger through:
> See what a rent the envious Casca made:
> Through this the well-beloved Brutus stabb'd;
> And as he pluck'd his cursed steel away,
> Mark how the blood of Caesar follow'd it,
> As rushing out of doors, to be resolved
> If Brutus so unkindly knock'd, or no;
> For Brutus, as you know, was Caesar's angel:
> Judge, O you gods, how dearly Caesar loved him!
> This was the most unkindest cut of all....[4]

Two types of visuals come into play during direct examination. One type of visual is the evidence itself, such as a weapon or a defective car part. The second type is an educational visual, such as a medical illustration, that can be employed to help the jurors understand the testimony.

In your trial preparation you seek to determine what visuals—what exhibits—prove your case in a persuasive way. As discussed in Chapter 3 "Opening Statement," a persuasive story is one about a human being and the values that the jurors have in common with the characters in the story. As discussed in both Chapter 3 "Opening Statement" and Chapter 4 "Closing Argument," we used the Michael Peterson case to illustrate how counsel employed visuals in a powerful way to prove the case. The prosecutor chose a photograph of the victim's scull with blunt trauma wounds and pictures of the blood on the stairs and walls to argue that Kathleen had been bludgeoned to death—murdered—by her husband. The photographs of Kathleen's skull were introduced during the medical examiner's direct examination, and the scene photographs were introduced during the detective's direct testimony. These exhibits went to the core of the prosecution's case. While your case may not have such dramatic evidence, look for visuals that serve the purposes of proving your case and doing so in a convincing manner.

As another illustration of how visuals can prove a case in a convincing way, consider the government's case against Paul Manafort, a case that became famous because Manafort was President Donald Trump's campaign manager. Manafort was convicted of five counts of tax fraud, one count of hiding a foreign bank account,

---

4. William Shakespeare, *Julius Caesar*, Funeral Oration, 3.2.

and two counts of bank fraud. This was a paper case. Where were the visuals with any human story and human values? Prosecutors called witnesses to testify concerning Manafort's extravagant spending of funds not disclosed to the Internal Revenue Service. On direct examination, witness Maximillian Katzman testified that Manafort was one of his best customers at a Manhattan menswear boutique, spending $929,000 at the store between 2010 and 2014. He further testified that Manafort paid by wire transfers from a foreign bank that prosecutors contended were not declared to the Internal Revenue Service. Now for the visuals. On direct examination, Katzman identified labels from the store on expensive clothes that had been seized from Manafort's residence, including the ostrich coat (below) valued at $15,000.[5] The pictures of his clothes helped prosecutors prove that Manafort's profligate lifestyle was financed with money from a nondisclosed foreign bank. The photographs constituted not only support for the criminal charges but also a compelling human story of deception.

Both of the previous examples involved photographs of existing evidence: the wounds on Kathleen Peterson's head and the clothing seized from Manafort's residence. An illustration of a created visual that constitutes substantive evidence is a summary chart. Summary charts are admissible under Federal Rule of Evidence 1006, which provides:

---

5. Julia Marsh, "This is the $15K ostrich coat purchased by Paul Manafort," New York Post, Aug. 1, 2018; Photograph courtesy of the Department of Justice.

The proponent may use a summary, chart, or calculation to prove the content of voluminous writings, recordings, or photographs that cannot be conveniently examined in court. The proponent must make the originals or duplicates available for examination or copying, or both, by other parties at a reasonable time and place. And the court may order the proponent to produce them in court.

A summary chart is not just useful as a visual aid to help jurors comprehend the content of a mass of writings, recordings, or photographs; it constitutes proof of the contents of the mass. Federal Rule of Evidence 1006 is an eminently sensible rule because it declares a visual—a summary chart—to be substantive evidence. Jurors don't have to wade through a mound of paper to determine its content; they can rely on the chart as evidence of what the paper contains.

Summary charts also create opportunities for counsel. Demonstrative exhibits do not go back to the deliberation room with the jury, but summary charts do. This creates the opportunity for counsel to get demonstratives into the jury room, by laying a foundation for them during witness testimony. To do that counsel must show that the chart, summary, or calculation tends to establish "the content of voluminous writings, recordings, or photographs that cannot be conveniently examined in court." To do this, counsel needs to plan ahead and think about what the summary chart should look like. It does not necessarily have to be just a list of things the witness would testify to. Rather, for instance, it could be a chart that summarizes transactions between two banks.

D. Displaying the Visual

I. Controlling the Jury's Focus

Now, we go into more depth on techniques for effectively displaying visuals to the jury during direct examination. To properly display a visual to a jury requires a clear understanding of the roles and functions of the players in the courtroom and of the visual. First, your role as counsel is subordinate to that of the witness. The witness, not you, should be the focus of the jurors' attention because the information you want the jurors to grasp is coming from the witness, not you. When the witness holds up an exhibit for the jurors to see, you want them concentrating on the visual, not you. The witness should be speaking directly to the jurors without any interference, and that means no interference by you too. You are like a juror who is curious to know what the witness has to offer. Your role is to elicit information from the witness with questions.

How do you accomplish this one-on-one dynamic of the witness communicating directly with the jury? Position yourself in the courtroom in such a way that the jurors are not looking at you when you ask questions but instead are looking at the witness in the witness chair. The ideal position for you on direct examination is at the far end of the jury box away from the witness's chair. This arrangement results in the jurors being bound to look at the witness. If you stand in front of the jury box, the jurors will look at you when you ask a question and then at the witness when an answer comes. Then, they will look back and forth like spectators at a tennis match until some jurors decide they like looking at one of you more than the other and you can only hope it is the witness. During witness preparation tell your witness that this is what you will do so your witness is not surprised when you do it. You can explain your placement to the jurors with a statement to your witness early in your direct that you are standing back there in order that the witness speak loud enough to be heard on that far end of the jury box. Once you have made this statement to alert the jury to your position during direct examinations, there's no need to repeat it over and over with other witnesses.

This staging of the courtroom with you conducting direct from the end of the jury box away from the witness (as shown above where you can see the back of the witness who is standing before the jury and the attorney is standing at the end of the jury box) assumes that the court's protocols allow it. Some courts do not permit such a positioning and confine counsel to a less favorable place in the courtroom. In some courts, such as North Carolina trial courts, counsel must sit when conducting direct examination.

In federal court, as shown in the next photograph, counsel will be restricted to standing behind a podium. In this federal court, visuals are displayed on the jurors' monitors.

2. Tell, Show, and Tell Again

a. Tell

First, counsel has the witness talk about whatever the visual shows. For instance, if the visual were a diagram of an apartment, counsel would have the witness describe the apartment. After the witness described the interior of the apartment to the jury, counsel hands a diagram of the apartment to the witness without showing it to the jury. Next, counsel asks predicate questions to lay a foundation for admitting the diagram into evidence and offers it into evidence. Note that this is the first "tell" stage; so far, the witness has only told about the appearance of the apartment; the diagram has not yet been shown to the jury.

b. Show and Tell Again

Once the judge has ruled the diagram is admissible, it is time for the show stage when counsel displays the diagram to the jury. You decide how you want the visual displayed. It is crucial that jurors be able to easily see whatever is in the visual. If the exhibit is small, such as an 8-by-11-inch photograph, you could ask the court's permission for either you or the witness to parade it in front of the jury or to have it passed hand-to-hand among the jurors. Simply state, "Your Honor, may defense exhibit 10 be published by having jurors pass it around?"

The alternative to parading or having the exhibit passed is to enlarge the image, and if you want to do this, you have a few options. First, you could have it enlarged and adhered to a board and place the board on an easel before the jury. Second, you could have it placed on a document camera so that the image could be enlarged on the screen. Third, you could copy the image into a computer and project it onto a screen.

Now, you want the witness in a position to point out and mark on places in the visual. Again, let us assume that the visual is a diagram of an apartment. You want the jurors to concentrate on the witness and what the witness has to say about the visual. To that end, you want to position the witness and the visual center stage where both can be seen. If you have placed a letter-sized diagram of the apartment on the document camera, ask the court's permission: "Your Honor, may the witness step down and come over to the document camera?" Or, you could ask that the witness step over to the easel where you have placed the board with the scene diagram. Pictured below is the staging with the witness on the left utilizing the scene diagram. Counsel stands on the right of the easel. You do not want the witness to stand in front of the visual, blocking the jurors' view of the diagram when marking it. Therefore, if the visual on the easel is a board with a large diagram of the apartment, you would have the witness stand to the side when marking the diagram. If the person is right-handed, have the witness stand on what would be the left side of the diagram from the jury's vantage point.

After you have properly positioned the witness, it is time for the witness to "tell again." This time the witness tells the jury about what can be seen in the visual. Your who-what-where-when-why questions direct the witness to describe what can be seen in the visual. For example, counsel asks, "Where were you standing when the shot was fired?"

During this "show and tell again" portion of the witness's direct examination, you are accomplishing the sixth purpose served by visuals: repeating the substance of portions of the witness's direct testimony. This repetition helps the jury retain the information better than if it were imparted only with testimony. While it is somewhat repetitive, any objection to the testimony should be overruled because the earlier testimony did not involve showing the jurors what the witness observed.

c. *Example of Tell, Show, and Tell*

Plaintiff's counsel:

Q. Ms. Styles, as you told us at 5 p.m. on April 11 of last year you were driving north on Eastlake to an intersection with Stewart Street. Was there a stoplight at that intersection?

A. Yes.

Q. Did you have a green light?

A. Yes, I did.

Q. What did you see happen?

A. A blue Chevy truck came from the left of me on Stewart Street, going really fast and ran the red light at the intersection and crashed into this silver Honda mini SUV that was coming my direction in the other lane on Eastlake. I slammed on my brakes and swerved onto the curb. [At this point counsel through questioning has Ms. Styles describe the intersection in more detail, how far from the intersection she was when she saw the collision, what she saw after the collision, and so on.]

[After counsel has elicited testimony about what Ms. Styles saw and heard at the time of the collision and afterward, counsel hands the witness a letter-sized diagram of the intersection. The exhibit is handled so that it is not visible to the jurors but is to the witness. If the diagram were on Sanction or another computer software program, the jurors' monitors would be turned off at this point.]

Q. I'm handing you what has been marked for identification as Plaintiff's exhibit number 31. Can you tell us what is it?

A. That's a diagram of the intersection of Eastlake and Stewart Street.

Q. How do you know that intersection?

A. I've been there.

Q. Is the diagram drawn to scale?

A. I don't think it is.

Q. Even though it is not to scale, does this diagram fairly and accurately show what the intersection looked like on April 11 of last year when you were there?

A. Yes, it does.

Q. Would this diagram assist you in explaining how the collision occurred?

A. It would.

Q. Your Honor, offer State's Exhibit 31.

Judge:

Any objection?

Defense counsel:

No objection.

Judge:

The exhibit will be admitted as Plaintiff's Exhibit 31.

Plaintiff's counsel:

Your Honor, may we publish the diagram on the document camera?

Judge:

You may.

[Plaintiff's counsel places the diagram on the document camera, and the diagram's image is projected onto the screen. Instead, if the diagram were stored on a software program, at this point the diagram would appear on the monitors in front of the jury.]

Plaintiff's counsel:

Your Honor, may we have Ms. Styles step over here to the document camera so that she can work with Exhibit 31?

Judge:

She certainly can.

[Ms. Styles walks over to the document camera where she stands next to the Plaintiff's counsel.]

Plaintiff's counsel:

Q. Ms. Styles, could you use the diagram to show the jurors where your car was when you first saw the blue truck approaching the intersection?

[Plaintiff's counsel has Ms. Styles describe what she saw by having her use the diagram as a visual aid.]

3.   Marking the Visual

The more interaction that the witness has with the visual the better. When the witness works with the visual, it brings the story to life and garners the jurors' attention. You may want to have the witness annotate the visual. If you plan on doing this, it is good practice to have other copies of the visual because the court may permit the opposing party to mark on the visual, and you likely will not want another witness to mar what your witness has done.

A witness can use a visual to tell the story of the case. For example, the witness Ms. Styles could mark on a scene diagram with dashes to show her car's path of travel or put an X where she first saw the blue Chevrolet truck heading toward the intersection. It is important to bear in mind the purposes to which the visual will be put when you have a witness mark on the exhibit. You want the markings on the diagram to be simple and easy to understand because the jurors are watching as the witness marks it, and you want them to comprehend what is being shown to them.

This interaction between witness and graphic can enhance the witness's performance as well. In fact, this is a good trial strategy commonly used to make an expert, who might otherwise come across as boring, more dynamic and interesting. It is not unusual for expert witnesses to come alive and really show off a great, educator side of themselves when they stand up and start interacting with a visual.

Another purpose is served by clearly marking the exhibit. The exhibit will be going to the jury room (unless it was offered for illustrative purposes only) and the jurors can look to it with its markings during deliberations to refresh their memories as to what the witness testified to during direct examination.

Yet another purpose is served by clear markings on the visual. If the case goes up on appeal, the exhibits as well as the transcript are available for review. Only when there are understandable markings on the exhibit will the appellate court be able to interpret them.

It is good practice to picture in your mind an appellate court judge trying to understand the markings when you question and direct the witness about what markings to put on the visual. Indeed, as you direct the witness regarding how to mark the exhibit, speak as though you were talking to that appellate court judge. For example, assume that the witness is marking a scene diagram. You could ask the witness to mark where he was standing at the time of the incident as follows: "I'm handing you a blue marking pen, could you put an X where your car was at the time of the collision, and also put your initials next to the X?" This approach would enable the appellate court judge reviewing the transcript of proceedings and the exhibit to understand where the witness indicated he was standing at the time of the collision.

E.   Expert Witness

This separate section is dedicated to the utilization of visuals during direct examinations of expert witnesses because their testimony can be difficult to comprehend, and visuals can aid the expert in explaining a scientific or technical field in an understandable way for the jury. A linear slideshow, such as a PowerPoint presentation, can be an excellent visual aid for the expert when teaching the jury about the field of expertise.

I.   The Teacher

We have stressed the importance of understanding the roles and functions played by you and the witness. Although you are eliciting information from the witness, the witness should be the primary focus of the jury's attention. This is paramount principle when you call an expert witness to testify. The expert's role is that of a teacher offering testimony about scientific or otherwise technical information that can be difficult for the jurors to comprehend if not presented properly.

Ideally, you want to station the expert at the front of the class as a teacher would be, speaking directly to the student-jurors, and using visual aids to impart the information in a manner that they will understand. If you can, you want the expert standing in front of the jury with a visual. For example, the expert's position can be standing by a visual that rests on an easel, next to the document camera, or at some other location clearly visible to the jury. You can position yourself so that you are inconspicuous while the expert addresses the jury. Naturally, this arrangement will not work if the court's protocol requires that you stand at a podium or be seated when questioning a witness. Again, during the direct examination, you are asking questions of the expert like a curious juror would.

You can utilize the tell-show-and-tell-again strategy during your direct examination of the expert because that will result not only in repeating the information but also highlighting important points in the testimony. A good teacher will repeat information in order to have the adult learners retain it better. Also, you want to ask as many broad, open-ended questions as possible because they allow the expert to teach, expounding on the field of expertise, findings, and opinions. For instance, during direct examination of a DNA expert, the questioner might ask, "Doctor, what was the result of DNA testing in this case?"

2.   The Visual Aids

Any good teacher relies on visual aids to get the material across, and this holds true for an expert witness. The types of visuals the expert can use to make the material comprehensible are innumerable, and in this section, we offer several examples of such visuals. You may be able to either replicate these visuals for your trial or they may serve as springboards for you to design visuals that will fit your case.

a. Computer Slideshow

Because your expert is a teacher delivering a lecture concerning the expert's field, findings, and conclusions, consider using a PowerPoint or Keynote computer presentation. For example, the plaintiff in an automobile tort case could call a doctor who on direct examination could both verbally describe and then tell and show the plaintiff's injuries with the aid of a slideshow of a series of medical illustrations, such as the following one.

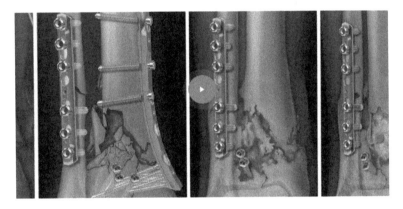

Hendricks v. State illustrates how an expert can utilize a computer slideshow to help the jury understand the expert's testimony. In *Hendricks*, the prosecution called Investigator Celestina Rossi, a blood spatter expert, who testified that a PowerPoint presentation would aid her in explaining her testimony to the jury. The first part of the slideshow showed definitions and descriptions of different blood stain patterns, and the second part consisted of photographs that Investigator Rossi took at the scene. The Texas Court of Appeals (Eastland) held:

> The trial court did not err in allowing Investigator Rossi's PowerPoint presentation. The presentation was only an aid for the jury to understand Investigator Rossi's testimony. A witness may be allowed to demonstrate before the jury so as to make her testimony more plain and clear.... Her testimony consisted of complex blood spatter analysis, and the presentation was used as a visual aid to assist the jury while she testified. Henricks had access to all the photographs used in the presentation, and they had already been entered into evidence. Further, the PowerPoint

presentation was not entered into evidence and was not available to the jury during its deliberations.[6]

Another benefit to having the expert witness use a slideshow is that it forces structure and organization into the testimony that might not otherwise be present. To create a slideshow with the expert, you and/or the expert have to think carefully about how each item is discussed, and where it makes the most sense to place it in the sequence of the questions and answers. This added organization and structure will only help jurors understand the important information your expert is trying to communicate.

b. Animation

In the Michael Peterson murder trial,[7] which was made into the documentary *The Staircase*,[8] the defense called injury biomechanics expert Dr. Faris Bandak to support the defense's contention that Michael Peterson did not bludgeon his wife to death, but instead she fell in a stairway several times, causing her fatal injuries. To illustrate his findings the expert used an animation that showed a stick figure that represented Kathleen Peterson repeatedly falling in the staircase, causing her injuries. In the following picture, Dr. Bandak can be seen showing a photograph of the wounds to the back of Kathleen Peterson's shaved head to the jury. Behind Dr. Bandak on the screen is the animation of the stick figure at the bottom of the stairs that was played during his direct examination. Also, another visual that played a role in the trial is the prosecution's model of the staircase, which can be seen in the background sitting on the floor of the courtroom.

---

6. *Henricks v. State*, 293 S.W. 3d 267, 276 (Tex. App. 2009).

7. https://www.netflix.com/title/80233441.

8. https://www.netflix.com/title/80233441.

Although no one witnessed Kathleen Peterson fall, the animation of the figure falling down the staircase turned the jurors into eyewitnesses to what the defense contended was the cause of her death. The same eyewitness effect can be generated for any case involving action—automobile tort, product liability involving an exploding hoverboard, or aviation with a crash after takeoff, which is shown in the following screenshot from the animation that and was created by High Impact.[9]

This kind of visualization can be extremely effective, particularly when the other side has not offered their own animation of how they believe the event happened. How jurors visualize events in their own heads is critical and often determines the outcome. If it is easier for them to visualize your theory of how something happened, they are more likely to embrace your theory over that of the other side.

c. *Medical Illustration*

If your expert witness is a doctor, the physician's testimony can be more easily understood and have greater impact when the doctor uses medical illustrations as visual aids. The illustration(s), such as the following one developed by High Impact, could be in a computer slideshow, projected on a screen with a document camera, or enlarged and adhered to a board(s) that can be placed on an easel. When

---

9. https://highimpact.com/.

the jurors can see what the doctor is testifying about, the evidence will be more effectively presented than if the doctor only verbally described the medical findings.

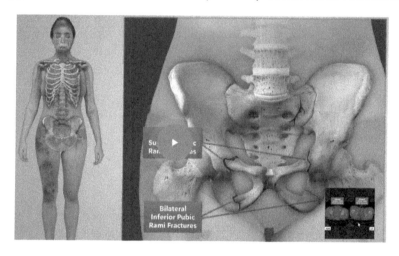

d.   *3D Laser Scanner Data*

Law enforcement is increasingly relying on 3D laser scanners to gather data at a crime scene and for later presentation at trial. Rather than having to take measurements at the scene, the laser scanner digitally preserves the crime scene.[10] This technology is a substantial time saver, and that is particularly important in vehicle collision cases where traffic can be brought to a stop for hours as the scene is processed. And, at trial, the scene can be accurately reconstructed for the jurors to see. The FARO Laser Scanner (below) is a popular brand of scanner.[11]

---

10. https://www.policeone.com/police-products/investigation/articles/how-3d-laser
-scanners-are-changing-crime-scene-investigations-yQC7H8A4Jd13ST8X/; https://www.youtube
.com/watch?v=Sav72l4qX7M.

11. https://www.youtube.com/watch?v=Sav72l4qX7M; https://public-safety.faro.com/us/
law-enforcement/.

From a trial lawyer's perspective, the most important aspect of being able to use this type of evidence in a trial is its ability to paint a complete picture of what the scene looked like in as close in time to the event as possible. The 3D scan allows witnesses to testify to precise locations in the scene and to show the jury what their sight lines were. Traditional photographs always have limitations because, for instance, the exact sight lines may not have been captured. However, with the scene scan, thousands of angles are captured, and this allow for a more in-depth recreation of the scene. When additional items are added, such as the trajectory of a bullet at a crime scene, and/or measurements, it permits the full picture of what happened to be presented to a jury.[12]

At the scene, the investigator will initially do a walk through to determine what needs to be included in the scan(s) and what the sight line(s) are. Once the scene has been scanned, SCENE2go, which consists of an app and a viewer, can be utilized. The app loads the scanned data into a USB flash drive that then can be transferred to most storage media, including either a Mac or Windows operating system.

SCENE2go's viewer is easy to navigate in the courtroom. An expert witness can use the scanner's images as visual aids to explain the expert's findings and conclusions regarding the scene. With pretrial practice, a lay witness can learn how to move the images around on the screen during direct or cross-examination. SCENE2go has different scene views. The scene can be in color or, with a click, it can be turned to grayscale. The 3D view shows measurements. There is a panoramic view. A clipping box can be used to remove distractions, such as a crowd, from the scene. A fly-through video can be created with an MP4 format. Also, annotations can be added to the image, such as videos shown in the image below.13

---

12. Communication with Mahmoud Awadallah, Assistant Prosecuting Attorney, Cuyahoga County, Ohio.

13. https://www.youtube.com/watch?time_continue=291&v=50fIMGGvtNU.

See pages 161-63 regarding how to lay a foundation at trial for admissibility of the 3D laser scanning images.

F.   Catalog of Visuals for the Case in Chief

I.   Day-in-the-Life Video

Often the plaintiff in a personal injury case will play a day-in-the-life video of the injured plaintiff to establish in concrete terms for the jury both the harm done and what the plaintiff has had to endure in the past and will have to endure in the future. The video should be confined to the facts—pain and the difficulties of the day—and not be designed to garner sympathy. It is a good idea to show the video to others during pretrial to gauge their reaction to the video. The video normally should not last more than ten minutes. Producers, such as Colton Legal Media,[14] specialize in personal injury day-in-the-life videos at a cost of between $6,500 and $8,500.

---

14. https://coltoncreative.com; https://publications.policeone.com/2018/Enhance
_the-accuracy_of_evidence_gathering_with_a_3D_laser_scanner_P1eBook.pdf.

2. Courtroom Demonstration

Courtroom demonstrations can be very effective if your witness and any other participants in the demonstration have been prepared pretrial. For example, in a criminal case involving an assault, the prosecutor could have the alleged victim of the assault along with another person show the jury how the defendant committed the assault.

Commonwealth v. Perryman[15] serves as an illustration of both how to conduct a courtroom demonstration and what the law requires for the demonstration to be conducted. Perryman was convicted of distribution of crack cocaine within 1,000 feet of a school zone, and he appealed, claiming that a demonstration of the police officer's surveillance telescope was improper. At trial, Detective Sergeant James Fong testified that he used the telescope to observe the defendant engage in what looked like he was delivering drugs. The trial judge permitted the jurors to look through the telescope to view a sign outside the courtroom. The demonstration was conducted over the defense objection that the lighting conditions were not the same as they were at the time Fong used it to conduct the surveillance.

The Appeals Court of Massachusetts affirmed the conviction and expressed the general rule regarding the admissibility of courtroom demonstrations as follows:

> A courtroom "experiment, demonstration, or reenactment" may be permitted by the trial judge so long as it "sufficiently resembles the actual event so as to be fair and informative.... Whether the conditions were sufficiently similar to make the observation [offered by the demonstration] *of any value in aiding the jury* to pass upon the issue submitted to

---

15. *Commonwealth v. Perryman*, 70 N.E.2d 1 (Mass. App. Ct. 2002).

them [is] primarily for the trial judge to determine as a matter of discretion. [The judge's] decision in this respect will not be interfered with unless plainly wrong."[16]

Although a courtroom demonstration during direct examination can bring the case narrative to life, it requires careful pretrial preparation. The O.J. Simpson demonstration with the glove is a cautionary warning to all trial lawyers about the need for thorough preparation. There are also a variety of examples of defense attorneys in product liability trials injuring themselves with the allegedly defective product while trying to demonstrate how they work to jurors. The key is to practice ahead of time.

3.   The Courtroom

Some witnesses are not very good at estimating time, distance, or a person's height and weight. If you asked a witness to estimate the distance between two objects at the scene, and the witness tells you they were 30 yards apart when you have been to the scene and know the distance is 10 yards, you know that you need a better way to have the witness communicate distance to the jury. Once you understand this, rather than asking the witness to tell the jurors the distance between the two points, you can have the witness assume that the witness chair is one of the points and have the witness point to another reference point in the courtroom to show the jurors the distance between the two points.

Checklist—Direct Examination Visuals

Six Reasons to Use Visuals During Direct Examination

1. Visuals breathe life into direct examinations;
2. Visuals can constitute evidence;
3. Visuals capture and keep the jurors' attention;
4. Visuals can simplify complicated and technical information;
5. Visuals help jurors retain information; and
6. Visuals can be used to repeat information.

---

16. *Id.* at 6.

Pretrial Preparation of Visuals

❑ Gather existing visuals with an aim toward collecting those that serve the above-listed purposes.

❑ Make short video clips from a long video for use on direct, cross, and/or closing, and consider making a disc of these clips to enter into evidence.

❑ Redact portions of video where necessary.

❑ Create demonstrative exhibits.

❑ Create demonstrative exhibits.

❑ Prepare evidence slideshows.

❑ Prepare summary exhibits.

❑ Prepare nonlinear case files.

❑ Prepare yourself by doing the following:

  ✓ Going to the scene where the incident took place as soon as practicable;

  ✓ Familiarize yourself with each exhibit that might be offered at trial;

  ✓ Prepare and practice the direct examination and cross-examination of your witness who will sponsor the exhibit;

  ✓ Marshal your exhibits so that they are ready for trial; and

  ✓ Follow any directives the court may have regarding exhibits.

❑ When you prepare your witness, including a discussion of not only the evidentiary foundation for the visual but also how it will be displayed.

Displaying the Visual

❑ Control the jury's focus by positioning the witness and visual center stage before the jurors.

❑ Follow this pattern of questioning—tell and show—so that the witness will repeat the information with the aid of the visual:

  1. Have the witness testify about what the visual shows.

  2. Lay the foundation for the exhibit and get it admitted into evidence.

  3. Display the visual.

  4. Have the witness describe the content of the visual.

❑ Have the witness mark the visual.

Expert Witness

❑ The expert is your teacher and should be placed in front of the class (jury), prompted with your questions, and lecture with the aid of visuals.

❑ Visual aids for experts can include animations, computer slideshows, and medical illustrations.

Chapter 6

Cross-Examination Visuals

> "Never, never, never, on cross-examination ask a witness a question you don't already know the answer to, was a tenet absorbed with my baby-food. Do it and you'll often get the answer you don't want, an answer that might wreck your case."
>
> Harper Lee, Atticus Finch in
> *To Kill a Mockingbird*

A. The Value of Visuals for Cross-Examination

Visuals can be extremely effective weapons for cross-examination. This chapter explains how concession visuals can be used to gain concessions supporting your case theory and undermining the other side's case theory. It also discusses how to impeach a witness with visuals. Techniques for getting the most out of visuals during cross-examination are illustrated with examples from criminal and civil cases.

Nothing can be more devastating to a witness's credibility than to be caught in a lie or misleading statement with irrefutable visual evidence. This is what happened in an 1858 murder trial when lawyer Abraham Lincoln cross-examined a prosecution witness. Lincoln represented William "Duff" Armstrong, who was charged with murdering James Metzker on August 29, 1857. At the trial, Lincoln cross-examined witness Charles Allen, who testified on direct examination that he saw Armstrong shoot Metzker. Lincoln's cross-examination locked the supposed eyewitness into testifying that he saw the shooting at 10:00 p.m. by moonlight.

Judge J.W. Donovan, who presided over the trial, described what happened next in his work *Tact in Court* as follows:

> The interest was now so intense that men leaned forward to catch the smallest syllable. Then the lawyer drew out a blue covered almanac from his side coat pocket—opened it slowly—offered it into evidence— showed it to the jury and court—read from a page with careful deliberation that the moon on that night was unseen and only arose at one the next morning.[1]

Lincoln's cross-examination destroyed the witness who, realizing that he had been caught in a lie, confessed to having killed Metzker. The visible proof—the almanac—exposed the lie for all to see.

B. Preparing the Visuals

Preparation of a cross-examination with visuals begins with an understanding of the three purposes of cross-examination. First, cross-examination can be designed to gather those concessions that support your legal and factual theories of the case. For instance, if you represent the plaintiff in a breach of contract case and you are cross-examining the defendant whom you claim breached a particular clause in the contract, you could project that clause in the contract onto a screen in the courtroom and have the witness concede that it was part of the contract he signed.

Second, cross-examination can be aimed at impeaching the witness. For example, during the cross-examination of a witness, you could introduce a certified copy of a judgment and sentence showing the witness's prior felony conviction and ask the witness whether the signature on the judgment and sentence is hers. The visuals you gather or create should serve one of these two purposes.

---

1. Francis L. Wellman, *The Art of Cross-Examination* 74-75 (Simon & Schuster 1997, 1st ed. 1903).

Third and finally, cross-examination can help reinforce the structure and internal logic of your key arguments through the use of sign-posting and other types of priming in the questions. It is often said that trial is a battle of salience, meaning that it is a battle for control over what jurors remember most, and cross-examination can play a significant role in winning that battle for you and your client.

How you gather and create visuals for cross-examination is identical to the methods described for accomplishing those tasks for direct examination at pages 79-80.

C. Preparing Yourself

1. Visit the Scene and Know Each Visual

To prepare yourself for cross-examination with visuals, you approach it in much the same fashion as you would to prepare yourself for direct examination. Visit the scene (see pages 80-81). Examine each exhibit and visual (see page 81).

2. Marshal Your Exhibits

You will also need to marshal your exhibits for the court just as you would for direct examination (see pages 82-83). However, how you prepare by storing your visuals and getting ready to retrieve them in court is different from direct examination. For direct examination, you can plan to introduce exhibits in the order you choose because the witness is yours and you control the direct examination. For cross-examination, you need to be more flexible and prepared to produce any visual you wish when you wish. This is where nonlinear software, such as Sanction or TrialDirector, prove invaluable.

PowerPoint is certainly capable of a nonlinear approach but requires a little more legwork in terms of building a menu slide and inserting hyperlinks that allow you to jump back and forth to different slides. Overall, TrialDirector or Sanction will give you the greatest flexibility to adjust on the fly.

D. Gaining Concessions

The primary purpose of cross-examination should be to gain concessions that support your case theory for at least three reasons. First, a concession from an adverse witness that supports your case theory is at least, if not more, valuable than eliciting the information from your witnesses. Jurors will give much more weight to admissions that go against the witness's own interests. Second, it is easier to obtain a concession from a witness than it is to impeach. Third, if you are able to get the adverse witness to make important concessions, you may be able to turn that witness into your own witness and not need to impeach.

The key to getting concessions that support your case is to ask: What must this witness admit that supports my case or undercuts my opponent's case? The key word in the question is "must." The witness must admit it because it is true. You can prove it is true by either direct evidence, circumstantial evidence, or just plain common sense. Therefore, the concession visuals that you should use during cross-examination are those that support your case or undercut your opponent's case theory and establish what the witness cannot deny.

The *Boudwin v. General Ins. Co. of America*[2] appellate opinion provides an illustration of how to use a visual to gain concessions. This was an appeal from a jury verdict for the defense in an auto accident case. At trial, two plaintiffs claimed physical disability and loss of enjoyment of life. The appellate court had no difficulty upholding the jury's decision that plaintiffs were not entitled to any damages because "(t)he record clearly shows that neither Jessi nor Lee have experienced any significant limitations or impairments as a result of the injuries they sustained in the May 31, 2008 accident."

Both plaintiffs testified on direct that they were in pain after the accident. On cross, defense counsel cross-examined them with their Facebook pages. The court described the cross of Lee in this way:

> …Lee acknowledged several entries from his Facebook page where he reported frequently "working out" and also playing sports such as basketball, tennis, "ultimate Frisbee," and softball, sometimes engaging in multiple sessions of sporting activities in a single day. He further acknowledged that he wrote on his Facebook page that he had participated in a softball tournament in the month before trial.…

As demonstrated in this example, social media has become an outstanding source for evidence that forces witnesses to admit certain facts. It is not unusual these days for witnesses to routinely post comments on social media that undermine their claims or arguments at trial, and jurors often treat these posts as moments of pure honesty on the part of the witness.

E. Impeaching the Witness

For lay and expert witnesses, there are seven areas for impeachment that lend themselves to the use of visuals on cross-examination:

---

2. *Boudwin v. General Ins. Co. of America*, unpublished opinion, 2011 WL 4433578 (La. App. Ct. 2011).

1. Prior inconsistent statement,
2. Contradiction,
3. Prior conviction,
4. Lack of personal knowledge,
5. Improbability,
6. Bias and interest, and
7. Learned treatise.

While the first six areas of impeachment apply to lay and expert witnesses, the seventh area—impeachment with a learned treatise is limited to an expert witness.

In this section, we discuss these six areas of impeachment that are especially suitable to the use of visuals, and we offer case examples of impeachment with visuals.

1. Prior Inconsistent Statement

Ordinarily a witness's prior inconsistent statement is admissible into evidence when it is not offered for the truth of the matter in the statement, and thus, it is not hearsay. Rather, the statement is offered to impeach the witness by showing that the witness has made a conflicting statement.

Impeachment with a prior inconsistent statement is particularly effective if done correctly. First and above all, never try to impeach a witness with a prior inconsistent statement on a trivial matter; jurors are likely to be offended because you are wasting their time. Furthermore, this can suggest desperation on your part, as jurors might be quick to conclude that you are reaching for anything because your case is so weak. Second, before you begin your impeachment with the prior statement, lock the witness into the testimony that the prior statement contradicts. It is a good practice to not tip off the witness to the fact that you are setting the witness up to be impeached with a prior statement. Keep your objective hidden.

Do you need to show the prior statement to the witness? Federal Rule of Evidence 613(a) on Witness's Prior Statement provides that you do not, as follows:

> **Showing or Disclosing the Statement During Examination.** When examining a witness about the witness's prior statement, a party need not show it or disclose its contents to the witness. But the party must, on request, show it or disclose its contents to an adverse party's attorney.

Third, as Rule 613(a) permits, you may refrain from showing the prior statement to the witness at this juncture. If you do show it to the witness, the witness may well attempt to revise his testimony. Although Evidence Rule 613(a) does not require that you do so, it is good practice out of fairness to confront the witness with the circumstances surrounding the giving of the prior statement, such as the date the statement was made and to whom it was made. In the alternative, you could ask, "Have you at any time in the past made a statement contrary to the one you just made?" And, although you are not required to do so by the rule, you could show the prior statement to the witness, but again this may lead the witness to revise his testimony.

Fourth, you want to confront the witness with the prior statement. For example, after having the witness identify and authenticate his prior witness statement, you could direct the witness's attention to the pertinent part of the prior statement in this way, "Please look at page 2, paragraph 2." Then, do not ask the witness to read the statement because the witness may attempt to undercut the impact of the statement by interjecting a comment or lowering his voice so it is not loud enough for the jury to hear. Rather, you should read the statement with authority, and follow that with this question, "Did I read the statement accurately?"

Fifth, instead of just reading the statement to the jury, you want to show the jury the prior statement. Are you allowed to introduce the prior statement (extrinsic evidence) into evidence? Federal Rule of Evidence 613(b) indicates that you may be able to under certain circumstances, as follows:

> **Extrinsic Evidence of a Prior Inconsistent Statement.** Extrinsic evidence of a witness's prior inconsistent statement is admissible only if the witness is given an opportunity to explain or deny the statement and an adverse party is given an opportunity to examine the witness about it, or if justice so requires. This subdivision (b) does not apply to an opposing party's statement under Rule 801(d)(2).

However, if the witness admits to having made the prior inconsistent statement and you offer the prior statement into evidence, opposing counsel may object on the grounds that the prior statement is cumulative and, therefore, inadmissible under Federal Rule of Evidence 403.

Note that Rule 613(b) does not apply to an opposing party's statements under Rule 801(d)(2). Rule 801(d)(2) states:

> A statement that meets the following conditions is not hearsay:
> (2) *An Opposing Party's Statement.* The statement is offered against an opposing party and:
> (A) was made by the party in an individual or representative capacity;
> (B) is one the party manifested that it adopted or believed to be true;
> (C) was made by a person whom the party authorized to make a statement on the subject;

(D) was made by the party's agent or employee on a matter within the scope of that relationship and while it existed; or

(E) was made by the party's coconspirator during and in furtherance of the conspiracy.

The statement must be considered but does not by itself establish the declarant's authority under (C); the existence or scope of the relationship under (D); or the existence of the conspiracy or participation in it under (E).

Therefore, under the Federal Rules of Evidence a party-witness's prior statement is non-hearsay, admissible as substantive evidence, and the prior statement may be shown to the jury.

Sixth, if the prior statement is admissible, you want to prominently display it to the jury. To achieve this, you need to be able to promptly locate and retrieve the document and then call out the particular prior inconsistent statement and project it on the screen in the courtroom. Computer software programs such as TrialDirector or Sanction are well suited to this task. Displaying the contradictory statement to the jurors is important because jurors often have to see things with their own eyes to believe them. If the jurors think the witness's prior contradictory statement was pretty plain and simple after seeing it, they may be quick to reject any explanation the witness has to offer for why it is not a contradiction.

The ideal way to display such contradictions is through video clips of the testimony rather than just showing a callout of the transcript. This would require the deposition to have been video-recorded, but this is commonly happening these days, particularly with party-witnesses.

2. Contradiction

A cross-examiner may impeach a witness by contradicting the witness's testimony with relevant visual evidence. Federal Rule of Evidence 401 states, "Evidence is relevant if: (a) it has any tendency to make a fact more or less probable than it would be without the evidence; and (b) the fact is of consequence in determining the action." However, if the evidence is only contradictory on a collateral matter or if it contravenes Federal Rule of Evidence 403 because its "probative value is substantially outweighed by a danger of one or more of the following: unfair prejudice, confusing the issues, misleading the jury, undue delay, wasting time, or needlessly presenting cumulative evidence," the evidence is inadmissible.

Baker v. Canadian National/Illinois Cent. RR[3] illustrates how to impeach a witness's testimony with a contradictory visual. In *Baker*, the plaintiff was injured

---

3. *Baker v. Canadian National/Illinois Cent. RR*, 536 F.3d 357 (5th Cir. 2008).

when the defendant Illinois Central's train struck a dump truck that Baker was driving. Baker claimed Illinois Central was negligent when it failed to provide a flagman or otherwise protect him when he was working on the track. A jury returned a verdict for Illinois Central deciding that it did not have to provide protection because Baker's work did not require him to place himself in a position where the train could strike him.

At trial, plaintiff's witnesses testified that Baker suffered severe post-accident limitations, including the inability to count money, make change, or be in crowds. On appeal, Baker contended that under Rule 403 the district court should have excluded a surveillance video because it was more prejudicial than probative. The opinion states, "Specifically, Baker notes that the surveillance footage shows him spending long periods of time in casinos and draws a connection between that footage and Illinois Central's closing argument, in which its attorney stated Baker had 'gambled with his life' by running the stop sign. Baker argues that this evidence informed jurors that he engaged in activities many people consider immoral." In affirming the trial court's verdict, the United States Court of Appeals for the Fifth Circuit held that the surveillance video was properly admitted to refute the witness's claims about Baker's post-accident limitations, stating:

> Rule 403 requires that the probative value of the evidence must be "substantially outweighed by the danger of unfair prejudice" before the court may exclude the disputed evidence. Unfair prejudice is not satisfied by evidence that is "merely adverse to the opposing party." For that reason, district courts should apply Rule 403 sparingly. Rule 403's "major function is limited to excluding matter of scant or cumulative probative force, dragged in by the heels for the sake of its prejudicial effect." Rule 403 is not designed to "even out" the weight of the evidence. Baker's post-accident quality of life was hotly disputed, and Baker's witnesses testified in detail regarding the allegedly severe post-accident limitations Baker faces, including the inability to count money, make change, or be in crowds. The video's probative value contradicting these statements weighs heavily against a hypothetical juror's moral aversion to gambling. The district court did not abuse its discretion by allowing the surveillance footage.[4]

There are other indirect ways to use visuals to contradict the testimony of a witness. For example, you can use a simple demonstrative to show a pattern of conduct on the part of the witness that contradicts what he or she has said in his testimony. In Chapters 3 and 4 we showed you this demonstrative, which visually highlighted the plaintiff's pattern of ignoring important warnings in the rail yard.

---

4. *Id*. at 369.

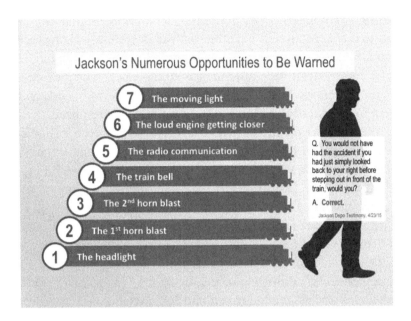

If the plaintiff were to testify that he is always attentive and aware of his surroundings while working in the rail yard, the attorney could use this demonstrative during the cross-examination to contradict those statements. The simplest way of doing this is to introduce the slide and gain the court's permission to publish it and then walk through each one of the seven warnings, asking the witness about them. Counsel could then conclude the cross with the plaintiff's deposition testimony appearing on the slide as follows:

> Q. You would not have had the accident if you had simply looked back to your right before stepping out in front of the train, would you?
> A. Correct.

3. Prior Conviction

Federal Rule of Evidence 609 governs the admissibility of a prior conviction to impeach a witness. Assuming that the prior conviction is admissible under Fed. R. Evid. 609, it is admitted only as impeachment evidence, going to the credibility of the witness. It may not be considered for any other purpose.

To authenticate the judgment and sentence document, which is the evidence of prior conviction, it will be either certified or exemplified. If the judgment and sentence document is offered in the state of the conviction, it will need to be certified, which means that the clerk of the court's certification states that it is a true and correct copy of what is in the document. An out-of-state judgment and sentence will need to be exemplified to be authentic, which means that the clerk of the court swears that the document is authentic; the presiding judge swears that it is authentic; and the clerk swears that the judge is the judge and the judge's signature is authentic. Under Federal Rule of Evidence 902, properly certified or exemplified judgments and sentences are self-authenticating. All counsel needs to do is offer the document into evidence; no testimonial foundation is required.

Is the prior conviction document, which is either a certified or exemplified copy of the judgment and sentence, admissible, and thus, evidence that the jury can see? If the cross-examiner asks the witness about the prior conviction and the witness admits that it is his, then the court may rule that the judgment and sentence document is inadmissible because it is merely cumulative.[5]

If the witness denies having the prior conviction, the cross-examiner will need to establish that the witness is the same person named in the judgment and sentence document. If the witness has the same name as the defendant on the judgment and sentence document, it is admissible in the absence of the sworn testimony of the witness to the contrary.[6] If the judgment and sentence document bears the defendant's fingerprints, the witness's fingerprints can be taken and compared with those on the document.

One other caveat: the law varies from jurisdiction to jurisdiction concerning the extent to which a cross-examiner may reveal information about the prior conviction. In some jurisdictions, the examiner may only ask about the type of crime and the punishment.[7]

4.   Lack of Personal Knowledge

A witness can be impeached by a cross-examination that reveals that the witness lacks personal knowledge of the subject about which the witness has testified.

Under Federal Rule of Evidence 104(a), the trial judge determines the preliminary question of whether the witness has sufficient personal knowledge of the matter about which witness will testify to permit the witness to testify. Federal Rule of Evidence 602 sets a low standard for determining whether a witness has personal knowledge, as follows:

> A witness may testify to a matter only if evidence is introduced sufficient to support a finding that the witness has personal knowledge of the matter. Evidence to prove personal knowledge may consist of the witness's

---

5. Federal Rule of Evidence 403.

6. *State v. Ammons*, 105 Wash. 2d 175, 190, 713 P.2d 719, 728 (1986).

7. *State v. Copeland*, 130 Wash. 2d 244, 285, 922 P.2d 1304, 1326-27(1996).

own testimony. This rule does not apply to a witness's expert testimony under Rule 703.

If you think that the witness lacks sufficient personal knowledge to testify on a subject, you can make a motion in limine to prohibit the witness from testifying. Even if the court determines that the witness has sufficient personal knowledge to testify on the matter, that does not preclude you from challenging the sufficiency of the witness's personal knowledge during cross-examination. Fed. R. Evid. 104(e) states that the "rule does not limit a party's right to introduce before the jury evidence that is relevant to the weight or credibility of other evidence."

An illustration of how to use a visual to impeach a witness by showing he lacked personal knowledge is Abraham Lincoln's cross-examination of Charles Allen (see page 106). Lincoln used an almanac to show that Allen could not have seen what he claimed because there was no moonlight by which he could see what happened.

5. Improbability

The cross-examiner may seek to show that the witness's testimony is improbable under the evidence or just contrary to common sense. Federal Rule of Evidence 401 defines relevant evidence as that which "has any tendency to make a fact more or less probable than it would be without the evidence; and ... is of consequence in determining the action." Relevant evidence may be excluded under Fed. R. Evid. 403 if it would cause confusion, waste time, or if unfair prejudice would substantially outweigh the probative value.

The cross-examination of Senator Ted Stevens is a good example of a cross-examination with a visual that exposed the implausibility of Stevens' testimony. In 2008, Stevens was convicted of seven corruption charges for failing to disclose more than $250,000 in gifts and free labor on the remodeling of his cabin. Because prosecutors failed to disclose exculpatory information, Stevens' conviction was vacated and dismissed.

One of the gifts that Stevens did not report on Senate disclosure forms was a $2,700 vibrating Shiatsu massage chair given to him by an Alaskan restaurant owner. Stevens claimed on direct examination that the chair had been loaned to him: "It's not my chair, it's not my chair. It's his chair, he put it in the house." On cross-examination, Assistant U.S. Attorney Brenda Morris asked Stevens if he had other furniture on loan. Stevens' testimony became steadily more ridiculous as the examination proceeded, finally losing all credibility as follows:

"That chair, it's still at your house?" Ms. Morris asked.

"Yes," Mr. Stevens replied.

"How is that not a gift?" she then asked.

Mr. Stevens said Mr. Persons "bought the chair as a gift but I refused it as a gift." He said he agreed to have the chair stored in his home for Mr. Persons.

"So, if you say it's not a gift, it's not a gift?" the prosecutor asked. She then confronted Mr. Stevens with a note he had written to Mr. Persons thanking him for the chair, saying how much he loved using the chair and even sometimes fell asleep in it.[8]

The senator's claim that the chair was not a gift became starkly improbable given his email stating that it was in his basement and that he enjoyed it.

6.   Bias and Interest

A party has a right to cross-examine an adverse witness to show bias or interest, and the defendant in a criminal case has a constitutional right to do so.[9] However, the U.S. Supreme Court has also held that the trial court can impose reasonable limitations on cross-examination to show bias or interest "based on concerns about, among other things, harassment, prejudice, confusion of the issues, the witness safety, or interrogation that is repetitive or only marginally relevant."[10]

United States v. Figueroa[11] is an example of a case where the trial court should have allowed defense counsel in a criminal case to cross-examine a witness about a striking visual. Edwin Figueroa was convicted of unlawful possession of a firearm. Prosecution witness Jonathan Wright testified that he sold the firearm to defendant Figueroa. Defense counsel sought to cross-examine Wright about his swastika tattoos because the defendant was a member of a racial or ethnic minority and the tattoos were evidence of bias. Defense counsel said that he intended to cross-examine Wright about them, arguing, among other things, that Figueroa was a member of a racial or ethnic minority, and the testimony would be used to impeach Wright as to his bias and credibility. The trial judge ruled that defense counsel could not cross-examine Wright about the tattoos. The United States Court of Appeals for the Second Circuit held:

> We think that the district court abused its discretion, however, when it ruled that Figueroa could not cross-examine Wright about his tattoos.

---

8. Neil A. Lewis, "Prosecutor Confronts Alaska Senator in Ethics Trial," New York Times, pg. 1, October 20, 2008, https://www.nytimes.com/2008/10/21/us/21stevens.html.

9. *Davis v. Alaska*, 415 U.S. 308, 315 (1974).

10. *Delaware v. Van Arsdall*, 475 U.S. 673, 679 (1986).

11. *United States v. Figueroa*, 548 F.3d 222 (2d Cir. 2008).

The record reflects that the defendant is a member of a racial or ethnic minority group. Wright, who testified against Figueroa, bore two tattoos depicting swastikas. Inasmuch as the tattoos suggested that Wright harbored animus against racial or ethnic minority groups and their members, they were relevant to and probative of Wright's credibility, bias, and motive to lie when testifying against Figueroa.[12]

Whether the trial court would have permitted the jury to see swastikas had the case verdict been reversed will never be known because the appellate court decided that the error was harmless.

Richardson v. State[13] is another example of a case in which a visual—a letter—should have been admitted at trial to show a witness's bias. In *Richardson*, the defendant was convicted of burglary with assault or battery. The defendant, Lowell Richardson, was the boyfriend of the alleged victim Christine Shine and the father of her child. On appeal, Richardson argued the trial court erred when it excluded Shine's letters to the defendant written after the events and while Richardson was incarcerated in the county jail. Specifically, the defense wanted the jury to read this particular passage: "Lowell I will make a serious ass promise to you and only you, if you ever in your fucking life *cheat on me again or even fix your mouth to say you don't want to be with me, I will kill you this time* and I will go to jail for the rest of my life and that's a promise." The defense offered the letters to prove Shine's bias against Richardson.

The Florida District Court of Appeals reversed the conviction, holding:

> In *Hair v. State*, 428 So.2d 760, 761–62 (Fla. 3d DCA 1983), this Court stated that a party may elicit facts tending to show bias, motive, prejudice or interest of a witness, a right that is particularly important in criminal cases because "the jury must know of any improper motives of a prosecuting witness in determining that witness' credibility." *Brown v. State*, 424 So.2d 950, 955 (Fla. 1st DCA 1983).
>
> *See Jones v. State*, 678 So.2d 890 (Fla. 4th DCA 1996); *Stanley v. State*, 648 So.2d 1268 (Fla. 4th DCA 1995); *Arias v. State*, 593 So.2d 260 (Fla. 3d DCA 1992); *Holt v. State*, 378 So.2d 106 (Fla. 5th DCA 1980); *See also* Charles W. Ehrhardt, Florida Evidence § 608.5, at 457 (2000 ed.) ("Interest, motive and animus are never collateral matters on cross-examination and are always proper").
>
> Shine's credibility was critical to the **state's** case. Her testimony concerning defendant›s use of a gun, even though corroborated by her "godsister," was obviously not believed by the jury, which acquitted him on the firearm aspect of the burglary charge. Shine's threat in her letter

---

12. *Id.* at 227-28.

13. *Richardson v. State*, 789 So.2d 1055 (Fla. App. 3 Dist. 2001).

to the defendant that if "you ever . . . cheat on me *again* . . . I will kill you *this time*," suggests, first, that the couple had already experienced one incident of infidelity. Given the timing of the letter, the jury could have reasonably inferred that it was this accusation of infidelity that led to the confrontation in this case. Second, it implies that she stabbed defendant with a knife during the incident, as the defense argued at trial. These interpretations could have led the jury to the conclusion that Shine was the actual aggressor during the argument, or that she was being untruthful about the details of the incident. Defendant had the right to have the jury hear this impeaching evidence.[14]

You can also use demonstratives to show biases of adverse witnesses, particularly expert witnesses. For example, you can develop a simple demonstrative that highlights key statistics about the opposing expert, such as how many times she has testified for the plaintiff or defense, compared to how many times she has testified in general. A simple demonstrative that shows that an expert has testified in 95 percent of the her cases for the plaintiff, and has made hundreds of thousands of dollars off of such testimony, visually reinforces that this witness may have a bias due to his or her relationship to the plaintiff's bar.

7. Learned Treatise

Opposing counsel has called an expert witness who testifies to something that is contrary to a statement in a learned treatise. Federal Rule of Evidence 803(18) provides you with authority to impeach the expert witness with the learned treatise as follows:

> The following are not excluded by the rule against hearsay, regardless of whether the declarant is available as a witness:
>
> (18) Statements in Learned Treatises, Periodicals, or Pamphlets. A statement contained in a treatise, periodical, or pamphlet if:
>
> (A) the statement is called to the attention of an expert witness on cross-examination or relied on by the expert on direct examination; and
>
> (B) the publication is established as a reliable authority by the expert's admission or testimony, by another expert's testimony, or by judicial notice.
>
> If admitted, the statement may be read into evidence but not received as an exhibit.

---

14. *Id.* at 1056-57.

The Comment to Fed. R. Evid. 803(18) states that while writers on evidence have favored the admissibility of learned treatises, "the great weight of authority has been that learned treatises are not admissible as substantive evidence though usable in the cross-examination of experts." Under the explicit language of the Rule, while the learned treatise will not be admitted into evidence, the pertinent information in the treatise can be read into evidence.

Can you show the information in the treatise to the jurors, for example, by projecting it on a screen or having it on a chart, so that they can read along with you, the cross-examiner, as you read the contents to them? *United States v. Mangan*[15] addressed this question in affirming the defendant's convictions for using the mail to defraud, filing a false tax return, and conspiring to file false claims against the United States. The Second Circuit's opinion describes how charts from a learned treatise were used effectively during cross-examination and the rationale for allowing counsel to utilize the charts on cross-examination as follows:

> An important element of the Government's proof against Kevin was the testimony of Douglas Cromwell, a handwriting expert with the United States Bureau of Alcohol, Tobacco and Firearms, that Kevin's handwriting appeared on various bank opening account cards and deposit and withdrawal tickets. The exemplars used by Cromwell as a basis for this testimony consisted of handwriting on checks of American Banquet Corporation, one of Kevin's enterprises, with which Bertsch had been associated, which Bertsch identified as Kevin's. Kevin claimed that the checks had been stolen by two former business associates in cooperation with state prosecutors. After an extensive suppression hearing Judge Stewart found that any illegal taking of the checks was the work of the individuals alone. Kevin attacks this finding but it surely was not clearly erroneous. The argument therefore fails....
>
> In cross-examining Cromwell, Kevin's counsel called his attention to several charts extracted from a learned treatise in an endeavor to show that the characteristics of handwriting which Cromwell had regarded as individual and identifying were generally recognized common characteristics. When counsel offered the charts in evidence, the judge rejected them, relying on the last sentence of "Learned Treatises" exception to the hearsay rule in Rule 803(18) of the Federal Rules of Evidence 18. It is not altogether clear to us how a chart can "be read into evidence," and good sense would seem to favor its admission into evidence, at least in a case where, as here, its significance had been fully explored with the expert. Still the trial judge permitted the jury to view the charts as they were being discussed, and we do not see how we can fault him for following the black letter as closely as he could.... If the jury had wanted

---

15. *United States v. Mangan*, 575 F.2d 32, 48 (2d Cir. 1978).

the charts during its deliberations, it could have asked for a reading of the relevant portion of Cromwell's testimony including their display. Other objections with regard to the handling of the handwriting testimony do not warrant discussion. (citations omitted)

In the *Journal of Civil Rights and Economic Development*, Robert F. McGill Jr. addresses the question of whether portions of learned treatises may be shown to the fact finder. McGill asserts:

> Rule 803(18) allows "statements contained in published treatises, periodicals, or pamphlets" to be admitted under the conditions of the Rule. What about charts and diagrams contained in books or periodicals? What about published films? There seems to be little problem with defining "statements" as including charts and diagrams taken out of published written work and in defining "read into evidence" as including "displayed in evidence."[16]

On the question of whether films should be able to be shown, McGill noted that appellate courts had split opinions on whether the films could be shown.[17]

F.   Displaying the Visual and Yourself

In Chapter 5 "Direct Examination Visuals," we stressed the importance of understanding the roles played by counsel who is conducting the direct examination and the witness. During direct examination, the witness should be the center of attention—the primary communicator with the jury. Counsel should be the inquisitive questioner guiding the witness. A veteran expert witness is even more the focal point; the expert is a teacher who should be at the front of the class—the jury. We suggested that if court practice and protocol allow counsel to move about the courtroom, it is best to stand at the end of the jury box furthest away from the witness chair. Counsel will want to position the visuals about which the witness will testify into the hands of the witness or in a place near the witness, such as on an easel near the witness stand.

On the other hand, the staging to display the visual and yourself during cross-examination ought to be much different (provided you are permitted to move around in the courtroom). Positioning in the courtroom for cross-examination as with direct examination should be guided by the roles played by counsel and

---

16. Robert F. Magill Jr., *Issues Under Federal Rule of Evidence* 803(18): The "Learned Treatise" Exception to the Hearsay Rule, Journal of Civil Rights and Economic Development: Vol. 9, Issue. 1, Article 4, 49-50 (1993), https://scholarship.law.stjohns.edu/jcred/vol9/iss1/4.

17. *Id.* at 50-51.

the witness. When properly done, cross-examination is not the time for counsel to satisfy counsel's curiosity and explore what the witness knows.

Cross-examination is the time for the cross-examiner to be the focus of attention. The cross-examiner should either know what the witness will answer or not care what the answer is going to be. The cross-examiner's goal is to elicit the information from the witness that the cross-examiner already knows the witness will either concede or be impeached. Often, the questions in cross-examination are more important than the answers, whether it is because of the suggestion that is being made in the question or because the questions are designed simply to guide jurors along and piece together the issues for them. Therefore, during your cross-examination, you and your visuals should be center stage in the courtroom because it is your time to testify and use visuals. When you are moving about the courtroom and want to approach the witness, if court practice calls for it, ask the court's permission: "May I approach the witness, Your Honor?" And do not get so close to the witness that you are invading the witness's zone of privacy.

On a final note about visuals and cross-examination, you should think about how you can employ simple visuals to help jurors organize the issues in the case. One of the most common complaints from jurors is that they have difficulty tracking the importance and/or relevance of certain testimony while a witness testifies. Attorneys can develop visual components to the cross-examination to deal with this issue. For example, if your goal were to convince jurors to think about the case as boiling down to three simple issues, one way to effectively utilize visuals in this instance is to color-code these issues. For example, green always signifies the first issue, blue always signifies the second issue, and red always signifies the third issue. During cross-examination, you can reinforce these three categories by using the colors in your corresponding visuals. In fact, you can take it even further and have colored file folders for various sets of questions. For example, you could begin the substantive questions in cross-examination by drawing on notes from a red file folder. When done discussing that issue with the witness, you can tell the witness you would like to move onto the next subject. You can walk back to your table, set the red folder down, and pick up the blue folder. These visual cues will help jurors understand how the testimony relates to the main issues in the case. It reinforces the simple, structured view of the case that you want them to adopt.

Checklist—Cross-Examination Visuals

Preparation

❑ Prepare clips from video depositions.
❑ Prepare clips of transcripts organized in nonlinear litigation software.
❑ Prepare clips of witnesses' prior statements in linear or nonlinear litigation software.

Concession Visuals

❑ Ask yourself: "What *must* the witness admit that supports my case theory or undercuts my opponent's case?"
❑ Identify visuals with content that the witness *must* admit or if the witness denies what is in the visual, the witness will be impeached.

Impeachment Visuals

Impeachment visuals include:

1. A prior inconsistent statement;
2. A visual that contradicts the witness's testimony;
3. A prior conviction—judgment and sentence document;
4. A visual that establishes that the witness did not have personal knowledge about that which the witness testified;
5. A visual that proves that the witness's testimony is improbable;
6. A visual that reveals the witness's bias or interest; and
7. A statement in a learned treatise that conflicts with the witness's testimony.

Displaying the Cross-Examination and Yourself

❏ Display the cross-examination visual so that it is clearly visible to the jury.

❏ To the extent the court allows, position yourself center stage because cross-examination is your opportunity to testify.

Chapter 7

Pretrial Visuals

"A picture is worth a thousand words."

Aphorism

A. Pretrial Visual Persuasion

Today's litigations predominantly end pretrial as a result of case dismissal or through some form of alternative dispute resolution (ADR)—settlement conference, arbitration, or mediation. Visuals can play an important role in your pretrial pleadings and in ADR. Visuals can be aimed at persuading your audience (your opponent, a mediator, an arbitrator, or a judge—not to mention the public) of the justness of your cause. In this chapter, we discuss incorporating visuals into your pleadings, selecting a mediator who favors visual presentations, using visuals in presenting your case during ADR, and what constitutes effective visuals for ADR.

B. Pleadings

In Chapter 3 on opening statements, we discussed the importance of using narrative visuals to communicate your compelling case story to a jury or a judge in a bench trial. In pretrial, your pleadings can communicate that compelling story to other audiences—your client, your opponent, an arbitrator or mediator, the judge, and the public. Like an opening-statement story, your pleadings should tell a story about human beings (a protagonist and an antagonist), values shared by the audiences. And the pleadings can have a case theme.

To illustrate how narrative visuals can effectively tell the case story, consider the original complaint[1] that was filed in what has been referred to as the "Ride The Ducks" case.[2] As we mentioned in previous chapters, Ride The Ducks (RTD) of Seattle was a tourist attraction in Seattle, Washington. Tourists aboard a World War II amphibian landing craft traveled from Seattle's downtown waterfront to Lake Union where it entered the water and traveled around the lake before returning to downtown. Along the route, the Captain (driver) entertained the passengers and described the city's sites.

The factual statement in the complaint powerfully told the plaintiff's story of what happened with visuals, as follows:

III. Facts

3.1   About 11:11 a.m. local time on Thursday September 24, 2015, a 1945 GMC DUKW No. 6—an amphibious military vehicle modified and remanufactured for tour operations by RTD International, and operated by RTD Seattle—was traveling northbound in the center lane on the SR 99 Aurora Bridge at approximately block no. 2900.00, 1000 feet from Raye Street.

3.2   DUKW No. 6 was occupied by Eric Bishop, its 54-year-old driver, and 36 passengers.

3.3   RTD Seattle created the route driven by Defendant Bishop, despite knowing that the SR 99 Aurora Bridge was unsafe to be traveled upon by a DUKW due to the bridge's narrow lane configuration, lack of center median, and posted speed limit.

3.4   At the same time, a 2009 MCI motor coach, operated by CWA Inc. dba Bellair Charters Hesselgrave South, was traveling southbound on the center lane on Washington Route 99 (SR) also known as the Aurora Bridge.

---

1. Complaint drafted by Karen Koehler of Stritmatter Kessler Koehler Moore law firm.

2. *Dinh v. Ride The Ducks Int'l*, No. 16-2-19995-0 SEA.

3.5   The motor coach was occupied by a 68-year-old driver and approximately 45 to 50 passengers.

3.6   The two vehicles were traveling in their respective lanes heading in opposite directions on the north span of the bridge when defendant Bishop reported hearing a loud "bang" and lost control of DUKW No. 6.

3.7   The DUKW crossed the center line of the SR 99 Aurora Bridge into the oncoming northbound lanes of traffic, then struck and penetrated the left side of the motor coach.

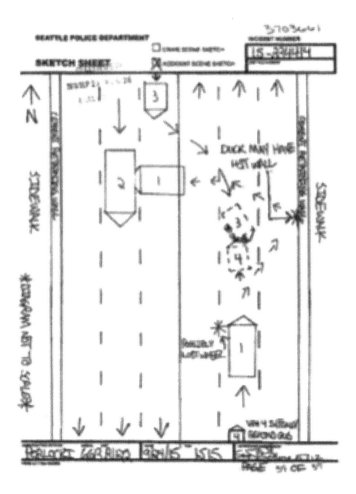

3.8   The National Transportation Safety Board documented the damage to the crash scene, the DUKW vehicle and motor coach using three-dimensional laser scanning technology. The following figures show the 3D scans of the left side of the DUKW and the left side of the motor coach.

3.9   RTD International manufactured, refurbished and modified DUKW No. 6 which was originally a 1945 military model. In approximately 2005, RTD International sold the DUKW to RTD Seattle.

3.10   On or before October 2013, RTD International determined that the axle housings in their manufactured, refurbished and modified DUKWs were dangerously defective.

3.11   On or about October 2013, RTD International issued a notice to purchasers of approximately 57 of its refurbished, manufactured and modified DUKW vehicles. The notice alerted the purchasers to dangerous defects in the axle housing. The notice provided guidance on a modification to strengthen the axle housing to prevent fractures.

3.12   RTD International took no further action to ensure that purchasers of its manufactured, refurbished and modified DUKW products had in fact remedied the dangerous defects.

3.13   RTD International did not issue a recall of its defective and dangerous DUKW products.

3.14 According to the NTSB: The left front axle that failed on the accident vehicle had an earlier modification to the axle housing that had been recommended by RTD International but did not have an associated service bulletin.

3.15 The "earlier modification" to the axle housing was not the same recommendation outlined in the October 2013 service bulletin as a recommended fix for the DUKW.

3.16 According to The Seattle Times story of September 29, 2015, RTD Seattle mechanic Dominick Anderson stated he had never seen the October 13, 2013, service bulletin.

3.17 RTD International issued a statement after the collision stating that it warned purchasers about potential failure of the front axle housing assembly on 57 vehicles in service throughout the country, and that it recommended specific inspections and repairs to reinforce the housing.

3.18 The NTSB has possession of the DUKW vehicle and component parts. It is currently performing metallurgical examinations of the axle components, review of the motor coach company's onboard video systems, and other investigatory acts.

3.19 Following the Crash, the Washington Utilities and Transportation Commission suspended RTD Seattle's operations pending a full examination into its fleet. The state's investigation team is still analyzing maintenance records and conducting physical inspection of the DUKW vehicles.

3.20 RTD Seattle has implored the State to act with "urgency" so that the vehicles can be placed back in service and the company's 130 employees sent back to work.

3.21 RTD Seattle has informed the State that it will now use a separate driver and tour guide instead of combining the two functions in one employee.

3.23 As a result of the collision, approximately 64 people were injured, five of whom were killed.

3.24 A total of 45 to 50 students and staff from North Seattle College were on the motor coach when it was struck. The College had organized an excursion for students in its international program.

3.25 Phoong Dinh, a new entering freshman, was seated in the window seat, on the left side just forward of the middle of the motor coach.

3.26 Phoong suffered numerous orthopedic injuries, complex facial lacerations and other injuries. She was transported to Harborview.

3.27 As of the date of this complaint, Phoong is still recovering at Keiro Nursing Home in Seattle.

This is just one example of the many ways that visuals can be inserted into pleadings. The images in this complaint help illustrate the severity of the crash. Other visuals can help the judge understand the timeline of events, how a process works, and how evidence relates to claims. One of the most common examples of these types of graphics in pleadings is in patent infringement claims, where attorneys routinely use diagrams of an invention to help judges understand a particular claim in the case. Often, these images are drawn from the actual patent. For example, here is an image from a Boeing patent for a water harvesting system that an attorney might include in the briefing to help the judge understand the different claims in the patent.

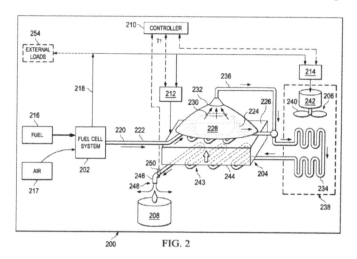

FIG. 2

In fact, visuals in patent briefing are critical when it comes to constructing claims and hearings over patent disputes. The use of graphics can help the judge understand the issue in a way that leads to a construction of a patent claim that is particularly favorable to the client.

Visuals are not just limited to complaints. Timelines and process graphics can be particularly helpful in summary judgment pleadings in order to simplify the issues and clarify a particular argument. For example, a desired summary judgment ruling may depend on the judge understanding the exact progression of events, which could necessitate a timeline such as the following.

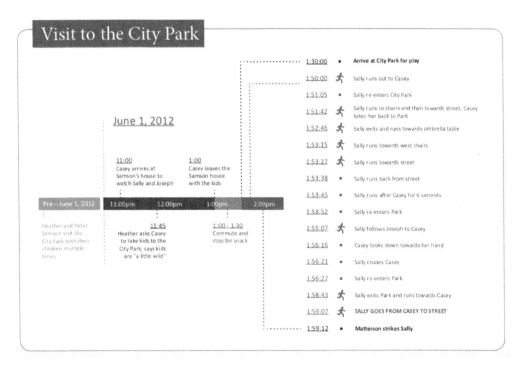

Sometimes, visuals are important to help the judge understand complex issues. For example, consider a case where one party believes it is critical that a judge understand how a synthetic fixed rate bond structure works. This is a complex idea for even the most educated individuals, and a visual might make it easier for the judge to understand the process. A visual that explains how this bond structure works, such as the following, along with corresponding witness explanations, may help the judge comprehend an otherwise complex and confusing fund-raising instrument.

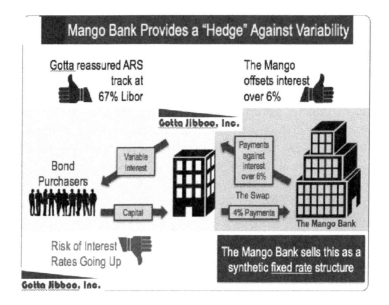

A key point in all this is that visuals are becoming more and more common in briefing. Too often, attorneys are quick to differentiate judges and jurors, concluding that the former, due to their education and experience, do not have the same needs as the latter. Judges are people too. Judges get confused. Judges get lost. Judges get bored. Judges get it wrong. After all, if judges were the perfect experts we often assume they are, there would be no need for appellate courts. Visuals are just one solution to these problems, and attorneys should look for opportunities to incorporate them into briefing when they can help advance the judge's inclination to favor a particular argument or issue.

C. Mediation

Mediation is presided over by a neutral third-party mediator selected by the parties. The mediator orchestrates the negotiations between the parties toward a voluntary settlement of the dispute. The mediator, unlike a judge, does not rule for one side or the other. Mediation is private. Mediation, unlike a trial, can be expeditious. Parties are not limited to legal remedies and can develop creative solutions to their disputes. Mediation is an informal process commonly conducted in a conference room.

You have two audiences at a mediation. The lawyer on the other side and the opposing party constitute one audience. In fact, we could break this down even further and argue that you sometimes have three audiences at a mediation because opposing attorneys and their clients are not always on the same page, or the opposing attorney has not effectively communicated the risks to his client. Persuasive visuals can bring them face-to-face with what will be shown at trial and help them appreciate how certain issues might be portrayed. After all, it is one thing to talk about an issue. It is another thing to see the elements of that issue visually organized in a compelling manner. Sometimes, the visual organization of an issue can help the other side appreciate the risk in a new and different way.

For example, the following visual, which was referenced in Chapter 4, was used in a mediation to help one of the parties appreciate the other party's ability to convince a jury that it had played a significant role in the growth of the company. The names have been changed, but the graphic helps organize the data to show the significant growth that Acme was responsible for.

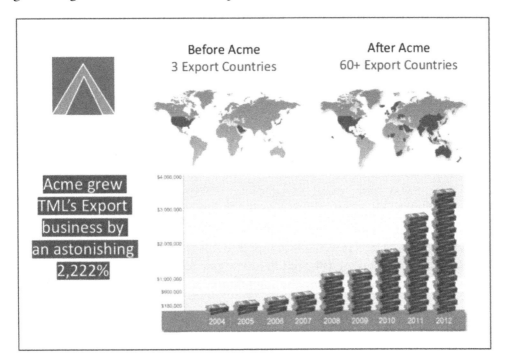

Obviously, there are a variety of factors at play in mediation, and you will not always convince the other side of the risks that they face, but visuals can certainly help achieve that goal. In fact, effective visuals can motivate the other side to reach a settlement with which you will be satisfied.

The second audience is the mediator. Your visuals can convince the mediator of the merits of your case, and, in turn the mediator can show your opposition what they are up against. This is important because mediators are not unlike jurors in the sense that you need to motivate and arm the mediator to convince the other side that it is wise to resolve the case through mediation rather than going to trial.

Visuals can be a powerful weapon for convincing the other side to settle. Sheldon J. Stark, a mediator and arbitrator, recounted what a federal judge told him about how effective visuals can be in disposing of criminal cases by guilty pleas as follows:

> A savvy federal district judge once told me that in his courtroom, the U.S. Attorney uses "Trial Director" presentation software. Trial Director is very powerful program that produces compelling visual document and photographic animations. In many cases, the federal prosecutor calls in the criminal defendant and counsel to show how they intend to present the case. In white-collar crime cases, Trial Director reduces the likelihood a jury will be bored by all the exhibits in the prosecutions paper trail. The percentage of cases that plead as a result has increased dramatically. "It's almost unfair," the judge told me.[3]

One question that counsel needs to consider is whether a visual should be held back until trial rather than being revealed during mediation. Because the great majority of cases are disposed of prior to trial, usually the better answer is to show the visual during mediation.

I.   Selecting the Mediator

How can you apply visual advocacy within the mediation process? You can begin with the selection of the mediator. Besides having confidence that the potential mediator has the competence to handle your case, you want to know whether the mediator will be receptive to visual presentations. If you are not familiar with the proposed mediator, you will need to investigate to determine the person's experience with visuals. Interviewing the mediator is an acceptable practice, and you should do so if you are not already knowledgeable about the person. During the interview, you can directly ask the person about whether the mediator finds visuals helpful. If the answer is "yes," ask how they proved useful. In assessing the proposed mediator, you can speak to other lawyers who have employed that mediator.

Another consideration in making your decision of whether to hire the mediator is whether the prospective mediator is a visual learner. In contrast to many lawyers who are auditory learners, non-lawyers are more likely to be visual learners than lawyers. Most states do not require mediators to be lawyers, and that may be a factor in your decision-making when selecting a mediator.

---

3. https://www.starkmediator.com/practice-tips/2014/05/01/making-use-demonstrative -visual-aids-mediation/.

2. Mediation Brief

The mediator may invite the parties to each provide a mediation brief. The brief should provide the law and facts of the case as well as an explanation of the dispute. While the mediator may require the parties to exchange their briefs, the mediator may also have the parties submit a confidential memorandum only to the mediator.

The mediation brief affords an opportunity for visual persuasion. Because you are trying to resolve the dispute through mediation, you want your mediation brief to sway both the mediator and your opposing party. Several of your visuals may be suitable to either insert into your mediation brief or attach to the brief. This is possible with Microsoft Word and other word processing software program. Suitable visuals, among others, that could be submitted as attachments to your brief include: a graph, photographs, a diagram, a chart, portions of a deposition, and bills.

3. Mediation Session

Ordinarily, a mediator starts the mediation session by explaining the process and having the participants sign an agreement to mediate that includes a confidentiality provision. The parties then may engage in a joint session with the opposing parties present. During the joint session, the parties make opening statements describing their case and offering a proposed settlement. Following the joint session, negotiations continue until a settlement is reached or they deadlock. If the parties have agreed to a joint session, this is when the lawyers can use visuals to impress the opposing party and the other lawyer with what they may face if the case goes to trial and thereby motivate them to settle.

If there is no joint session, which is often the case because they can aggravate hostility and are disfavored by many mediators, it is common for the parties and their lawyers to be placed in separate rooms. The mediator shuttles back and forth carrying messages and presenting his or her own view on the proposals. If the parties are in separate rooms, you can ask the mediator to take your visuals to the other side and display them.

When you intend to show electronic visuals and the necessary hardware (usually a computer and a screen) is not provided at the mediation venue, you will need to have the equipment with you.

The sorts of visuals that you would use during the mediation are along the same lines as those that you would employ during opening statement and closing argument at trial. However, legal evidence and procedural rules do not apply to mediation, and therefore, you can devise visuals that would be inadmissible at trial.

D. Arbitration

In arbitration the parties present their case to a third person or persons who are neutral. As opposed to mediation, which is an informal, voluntary process aimed at achieving an agreed to settlement, arbitration is more like a trial with the arbitrator authorized to hear the evidence and render a decision in the case.

Usually, the parties select a single arbitrator, but some contracts call for a panel of three. The arbitration proceedings operate along the same lines as a trial with opening statements, direct examination and cross, and closing argument. However, the rules are less rigid, meaning that you can usually be much more argumentative in opening than you can at an actual trial, which creates more opportunities to employ visuals that might prime the arbitrators to look at an issue in a particular way.

Arbitration commonly has been agreed to in a contract. However, many arbitration agreements have been criticized as being coerced, rather than voluntary, because of the unequal bargaining power between businesses and consumers. Arbitration can be preferable to a trial because arbitration is less expensive and less time consuming than trial. Some arbitration is mandatory. For example, in order to relieve the court of a burdensome caseload, court rules provide that the parties engage in arbitration if the relief that is requested falls below the benchmark set by the court rules, such as below $100,000.

The arbitrator's decision can be appealed, but the grounds for appeal are limited and specified by statute.

Arbitration can be governed by rules, such as the Commercial Arbitration Rules and Mediation Procedures that provide in part as follows:

R-30. Conduct of Proceedings

(a) The claimant shall present evidence to support its claim. The respondent shall then present evidence to support its defense. Witnesses for each party shall also submit to questions from the arbitrator and the adverse party. The arbitrator has the discretion to vary this procedure, provided that the parties are treated with equality and that each party has the right to be heard and is given a fair opportunity to present its case.

R-31. Evidence

(a) The parties may offer such evidence as is relevant and material to the dispute and shall produce such evidence as the arbitrator may deem necessary to an understanding and determination of the dispute. Conformity to legal rules of evidence shall not be necessary. All evidence shall be taken in the presence of all of the arbitrators and all of the parties, except where any of the parties is absent, in default or has waived the right to be present.

(b) The arbitrator shall determine the admissibility, relevance, and materiality of the evidence offered and may exclude evidence deemed by the arbitrator to be cumulative or irrelevant.

(c) The arbitrator shall take into account applicable principles of legal privilege, such as those involving the confidentiality of communications between a lawyer and client.[4]

Notably, under arbitration rule R-31(a), strict compliance with the legal rules of evidence may not be required, but the arbitrator, under R-31(b) has the discretion to decide what evidence is admissible and exclude cumulative and irrelevant evidence. As R-30(a) indicates, the arbitration proceeds like a bench trial with the addition of the arbitrator, who is a quasi-judicial officer, questioning the witnesses.

As with a bench trial, the goal of a party involved in arbitration is to convince the arbitrator to rule in the party's favor. A powerful way to persuade an arbitrator is with visuals. The arbiter, who is likely to be a retired judge, will be receptive to visuals if they are helpful in providing: a case narrative laying out the key facts; a statement of the applicable law; a tutorial regarding technical matters; and/or an explanation of the case problems and how they may be resolved.

The visuals that are discussed and shown in the previous four chapters on opening statements, direct examination, cross-examination, and closing argument would likewise be powerful persuasion visuals for an arbitration hearing. Examples of a few of those visuals are as follows: an animated video of the incident that is at the heart of the case; pertinent clips from a video deposition; a PowerPoint presentation; a summary chart; and photographs.

Because strict compliance with legal evidence rules is not required in an arbitration or mediation, the types of visuals that may be offered during an arbitration and mediation are broader than those that would be admissible at trial. Indeed, the Commercial Arbitration Rule R-31(a) specifically states that the parties may offer any relevant and material visuals that will help the arbitrator understand and determine the dispute.

E. Catalog of Effective Visuals for ADR

In this section we offer what can be very effective visuals that can be used during mediation, arbitration, and settlement conferences. As with illustrations of visuals that can be utilized during phases of trial, this catalog is non-exclusive.

---

4. https://www.adr.org/sites/default/files/Commercial%20Rules.pdf.

1. Day-in-the-Life Videos

Although you can show visuals at a mediation that would be inadmissible at trial, is it advisable to do so? For example, should you show a day-in-the-life video at a mediation that contains visuals that would be inadmissible at trial? There are conflicting views on this question. David Ball, trial consultant, author, and plaintiffs' guru on damages in civil cases, bluntly states his opinion as follows:

Show a Day-in-the-Life Video That is 100 Percent Admissible

Your settlement video can go farther, to some extent, but the day-in-the-life video should be a realistic threat.

In mediation conferences, whether showing a day-in-the-life or a mediation video, ixnay on the drippy, sappy, sentimental announcers and soft-focused views and emotional cross-fades and all the other soap-opera gimmicks! Especially get rid of the syrupy music. That stuff fools no one.[5]

Morgan C. Smith, owner of Cogent Legal, which is a legal graphics and consulting firm, holds a different opinion, as follows:

However, since the rules of evidence do not apply in mediation, a creative mind is free to expand the presentation to include things like interviews with family members and music that bring the person's injuries or death to light in a way that no paper presentation ever could. Well-done interviews of people talking about what a life-changing event the incident was to the plaintiff, or the loss of comfort, care and companionship of a loved one who has died, are extremely moving. While these interviews would not be admissible in court, you can tell the opposing counsel that each and every witness will be called at trial to testify in the same manner.[6]

All sorts of viewpoints exist on this issue, but the bottom line is that, if your visual can help the opposing attorney or party appreciate the risk of trial in a new or different way, the visual adds value to the mediation. The key is to understand your opposition and tailor your visual message to them. Sometimes, it is as simple as realizing that the opposing attorney has not been forthright with his clients about the true risk in the case, and you need to find a way to send a clear message to the client. Regardless of the scenario, visuals are just one more tool in your toolbox for accomplishing your goals.

---

5. David Ball, *David Ball on Damages* 3, 194 (National Institute of Trial Advocacy 2011).

6. Morgan C. Smith, *Go Graphics in Mediation, Not Just in Trial,* Plaintiff Magazine, June 2011, at 2-3.

Colton Legal Media is an example of a producer of day-in-the-life videos that can be shown pretrial and at trial.[7] Following is a frame shot from a Colton day-in-the-life video in which a prosthesis is attached to the plaintiff. Andrew Colton is a former national network news correspondent now retained by more than 200 law firms for legal video productions and media relations. Pricing for his "day in the life video," "legal settlement documentary," and trademarked "Life After Loss®" productions start around $6,000 and can exceed $30,000. Andrew Colton has said, "Lawyers turn to me when they want the right mix of technology and professional storytelling. It's one thing to write in a memo or brief how someone is handling the loss of a limb but seeing them live post-amputation—while talking about it—adds depth that even the best written brief can't convey."

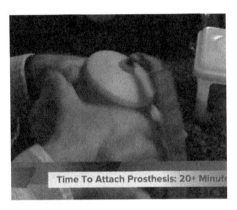

2. Video Simulation or Animation

A short video that shows what happened, such as the video developed by High Impact of a product—a chair leg—malfunctioning and injuring the plaintiff's head, which is illustrated with the following screenshot, can have a dramatic impact on the opposing party at a mediation or arbitration.

---

7. https://coltoncreative.com.

In Chapter 8 Evidentiary Predicates, we discussed the evidentiary foundations that must be laid for an animation or a simulation before they can be admitted into evidence (see pages 154-59). However, evidence rules do not apply at a mediation, and at an arbitration the arbitrator may decide that it is not necessary to conform to the legal rules of evidence. Consequently, the animation or simulation may be shown without having to call the experts that the proponent would be required to call at trial.

3.   Visual Brief

You can easily create a visual brief with PowerPoint or Keynote. You can insert pictures, videos, and audio clips into your PowerPoint slideshow. The videos can be of witness interviews, a day-in-the-life, or whatever other visuals communicate your case theory. The PowerPoint you create for your opening statement is a good place to start creating the visual brief.

Once you have crafted the PowerPoint presentations, you have at least two choices of how you can deliver it to the mediator, arbitrator, and/or your opponent. First, you could provide the visual brief as a PowerPoint slideshow presentation. The viewer would only have to click though the slides or, if you wished, you could set the times for slides. A second alternative is to convert the PowerPoint into a movie. With a Mac, all you need to do is click on **File** and then click on **Save as Movie** and you will be able to select movie options that you want. Then click **Save** and you have created a movie visual brief.

Checklist—Alternative Dispute Resolution Visuals

Pleadings

❑   Incorporate impactful narrative visuals into your pleadings.

Mediation

❑   Ask yourself: "What visuals will convince the mediator of the merits of your case and motivate the other side to settle?"
❑   Ask the mediator whether he or she finds visuals helpful to the process.
❑   Avail yourself of the opportunity to include visuals in the mediation brief.

Arbitration

❑   Use trial visuals during mediation and arbitration.
❑   Because evidence rules are not applicable in a mediation and are relaxed in arbitration, consider using visuals that are persuasive even though they would be inadmissible at trial.

Catalog of Visuals for Opening Statement

❑   Consider using these visuals, among others, during ADR:
    ✓   Day-in-the-life video
    ✓   Video simulation or animation
    ✓   A visual brief

Chapter 8

Evidentiary Predicates

N. Electronic Communications
   1. Social Media
   2. Emails and Text Messages

> "For our purposes, the most important procedural rule is that the proponent of an item of evidence must ordinarily lay the foundation before formally offering the item into evidence."
>
> Edward J. Imwinkelried,
> *Evidentiary Foundations* 3,
> (Carolina Academic Press) (10th ed. 2018)

A. Overview

This chapter discusses evidentiary law pertinent to either introducing visuals into evidence or having them shown to the jury for illustrative purposes. Further, the chapter offers case examples involving common trial visuals and of pattern predicate questions that can be used to lay proper foundations. It examines trial techniques that can be used to facilitate the introduction of visuals into evidence. Also, this chapter provides legal authority for the admissibility of most types of trial visuals from a photograph to electronic communications. Finally, this chapter is supplemented by Appendix 8.1 found on this book's companion website http://www.fastcase.com/visuallitigation that contains an extensive outline of cases nationwide that have addressed some of the most common evidentiary issues regarding visual evidence, and this list includes not only published but also unpublished appellate opinions.

We refer to the Federal Rules of Evidence throughout the chapter because forty-two states have adopted them, sometimes with variations.

B. Laying an Evidentiary Foundation

Generally, before a trial lawyer can introduce anything, including visuals, into evidence, the lawyer must lay an evidentiary foundation. For example, if a lawyer wants to introduce a contract into evidence, the lawyer must establish that the contract was authentic and that it was relevant to the lawsuit. The trial judge under Federal Rule of Evidence 104(a) decides the preliminary question of admissibility. Fed. R. Evid. 104(a) states: "The court must decide any preliminary question about whether . . . evidence is admissible. In so deciding, the court is not bound by evidence rules, except those on privilege." While the judge decides the admissibility question, the jury decides what weight to give to the piece of evidence.

An exception to the proposition that the lawyer must lay an evidentiary predicate before an exhibit is admitted occurs when the judge exercises discretion and admits the evidence subject to counsel later completing the proof of the foundation. Often evidence is admitted before the full foundation has been established when the evidence is not readily identifiable and requires a chain of custody be established by multiple witnesses. Faced with the predicament that the witness on the stand cannot supply all the links in the chain and yet counsel wants the witness to testify about the exhibit and does not want to recall the witness later, counsel may offer the exhibit. If opposing counsel objects, the proponent of the exhibit informs the judge, "I'll tie it up later, Your Honor." If the court allows the exhibit into evidence at this juncture and there is a later failure of proof, the court may instruct the jury to disregard what they saw and/or heard. On the other hand, if the damage that was done by admitting the evidence is significant, the court may be compelled to declare a mistrial.

C. The Fundamentals

Before any visual exhibit is admitted into evidence, the proponent must lay a foundation by establishing three fundamentals. First, the exhibit must be relevant. Second, the exhibit must pass the requirements of Federal Rule of Evidence 403. Third, the exhibit must be authentic.

I. Relevant

Whether a visual exhibit is relevant is governed by Federal Rules of Evidence 401 and 402. Fed. R. Evid. 401 provides: "Evidence is relevant if: (a) it has any tendency to make a fact more or less probable than it would be without the evidence; and (b) the fact is of consequence in determining the action." Fed. R. Evid. 402 states, "Relevant evidence is admissible unless any of the following provides otherwise: the United States Constitution; a federal statute; these rules; or other rules prescribed by the Supreme Court. Irrelevant evidence is not admissible."

2. Rule of Evidence 403

Even if an exhibit is relevant, it may be excluded from evidence if it does not pass the tests stated in Fed. R. Evid. 403 that provides: "The court may exclude relevant evidence if its probative value is substantially outweighed by a danger of one or more of the following: unfair prejudice, confusing the issues, misleading the jury, undue delay, wasting time, or needlessly presenting cumulative evidence."

In laying a foundation for a visual, counsel should make every effort to alleviate any of the possible concerns expressed in Rule 403. For example, if counsel wants a jury to view a PowerPoint presentation prepared by an expert and is concerned that opposing counsel could object on the grounds that the slideshow would waste the court's time and present cumulative evidence, counsel could elicit testimony from the expert that the slideshow will assist in explaining the technical field and that it does not repeat what the expert has or will testify to.

3.   Authentic

The proponent of a visual must establish that the visual, which could be a photograph, a document, diagram, and so on, is authentic. Federal Rule of Evidence 901(a) states what the lawyer must establish in order to authenticate an exhibit, as follows: "To satisfy the requirement of authenticating or identifying an item of evidence, the proponent must produce evidence sufficient to support a finding that the item is what the proponent claims it is."[1]

Fed. R. Evid. 901(b) provides these examples of sufficient evidence that comply with the Rule. The following are examples that apply to visuals:

(1)   Testimony of a Witness with Knowledge. Testimony that an item is what it is claimed to be.

(2)   Nonexpert Opinion About Handwriting. A nonexpert's opinion that handwriting is genuine, based on a familiarity with it that was not acquired for the current litigation.

(3)   Comparison by an Expert Witness or the Trier of Fact. A comparison with an authenticated specimen by an expert witness or the trier of fact.

(4)   Distinctive Characteristics and the Like. The appearance, contents, substance, internal patterns, or other distinctive characteristics of the item, taken together with all the circumstances.

. . .

---

1. See *People v. Hence*, 110 Mich. App. 154, 162, 312 N.W. 2d 191 (1981), for an example of a situation where circumstantial evidence provided by multiple witnesses established that a revolver was similar to one in the defendant's possession—it was what the proponent—the prosecution—claimed it was.

(7)   Evidence About Public Records. Evidence that:
(A)   a document was recorded or filed in a public office as authorized by law; or
(B)   a purported public record or statement is from the office where items of this kind are kept.
(8)   Evidence About Ancient Documents or Data Compilations. For a document or data compilation, evidence that it:
(A)   is in a condition that creates no suspicion about its authenticity;
(B)   was in a place where, if authentic, it would likely be; and
(C)   is at least 20 years old when offered.
(9)   Evidence About a Process or System. Evidence describing a process or system and showing that it produces an accurate result.

If no witness can readily identify the exhibit—say it is what the proponent claims it is—you must develop through witness testimony a chain of custody. By proving the chain of custody, you establish for the court the ultimate fact you that the real evidence is what it is claimed to be.

Some visuals are self-authenticating, such as a certified copy of a public record. When the visual is self-authenticating, counsel need not produce extrinsic evidence of authenticity, such as by eliciting testimony from a witness as to the exhibit's authenticity. Rather, if the visual is relevant and passes Fed. R. Evid. 403 tests, counsel merely offers the exhibit into evidence. Fed. R. Evid. 902 provides that the following evidence is self-authenticating:

The following items of evidence are self-authenticating; they require no extrinsic evidence of authenticity in order to be admitted:
(1)   Domestic Public Documents That Are Sealed and Signed.
(2)   Domestic Public Documents That Are Not Sealed but Are Signed and Certified.
(3)   Foreign Public Documents.
(4)   Certified Copies of Public Records.
(5)   Official Publications.
(6)   Newspapers and Periodicals.
(7)   Trade Inscriptions and the Like.
(8)   Acknowledged Documents.
(9)   Commercial Paper and Related Documents.
(10) Presumptions Under a Federal Statute. A signature, document, or anything else that a federal statute declares to be presumptively or prima facie genuine or authentic.
(11) Certified Domestic Records of a Regularly Conducted Activity.
(12) Certified Foreign Records of a Regularly Conducted Activity.

(13) Certified Records Generated by an Electronic Process or System.

(14) Certified Data Copied from an Electronic Device, Storage Medium, or File.

D. Hearsay and the Original Writings Rules

When the visual exhibit contains words, such as documentary evidence (a will, contract, and so on), the hearsay and/or the original writings rule can come into play when laying an evidentiary foundation. Hearsay is defined in Fed. R. Evid. 801, and exceptions to the hearsay rule are listed in Rule 803. Federal Rules of Evidence 1001-1004 specify that a duplicate of the original may be admitted into evidence provided that neither a genuine question is raised as to the document's authenticity nor would it be unfair to admit the duplicate.

E. Real Evidence

1. Authentic

Real evidence, also referred to as "physical evidence," is evidence that was involved in the case. If the exhibit is readily identifiable by a witness (the witness's wallet containing the witness's driver's license and credit cards), rather than a fungible exhibit—one that is able to be replaced by another identical item (a dollar bill if the witness did not know the serial number on the bill), then counsel only needs that witness to authenticate the exhibit. Under Fed. R. Evid. 901(a), counsel need only elicit testimony that the witness can identify it to establish authenticity. For example, Mr. Miller, the victim of a robbery, testifies: "That's my wallet that was taken from me. It has my driver's license, credit cards, and the amount of cash I had in it when it was taken." The rule can be satisfied by producing "evidence sufficient to support a finding that the item is what the proponent claims it is."

Fed. R. Evid. 901(b) provides examples of evidence that satisfies Rule 901(a). Indeed, the testimony of Mr. Miller comports with the example in Fed. R. Evid. 901(b)(1): "Testimony that an item is what it is claimed to be" (the wallet and its contents).

By contrast, a chain of custody of the evidence must be established if the evidence is not readily identifiable by a witness. For example, assume that a witness identified the defendant in a robbery case as the person who pulled a knife out of his pocket, threatened the victim with it, and took $40 (two $20 bills) from him. If the prosecutor showed the witness two $20 bills that a police officer recovered from the defendant's pocket when he arrested the defendant on the night of the robbery, the witness would not be able to authenticate that they were the bills taken from him let alone that the bills were recovered from the defendant. To establish a chain of custody, the prosecutor would need to call the officer who arrested the defendant, took custody of the bills, put them in an evidence envelope, initialed the envelope (thus making the evidence readily identifiable to the officer), and took the envelope to the evidence room. Further, the prosecutor would call the detective who brought the envelope from the evidence room to the courtroom.

2. Relevant

Continuing with the robbery illustration, when laying the foundation for the two $20 bills counsel would seek to establish that the two bills are relevant to the robbery of the witness. The prosecutor would want to, in the language of Fed. R. Evid. 901(b) "make a fact more… probable than it would be without the evidence." Here, the fact that the defendant had the exact amount of money that was taken, and the cash was in the same denomination are relevant because it makes it more probable that not only was the witness robbed but also that the defendant was the robber.

3. Rule of Evidence 403

Defense counsel in the robbery illustration might object to the admissibility of the two $20 bills on the grounds that the exhibit is unfairly prejudicial because any probative value is outweighed by its unfair prejudice. The defense could argue that there is no way of knowing that the $40 belonged to the victim and it would be unfairly prejudicial to assume it did. The prosecutor would argue that the bills are probative because they are circumstantial evidence that the defendant took the money and that while the evidence is prejudicial to the defendant, it is not *unfairly* so.

In *Diamond Offshore Servs. Ltd. v. Williams*,[2] plaintiff sued for negligence and un-seaworthiness when his back was injured on an offshore drilling rig. The case illustrates how courts can apply the Rule 403 test of whether probative value is outweighed by its unfair prejudice. The Texas Supreme Court held that the trial court should not have excluded an 80-minute video showing plaintiff performing various outdoor tasks, such as using his excavator to haul debris and working on a vehicle, over the course of three days. The Texas Supreme Court's analysis of the application of Rule 403 was as follows:

---

2. *Diamond Offshore Servs. Ltd. v. Williams*, 542 S.W.3d 539 (Texas 2018).

Williams contends the video unfairly prejudices him by suggesting he can work without rest and without pain. That is exactly why Diamond offered the evidence—to show Williams and his witnesses overstated the extent of his physical limitations and pain. Mere damage to an opponent's case does not constitute unfair prejudice. The video does not encourage the jury to decide on any improper basis, but rather on the basis that Williams's condition is not as severe as he claims. That is not unfair.

Williams's chief complaint is that the video misleads the jury by falsely portraying him as able to be physically active for long periods without pain. Videos of injured plaintiffs will, by their very nature, be incomplete. It is impractical if not impossible to record all of a plaintiff's post-injury life. Parties select what to record, or what part of a recording to show, to best help their case. That is inherent in our adversarial system. A video is not misleading just because it does not support the opponent's view of the case. Alleged omissions or inaccuracies typically go to the weight of the evidence, not its admissibility.[3]

4.   Illustration—Laying a Foundation: Real Evidence

In the robbery example where the property stolen was the witness's wallet, the prosecutor would have the clerk mark the envelope containing the wallet with an exhibit number and party identification, such as State's Exhibit #5. The questions and answers could be as follows:

Prosecutor (handing as State's Exhibit #5 to the witness Miller who is the alleged victim of the robbery):

Q.   Mr. Miller, I am handing you what has been marked for identification as State's Exhibit 5. Can you identify the bag?

A.   Yes.

Q.   How do you recognize it?

A.   I've seen the bag before and my initials are on the bag, right here?

Q.   Could you open the bag and look at what is in it, but do not show the contents of the bag to the jury. Can you tell us whether you recognize what is in the bag?

A.   Yes.

Q.   What is it?

A.   It is my wallet.

Q.   How do you know it is your wallet?

A.   I've examined it before at the police station. It has my driver's license in it, my credit cards, and the same amount of cash that I had in it

---

3. *Id.* at 549-550.

when it was taken from me. After I examined it at the police station,
I put it back in this envelope and initialed the envelope.

Prosecutor:
Your Honor, I offer State's Exhibit 5.

Judge:
Any objection?

Defense Counsel:
No, Your Honor.

Judge:
Plaintiff's Exhibit 5 will be admitted.

Prosecutor:
Mr. Miller, will you remove your wallet from the envelope and hold it up so the jurors can see it.

F. Demonstrative Evidence

As opposed to real evidence that can be linked to the occurrence that led to the lawsuit, demonstrative evidence was not involved in the occurrence. Demonstrative evidence demonstrates a matter to be proved in the lawsuit and typically helps a witness illustrate the testimony. For example, a defectively designed toy that is an exhibit and the focal point of a product liability case is an example of real evidence. On the other hand, a diagram of an intersection where a car crash occurred that is introduced as an exhibit in an automobile tort case as a visual aid that a witness to the crash could use to show the jury what happened is an example of demonstrative evidence. Some other examples of demonstrative evidence include charts, models, anatomical drawings, courtroom demonstrations, and animations.

As with all exhibits, the three fundaments (authentication, relevancy, and passing Rule 403 test) must be established for the court to allow visual demonstrative evidence to be shown to the jury. For example, assume that the plaintiff in an automobile tort case wants to introduce a diagram of the intersection where the collision occurred because an eyewitness would use it as a visual aid in communicating what happened to the jury.

To establish the three fundamentals, counsel would elicit testimony from the witness that she is familiar with the intersection because she was there when the accident happened. Further, the witness should testify that the diagram is a fair and accurate depiction of the intersection as it looked at the time of the collision. By testifying that she is familiar with the intersection and that it shows the intersection as it looked at the time of the collision, the witness authenticates the diagram under Fed. R. Evid. 901(a), which requires the proponent produce "evidence sufficient to support a finding that the item is what the proponent claims it is."

More to the point, the testimony complies with Fed. R. Evid. 901(b)(1), which states that the following is an example of evidence satisfying Rule 901(a): "Testimony that an item is what it is claimed to be." The testimony about the diagram showing the intersection as it looked at the time of the collision is essential to fulfill the relevancy requirement because under Fed. R. Evid. 401 the proponent must show that the exhibit has "any tendency to make a fact more or less probable than it would be without the evidence." Without testimony connecting the diagram to the collision, the diagram would be irrelevant and thus inadmissible.

Does the diagram need to be to scale to be admissible? If the witness can testify that it is a fair and accurate depiction, it should be admissible. The testimony that the diagram is a fair and accurate depiction is sufficient to meet the requirement that it is authentic (the witness provides testimony that the diagram shows the intersection) and relevant (at the time of the collision). If the witness is unable testify that the diagram is a fair and accurate depiction of the intersection, the diagram would be inadmissible under Fed. R. Evid. 403 because the diagram would be misleading, and its unfair prejudice would outweigh its probative value.

Another example of demonstrative evidence is a courtroom demonstration. If the demonstration is relevant, a fair and accurate representation of what the witness saw, and passes the Fed. R. Evid. 403 tests, the court has the discretion to allow it. The following is an example of how a foundation could be laid for a courtroom demonstration in the robbery case:

> Prosecutor:
>> Mr. Miller, could you please come over here in front of the jury. I'm handing you a ruler and ask that you assume that this is a knife that you have previously described. Assume that I am the man who pointed the knife at you. Please show the jury, using the ruler, how the defendant pointed it at you.
>
> Defense Counsel:
>> Objection. 403. Waste of time and cumulative.
>
> Prosecutor:
>> Your Honor, the jury should have an opportunity to see how Mr. Miller said the knife was pointed at him.
>
> Judge:
>> Objection is overruled. You may proceed.

Demonstrative evidence may be admitted into evidence. *Clark v. Cantrell*,[4] explains:

> Demonstrative evidence often is admitted only for use in the courtroom to explain and illustrate a witness's testimony, but it also may be

---

4. *Clark v. Cantrell*, 339 S.C. 369, 529 S.E.2d 528, 535-36 (2011).

admissible as an exhibit for the jury to examine and consider during deliberations. *E.g.*, *State v. Kelsey*, 331 S.C. 50, 502 S.E.2d 63, 76 (1998) (photographs and diagram of crime scene properly admitted in evidence); *Holmes v. Black River Elec. Co-op., Inc.*, 274 S.C. 252, 258, 262 S.E.2d 875, 878 (1980) (photographs of plaintiff's injured arm properly admitted in evidence); *State v. Barrs*, 257 S.C. 193, 199, 184 S.E.2d 708, 711 (1971) (upholding admission of coil of copper wire that was like the one allegedly stolen by defendants as proper demonstrative evidence); Mueller & Kirkpatrick, *supra* §9.31.

If requested, the trial judge may instruct the jury under Federal Rule of Evidence 105 that the demonstrative evidence may only be considered by the jury for a limited purpose. Fed. R. Evid. 105 states: "If the court admits evidence that is admissible against a party or for a purpose—but not against another party or for another purpose—the court, on timely request, must restrict the evidence to its proper scope and instruct the jury accordingly." The following is the type of limiting instruction that the court could give orally during the trial when the demonstrative exhibit is introduced for illustrative purposes only:

> I am allowing this exhibit to be used for illustrative purposes only. This means that its status is different from that of other exhibits in the case. This exhibit is not itself evidence. Rather, it is one *[party's] [witness's] [summary] [explanation] [illustration] [interpretation]*, offered to assist you in understanding and evaluating the evidence in the case. Keep in mind that actual evidence is the testimony of witnesses and the exhibits that are admitted into evidence.
>
> Because it is not itself evidence, this exhibit will not go with you to the jury room when you deliberate. The lawyers and witnesses may use the exhibit now and later on during this trial. You may take notes from this exhibit if you wish, but you should remember that your decisions in the case must be based upon the evidence.[5]

For an illustration of predicate questions for a diagram that is a demonstrative exhibit, see pages 91-92. You can tailor those model predicate questions to almost every type of demonstrative exhibit.

---

5. Washington Pattern Jury Instruction 6.06—Civil.

G. Animations

If you want the jury to see the occurrence, such as a plane crash, as it happened, you can have a computer animation of the event created. The impact that a computer animation can have on a jury was discussed in *Clark v. Cantrell*:[6]

> Attempts to use computer-generated video animations at trial, although not an everyday occurrence, are increasing. Computer animation is likely to become more prevalent, especially as the price of preparing such animations falls. G. Ross Anderson, Jr., *Computer Animation; Admissibility and Uses*, South Carolina Trial Lawyer Bulletin 9 (Fall 1995).
>
> Computer animation allows attorneys to convert witnesses' verbal testimony into dynamic, visual demonstrations capable of mentally transporting jurors to the scene. However, a computer animation can mislead a jury just as easily as it can educate them. An animation is only as good as the underlying testimony, physical data, and engineering assumptions that drive its images. The computer maxim "garbage in, garbage out" applies to computer animations.

Anderson, *supra*, at 9. As the Louisiana Supreme Court further explains,

> The extreme vividness and persuasiveness of motion pictures is a two-edged sword. If the film does not portray original facts in controversy, but rather represents a staged reproduction of one party's version of those facts, the danger that the jury may confuse art with reality is particularly great. Further, the vivid impressions on the trier of fact created by the viewing of the motion pictures will be particularly difficult to limit or, if the film is subsequently deemed to be inadmissible, to expunge by judicial instruction.

An animation is demonstrative evidence, which was discussed in the preceding section. The evidentiary predicate is the same as that described in that section. In *People v. Cauley*,[7] the Colorado Court of Appeals outlined the elements required to lay a foundation for a computer animation as follows:

> A computer animation is admissible as demonstrative evidence if the proponent of the video proves that it: 1) is authentic under CRE 901; 2) is relevant under CRE 401 and 402; 3) is a fair and accurate representation of the evidence to which it relates; and 4) has a probative value that is not substantially outweighed by the danger of unfair prejudice under CRE

---

6. *Clark v. Cantrell*, 529 S.E.2d 528, 536 (SC 2011).

7. *People v. Cauley*, 32 P.2d 602 (Col. 2001). *See also People v. Castillo*, 584 N.W.2d 606, 608 (Mich. 1998).

403.... An item of demonstrative evidence is authenticated if there is evidence to support a finding that the item is what its proponent claims it to be. CRE 901. Once authenticity is established, defects in physical evidence go to the weight of that evidence, not its admissibility....

In addition, appellate courts have encouraged trial courts to give cautionary or limiting instructions to the jury when admitting computer generated evidence.[8]

When a person witnessed the event, the evidentiary foundation for authenticating the animation would be similar to the foundation that would be laid by a witness who was called to authenticate a video of an event. The witness testifies that the animation fairly and accurately portrays what the witness saw.

An expert may authenticate an animation when the expert testifies that it illustrates the expert's testimony. For example, in *People v. Bulmer,*[9] an expert on shaken-baby syndrome[10] utilized a computer-animated slideshow to explain what happens to an infant's brain during a shaking episode. The Michigan Appellate Court, in *Bulmer,* held that the jury was properly instructed that the slideshow was a demonstration and not a reenactment of what happened. Further, the court held that the slideshow was demonstrative evidence admissible under Michigan Rules of Evidence 701 and 702 because it was relevant and probative of the issue that the jury was to decide—whether the baby was gently or severely shaken.[11]

The animation used by an expert to explain the expert's testimony must meet the foundational requirements. In *State v. Farner,*[12] a negligent homicide case, an accident reconstructionist used a computer animation to illustrate and explain the expert's testimony about how the accident occurred. The Supreme Court of Tennessee discussed the necessary evidentiary predicate for an animation in depth as follows:

> At the risk of stating the obvious, we note that a computer animation offered to illustrate an expert's opinion will not be admissible unless the expert testimony is itself admissible pursuant to *McDaniel* and the applicable Tennessee Rules of Evidence....
>
> The proponent must further establish that the computer animation is a fair and accurate depiction of the event it purports to portray....
>
> Because the jury may be so persuaded by its life-like nature that it becomes unable to visualize an opposing or differing version of the

---

8. *Id.* at 607.

9. *State v. Bulmer,* 662 N.W.2d 117 (Mich. 2003).

10. The validity of shaken-baby syndrome has been called into question. See https://www.washingtonpost.com/graphics/investigations/shaken-baby-syndrome/.

11. *Id.* at 119.

12. *State v. Farner,* 66 S.W.3d 188, 208-09 (Tenn. 2002).

event, the requirement that the animation fairly and accurately portray the event is particularly important when the evidence at issue is a computer animated recreation of an event. *See, e.g., State v. Trahan*, 576 So.2d 1, 8 (La. 1990) (discussing a motion picture and stating "[t]he vivid impressions on the trier of fact created by the viewing of the motion pictures will be particularly difficult to limit"); *Clark*, 529 S.E.2d at 536 (recognizing that if the portrayal is inaccurate, computer animations pose a high potential to mislead the jury and to create lasting impressions that unduly override other evidence); *Sommervold*, 518 N.W.2d at 737 (stating that because a video reconstruction has a substantial impact on the jury which will tend to view it as true, to be admissible, such reconstructions must be "nearly identical" to the actual event); *Hinkle v. City of Clarksburg*, 81 F.3d 416, 424–25 (4th Cir.1996) (stating that because of its unusual persuasive value, to be admissible, a computer animated visualization must be substantially similar to the actual event).

Like all evidence in Tennessee, a computer animation is subject to exclusion if "its probative value is substantially out-weighed by the danger of unfair prejudice, confusion of the issues, misleading the jury, or by considerations of undue delay, waste of time, or needless presentation of cumulative evidence." . . . If a computer animated portrayal is inaccurate, its probative value decreases and the likelihood that it will be subject to exclusion under Rule 403 increases. Like other evidence, the admissibility of computer animations generally rests within the sound discretion of the trial court, with the rules of evidence governing the exercise of the trial court's discretion.

Applying these rules to the facts in this record, we conclude that the trial court abused its discretion in admitting the computer animated visualization in this case because it is not a fair and accurate portrayal of the event depicted, and as a result, its probative value was substantially outweighed by the danger of unfair prejudice. (citations omitted)

When an animation is shown to the jury, a limiting instruction such as this one given in *Hinkle v. Clarksburg*[13] may be given:

This animation is not meant to be a recreation of the events, but rather it consists of a computer picture to help you understand Mr. Jason's opinion, which he will, I understand, be giving later in the trial. And to re-enforce the point, the video is not meant to be an exact recreation of what happened during the shooting, but rather it represents Mr. Jason's evaluation of the evidence presented.

---

13. *Hinkle v. Clarksburg*, 81 F.3d 416, 425 (1998).

H. Simulations

In 2011, *Bullock v. Daimler Trucks No. America* not only differentiated computer animations from computer simulations but also described the required evidentiary predicate for each by favorably quoting 5 Federal Evidence §9:26 (3d ed. 2010) as follows:

> The rapid advances in computer technology have made possible a dramatic new type of demonstrative evidence in the form of on-screen computer animations or simulations. Animations are visual depictions that serve to illustrate or clarify such things as an expert's opinion as to what occurred. Animations, therefore, are usually offered as illustrative evidence.
>
> Simulations, on the other hand, are created by entering known data into a computer program, which analyzes those data according to the rules by which the program operates (e.g., the laws of physics or mathematics) to draw conclusions about what happened and to recreate an event at issue. The program itself, rather than witness testimony, is the source of the visual images depicted and may actually serve as the basis for opinion testimony. Simulations are therefore usually classified as substantive evidence.
>
> Because animations are typically used to illustrate witness testimony, if a computer-generated animation is offered into evidence, usually the only foundation necessary is that required of other forms of demonstrative evidence—the testimony of a knowledgeable witness that the animation fairly and accurately depicts what its proponent claims. [A] limiting instruction should be given telling the jury the purpose for which the animation is admitted and that it is not to be considered as substantive evidence. Usually illustrative evidence is not sent to the jury room.
>
> A simulation designed to recreate an event at issue is normally offered as substantive evidence and requires a much more rigorous foundation, because the jury is being asked to accept the simulation, which may go beyond anything a witness observed, as evidence of what actually happened. A simulation normally must be authenticated by showing: (1) the qualifications of the expert who prepared the simulation; (2) the capability and reliability of the computer hardware and software used; (3) the calculations and processing of data were done on the basis of principles meeting the standards for scientific evidence under Fed. R. Evid. 702; (4) the data used to make the calculations were reliable, relevant, complete, and properly inputted; and (5) the process produced an accurate result. Simulations which are not properly authenticated are excluded.[14] (citations omitted)

---

14. *Bullock v. Daimler Trucks No. America*, 819 Fed. Supp. 2d 1172, 1176 (2011).

Because a computer simulation constitutes substantive evidence, the proponent must lay a foundation that the simulation meets reliability and relevance requirements under the standard for admissibility of expert evidence in the jurisdiction where it is offered. For federal courts, the standard is that stated in *Daubert v. Merrell Dow Pharmaceuticals, Inc.*[15] Under *Daubert*, the court, acting as gatekeeper, considers five factors: (1) whether a method can or has been tested; (2) the known or potential rate of error; (3) whether the methods have been subjected to peer review; (4) whether there are standards controlling the technique's operation; and (5) the general acceptance of the method within the relevant community. Some jurisdictions use the *Frye* test for admissibility. Under *Frye v. United States,*[16] the evidence "must be sufficiently established to have gained general acceptance in the particular field in which it belongs" Yet other jurisdictions apply a modified *Daubert* test, a mix of *Daubert* and *Frye* and other state standards.[17]

In *In re Yamaha Motor Corp.*,[18] the U.S. District Court for the Western District of Kentucky explained why the *Daubert* standard must be met and applied it to the simulation. Expert witness Ronald Carr's computer simulation was created by a software program known as HVE-SIMON (HVE). Engineering Dynamics Corporation (EDC) created HVE to simulate traditional on-road accidents. The court held:

> Computer simulations are substantive evidence subject to *Daubert* reliability and relevance requirements.... Courts analyzing computer simulations under *Daubert* ask whether the simulation has been tested, subjected to peer review, has a known error rate, and has general acceptance in the scientific community.... However, courts also acknowledge that these factors do not always apply to computer simulations in the same way that they apply to typical expert testimony.
>
> Yamaha objects that Carr's Rhino model is unreliable under *Daubert.* According to Yamaha, the model has not been validated or tested, has no known error rate, has not been peer-reviewed, is not accepted in the scientific community, and was created specifically for the purposes of litigation. The appropriate inquiry, however, is whether the HVE suite passes *Daubert's* reliability requirements. As described earlier, EDC has created HVE models for hundreds of different vehicles. It would make little sense to require each and every model to be tested, subjected to peer review, and gain general acceptance in the scientific community. It

---

15. *Daubert v. Merrell Dow Pharmaceuticals, Inc.*, 509 U.S. 579 (1993).

16. *Frye v. United States*, 293 F. 1013, 1014 (D.C. Cir. 1923).

17. *Christine Funk*, Daubert Versus Frye: A National Look at Expert Evidentiary Standards, The Expert Institute (2018), lists the standards for each state https://www.theexpertinstitute.com/daubert-versus-frye-a-national-look-at-expert-evidentiary-standards/.

18. *In re Yamaha Motor Corp.*, 816 F. Supp. 2d 442, 460-61 (2011).

is sufficient that HVE meets these requirements, and Yamaha agrees it does. R. 2507 at 4 ("Nowhere has Yamaha attacked the validity of the HVE–SIMON suite in general.").

Besides challenging the simulation as unreliable under *Daubert* or another standard for the admissibility of expert evidence, opposing counsel may argue that the input into the computer program was flawed or insufficient, making the simulation inadmissible. *In re Yamaha Motor Corp.* addressed this objection as follows:

> In addition to the traditional *Daubert* requirements of testing, peer-review, error-rate and general acceptance, Yamaha also argues that the simulated Rhino is unreliable because key inputs were estimated by Carr. In support of this argument, Yamaha sponsored a third-party examination of Carr's simulation. This report is highly critical of Carr's simulation. Indeed, it notes a panoply of serious shortcomings with the Rhino model. However, the mere fact that an expert's opinion has flaws does not mean that the opinion is unreliable.
>
> Courts have treated challenges to the data or inputs underlying a computer simulation in differing ways. Typically, where an expert seeks to testify regarding a program or simulation that itself passes *Daubert*, an objection to the particular *inputs* utilized by the expert will not result in the testimony being stricken. In *Shadow Lake Management Co. Inc. v. Landmark American Ins. Co.*, 2008 WL 2510121 (E.D. La. June 17, 2008), the court noted that a computer program utilized by an expert was "commonly used" and "sufficiently reliable" and that "[t]he Defendant's concerns about the factual basis of [the expert's] reports and opinions are best resolved by vigorous cross-examination and the presentation of contrary evidence." Similarly, in *Phillips v. The Raymond Corp.*, the plaintiff challenged a computer simulation offered by the defendant's expert. The court held that "the miscalculations and inaccuracies Phillips contends he has identified go to the weight of the evidence and not its admissibility." In *Turner v. Williams*, the court considered a challenge to expert testimony regarding an accident-reconstruction program. 326 Ill. App. 3d 541, 260 Ill. Dec. 804, 762 N.E.2d 70, 81–82 (2001). According to the court, "[the expert] testified that the computer programs used, EDCRASH and EDSMAC4, are 'widely used and accepted in the field of crash analysis.' In our view, the information used or not used by [the expert] was not a sufficient basis to bar his testimony. This issue could have been adequately brought to light before the jury on cross-examination." However, in *Reali v. Mazda Motor of America, Inc.*, the court concluded that a critical input into a computer simulation was "unreliable" and struck the testimony on that basis. 106 F. Supp. 2d 75 (D.Me. 2000).[19]

---

19. *Id.* 461-62.

I. Photographs, Models, and Videos

1. Elements of the Foundation

The evidentiary foundation for photographs, models, and videos are essentially the same as the one described in section F for demonstrative evidence (see pages 151-53). The proponent of the photograph, model, or video asks predicate questions to elicit the following information: (1) the photograph, model, or video is relevant because it shows something that would "make a fact more... probable than it would be without the evidence" ("That is the intersection where the collision occurred"); (2) the witness is familiar with and can identify the exhibit ("I know it's the intersection where the collision occurred because I was there and witnessed the collision."); (3) the exhibit fairly and accurately depicts what the witness claims it to be, and thus, it is authentic; and (4) if there is a change in the exhibit from how it looked at a relevant time, the difference is explained ("The collision happened in the evening and the picture was taken during the daytime so it isn't as dark in the picture, but otherwise it is a fair and accurate picture of the intersection.").

2. Enlarged Photograph

An enlargement of a photograph may be displayed to the jury if the photograph is admissible. In *Browning v. State*,[20] the defense objected to the prosecutor using a PowerPoint slideshow that included photographs that had been admitted into evidence along with the prosecutor's talking points. The Oklahoma Court of Appeals held:

> Exhibits properly admitted at trial may be used in closing argument. The parties' wide latitude in argument includes latitude to use visual aids. We have upheld the prosecution's use of large projections of color slides and photographs throughout the trial, as the display of otherwise admissible photographs is within the trial court's discretion.[21]

3. Surveillance Video or Photograph

Even when no witness can establish the accuracy of a surveillance video, it can be admitted into evidence if sufficient evidence exists to establish the reliability

---

20. *Browning v. State*, 134 P.3d 816, 839 (Okla. Crim. App. 2006).

21. *Id.* at 839. *See also North Carolina v. Snider*, 168 N.C. App. 701, 706 (2005) and *People v. Watson*, 245 Mich. App. 572, 582 (2005).

of the process that produced it. This has been referred to as the "silent witness theory." The Illinois Supreme Court discussed the foundational elements for a surveillance video in *People v. Taylor*[22] as follows:

> Similar to the foregoing cases, the appellate court in the case at bar looked to several factors in determining whether a proper foundation had been laid for the admission of the VHS tape: (1) the device's capability for recording and general reliability; (2) competency of the operator; (3) proper operation of the device; (4) showing the manner in which the recording was preserved (chain of custody); (5) identification of the persons, locale, or objects depicted; and (6) explanation of any copying or duplication process. We agree that these factors may be considered when determining whether the process by which a surveillance videotape was produced was reliable. However, like other jurisdictions, we emphasize that this list of factors is nonexclusive. Each case must be evaluated on its own and depending on the facts of the case, some of the factors may not be relevant or additional factors may need to be considered. The dispositive issue in every case is the accuracy and reliability of the process that produced the recording.[23]

J. 3D Laser Scanner Images

In Chapter 5 on "Direct Examination," we discussed the 3D laser scanner that can be used to record data at a scene and to create a dynamic presentation of that scene for trial. Here, we focus on the admissibility of 3D laser scanner images and predicate questions that can be asked to lay a proper foundation.

1. Reliability of the 3D Laser Scanner

Challenges may be made to the reliability of the 3D laser scanner and any images it produced as well as to an expert, such as an accident reconstructionist, who would testify in reliance upon the scanner. Reliability may not be a major issue in your jurisdiction because 3D laser scanners are commonly used in construction and/or because opposing counsel is familiar with widely used technology, like Google Maps, and recognizes that the likelihood that a motion to exclude the scanner evidence would be granted is unlikely.

If the 3D laser scanner evidence is challenged, its admissibility will be determined by the jurisdiction's test(s). If the jurisdiction applies the *Frye v. United*

---

22. *People v. Taylor*, 956 N.E.2d 431 (Ill. 2011).

23. *Id.* at 439. *See also State v. Pickens*, 24 N.E.3d 1023, 1055 (Ohio 2014).

States[24] test, the proponent of the evidence is required to establish that the 3D laser scanner in question is generally accepted in the scientific community.

On the other hand, if the jurisdiction follows *Daubert v. Merrell Dow Pharmaceuticals Inc.*,[25] the court will consider these factors: (1) whether the theory or technique can be and has been tested; (2) whether the theory or technique has been subjected to peer review and publication; (3) the known or potential rate of error and the existence and maintenance of standards controlling the technique's operation; and (4) the level of acceptance in the scientific community.

While federal courts adhere to the *Daubert* standard, some state courts also follow *Daubert*, some states follow *Frye* and others follow an amalgam of *Daubert* and *Frye*.

No matter which of these tests the court applies, ample evidence exists to establish the reliability of 3D laser scanner evidence. It has been generally accepted in the scientific community. It has been subject to peer review, and FARO will provide validation papers upon request. The FARO scanner provides error rate reports. Consequently, courts have accepted 3D laser scanner evidence, and on this book's companion website http://www.fastcase.com/visuallitigation. Appendix 8.2 is a list of cases where this evidence has been admitted. FARO will provide an updated list of cases upon request.

2. Laying the Foundation

To lay a foundation for 3D laser scanner evidence, counsel should elicit testimony that the operator of the scanner was qualified; that the equipment was calibrated; and that it was properly operated. FARO has courteously provided the following predicate questions for laying the foundation for the admissibility:

Concerning the Case:
- What examinations have you conducted concerning this case?
- What were the results of this examination?
- Did you write a report regarding the results of this examination?

---

24. *Supra* note 16.

25. *Supra* note 15.

- What did the examination entail?
  - o Photographs
  - o Notes
  - o Videos
  - o Measurements

Concerning the Scanner
- Has the FARO Laser Scanner been tested in scientific setting and public settings?
- Is FARO data peer reviewed?
- Is there acceptance within the scientific community?
- Is this an accurate representation of what you witnessed or saw at the scene in question?

Concerning Measurements
- How did you obtain measurements?
- What instrument was used to obtain these measurements?
- Is the instrument calibrated to international standards?
- When was the last time the instrument was calibrated?
- Do you maintain calibration certificates?
- What is the measurement error rate of the instrument?
- What is the measurement standard deviation of this specific project/case?
- Have you or are you able to generate a report documenting the standard deviation?
- Is the raw data secured?
- What is your data security protocol?
- Was a 3D reconstruction generated from the measurement data?
- What software was used to generate the reconstruction?
- What specific measurements were obtained from the raw data that aided your reconstruction of events?
- Are your results reproducible?
- What training do you have relating to this instrument?
- How many scenes have you used this instrument in?
- How many reconstructions have you done using this instrument?

K. Summary Charts

Two kinds of summary charts exist: (1) a Fed. R. Evid. 1006 chart and a Fed. R. Evid. 611(a) chart. The evidentiary predicates and the extent to which a jury can consider them are different.

I. Fed. R. Evid. 1006 Chart

Fed. R. Evid. 1006 provides:

> The proponent may use a ... chart.... to prove the content of volumi-
> nous writings, recordings, or photographs that cannot be conveniently
> examined in court. The proponent must make the originals or dupli-
> cates available for examination or copying, or both, by other parties at
> a reasonable time and place. And the court may order the proponent to
> produce them in court.

Rule 1006 makes common sense. If there are too many writings, recordings,
or photos for the jury to conveniently examine, they can be summarized on a chart.
To lay an evidentiary foundation for a summary chart, the proponent must establish that the original writings, recordings, or photographs would be admissible,
that they cannot be conveniently examined in court, and that the chart accurately
summarizes the originals.

United States v. Milkiewicz,[26] is an example of how to lay a foundation for a
Rule 1006 chart and its benefits. In *Milkiewicz*, the defendant appealed a conviction of defrauding a federal court when he collaborated with a court administrator,
sold office supplies to the court at inflated prices, and billed it for more products
than he delivered. At trial two summary charts were admitted into evidence, one
showing the allegedly fraudulent sales transactions and the other showing discrep-
ancies in defendant's income tax reporting. The United States Court of Appeals for
the First Circuit discussed what must be established as an evidentiary predicate for
a summary chart to be admissible:

> Rule 1006 allows "[t]he contents of voluminous writings which can-
> not conveniently be examined in court [to] be presented in the form
> of a chart, summary, or calculation." Fed. R. Evid. 1006. It creates an
> exception to Rule 1002, which requires that originals be used to prove
> the content of writings, recordings and photographs. Evidence admit-
> ted under Rule 1006 must be otherwise admissible and remains subject
> to the usual objections under the rules of evidence and the Constitu-
> tion. "Most notably, Rule 1006 evidence normally is objectionable if the
> voluminous source material on which it is based is inadmissible." ... The
> proponent must show that the voluminous source materials are what the
> proponent claims them to be and that the summary accurately summa-
> rizes the source materials.
>
> Under Rule 1006, the underlying documents must be made
> available to the other parties, and "[t]he court may order that they be

---

26. *United States v. Milkiewicz*, 470 F.3d 390 (1st Cir.).

produced in court." The discretion accorded the trial court to order production of the documents means that the evidence underlying Rule 1006 summaries need not be introduced into evidence ... but nothing in the rule forecloses a party from doing so. For example, we can imagine instances in which an attorney does not realize until well into a trial that a summary chart would be beneficial, and admissible as evidence under Rule 1006, because the documents already admitted were too voluminous to be conveniently examined by the jury.

Most often, however, we think it likely that an attorney would anticipate the benefits of summarizing voluminous writings and would take advantage of the opportunity offered by Rule 1006 to present only the summary at trial. Consequently, while in most cases a Rule 1006 chart will be the *only* evidence the fact finder will examine concerning a voluminous set of documents,... in other instances the summary may be admitted *in addition to* the underlying documents to provide the jury with easier access to the relevant information....

This latter practice has drawn criticism as inconsistent with the purpose of Rule 1006 to provide an exception to the "best evidence rule" because, "[i]f the underlying evidence is already admitted, there is no concern that a summary is used in lieu of the 'best evidence.'"... We agree with the Fifth Circuit, however, that "[t]he fact that the underlying documents are already in evidence does not mean that they can be 'conveniently examined in court.'"... Thus, in such instances, Rule 1006 still serves its purpose of allowing the jury to consider secondary evidence as a substitute for the originals.[27] (citations omitted)

2.   Fed. R. Evid. 611(a) Chart

Fed. R. Evid. 611(a) makes no mention of summary charts. Instead, Rule 611(a) empowers a judge to permit summary charts to be used under the judge's authority under Rule 611(a) to "exercise reasonable control over the mode... of... presenting evidence so as to (1) make those procedures effective for determining the truth; (and) (2) avoid wasting time."

A Rule 611(a) chart is different from a 1006 chart. While a 1006 chart is substantive evidence that may go to the jury room for consideration during deliberations, a 611(a) chart is demonstrative evidence that does not come into evidence. The *United States v. Milkiewicz*[28] case, which was discussed in the previous section and laid out the evidentiary predicate for a 1006 chart, also covered not only the

---

27. *Id.* at 396-97.

28. *United States v. Milkiewicz*, 470 F.3d 390 (1st Cir.)

difference between it and a 611(a) chart but also how the lines between the two are indistinct:

> A trial judge also may allow use of a chart or other summary tool under Fed. R. Evid. 611(a), which gives the trial court "control over the mode [of] presenting evidence."... Such summaries most typically are used as "pedagogical devices" to "clarify and simplify complex testimony or other information and evidence or to assist counsel in the presentation of argument to the court or jury."... A summary chart used as a pedagogical device must be linked to evidence previously admitted and usually is not itself admitted into evidence....
>
> The lines between these two types of summary documents are easily blurred. A summary that is admissible under Rule 1006—and is thus most appropriately introduced under that rule—could properly be offered under Rule 611(a) if the supporting material has been admitted into evidence. Likewise, a chart that originally was offered as a jury aid to assist with review of voluminous underlying documents already in evidence—and which accurately summarizes those documents—alternatively could be admitted under Rule 1006 if the court concluded that the supporting documents could not be examined conveniently in court. To complicate matters, a court also has discretion under Rule 703 to provide the jury in some circumstances with the "facts or data" underlying an expert's opinion, and such material may be presented in the form of a summary chart.[29] (citations omitted)

Because a 611(a) summary chart is merely a pedagogical device, the court may give the jury a limiting instruction along this line:

> Certain charts and summaries have been shown to you solely to help explain the facts disclosed by the books, records and documents which are evidence in this case. These charts and summaries are not evidence or proof of any facts. You should therefore determine the facts from the evidence.[30]

United States v. Baker[31] is an example of how Rule 611(a) can be utilized in trial. In that case, an FBI agent testified to the values of drug transactions with the aid of summary charts that were based on her notes of the trial testimony. The summary charts were admitted for illustrative purposes to aid the agent's testimony.

---

29. *Id.* at 397-98.

30. *United States v. Ogba*, 526 F.3d 214, 225 (5th Cir. 2008).

31. *United States v. Baker*, 10 F.3d 1374 (9th Cir. 1993).

L. Documentary Evidence

Some documents, such as a certified copy of a court document, are self-authenticating, and, thus, the proponent need not call a witness to lay a foundation as to its authenticity. You just offer the self-authenticating document into evidence, provided it is relevant and passes Rule 403 and other applicable evidence rules.

However, for other documents the proponent will need to have a witness verify that it is an authentic document, and Fed. R. Evid. 901(b) provides three examples of how to do that. First, this can be accomplished by having a witness testify to being familiar with the writer's handwriting and that the writing on the document is that of the writer.[32] Second, a witness who saw the person write the document could testify to the document's authenticity.[33] A third way to authenticate the document would be to call a handwriting expert who compared the handwriting on a document known to be that of the writer with the handwriting on the questioned document to render an opinion that the handwriting on the document is authentic.[34]

Also, as was covered earlier, other common issues relating to the admissibility of a document concern the hearsay and original writings rules.

M. Video Depositions

1. Court Rules and Compliance

State and federal court rules govern the videoing of depositions, and failure to comply with those rules can result in the exclusion of the video deposition from a hearing or trial. Here we discuss not only those rules but also the best practices to ensure compliance with them.

The following is an example of a Washington civil court rule governing videoing a deposition:

Washington State Court Civil Rule 30 Depositions Upon Oral Examination
(8) Videotaping of depositions.
(A) Any party may videotape the deposition of any party or witness without leave of court provided that written notice is served on all parties not less than 20 days before the deposition date, and specifically states that the deposition will be recorded on videotape.

---

32. Fed. R. Evid. 901(b)(2).

33. Fed. R. Evid. 901(b)(1).

34. Fed. R. Evid. 901(b)(3).

Failure to so state shall preclude the use of videotape equipment at the deposition, absent agreement of the parties or court order.

(B) No party may videotape a deposition within 120 days of the later of the date of filing or service of the lawsuit, absent agreement of the parties or court order.

(C) On motion of a party made prior to the deposition, the court shall order that a videotape deposition be postponed or begun subject to being continued, on such terms as are just, if the court finds that the deposition is to be taken before the moving party has had an adequate opportunity to prepare, by discovery deposition of the deponent or other means, for cross examination of the deponent.

(D) Unless otherwise stipulated to by the parties, the expense of videotaping shall be borne by the noting party and shall not be taxed as costs. Any party, at that party's expense, may obtain a copy of the videotape.

(E) A stenographic record of the deposition shall be made simultaneously with the videotape at the expense of the noting party.

(F) The area to be used for videotaping testimony shall be suitable in size, have adequate lighting and be reasonably quiet. The physical arrangements shall be fair to all parties. The deposition shall begin by a statement on the record of:

     (a) the operator's name, address and telephone number,

     (b) the name and address of the operator's employer,

     (c) the date, time and place of the deposition,

     (d) the caption of the case,

     (e) the name of the deponent, and

     (f) the name of the party giving notice of the deposition. The officer before whom the deposition is taken shall be identified and swear the deponent on camera. At the conclusion of the deposition, it shall be stated on the record that the deposition is concluded. When more than one tape is used, the operator shall announce on camera the end of each tape and the beginning of the next tape.[35]

---

35. Wash. CR 30(b)(8) https://www.courts.wa.gov/court_rules/?fa=court_rules .display&group=sup&set=cr&ruleid=supcr30.

Sections of Federal Rule of Civil Procedure 30 Deposition by Oral Examination that are pertinent to videoed depositions are as follows:

(3) *Method of Recording.*

(A) *Method Stated in the Notice.* The party who notices the deposition must state in the notice the method for recording the testimony. Unless the court orders otherwise, testimony may be recorded by audio, audiovisual, or stenographic means. The noticing party bears the recording costs. Any party may arrange to transcribe a deposition.

(B) *Additional Method.* With prior notice to the deponent and other parties, any party may designate another method for recording the testimony in addition to that specified in the original notice. That party bears the expense of the additional record or transcript unless the court orders otherwise.

(4) *By Remote Means.* The parties may stipulate—or the court may on motion order—that a deposition be taken by telephone or other remote means. For the purpose of this rule and Rules 28(a), 37(a)(2), and 37(b)(1), the deposition takes place where the deponent answers the questions.

(5) *Officer's Duties.*

(A) *Before the Deposition.* Unless the parties stipulate otherwise, a deposition must be conducted before an officer appointed or designated under Rule 28 Rule. The officer must begin the deposition with an on-the-record statement that includes:

(i)   the officer's name and business address;

(ii) the date, time, and place of the deposition;

(iii) the deponent's name;

(iv) the officer's administration of the oath or affirmation to the deponent; and

(v)   the identity of all persons present.

(B) *Conducting the Deposition; Avoiding Distortion.* If the deposition is recorded nonstenographically, the officer must repeat the items in Rule 30(b)(5)(A)(i)–(iii) at the beginning of each unit of the recording medium. The deponent›s and attorneys' appearance or demeanor must not be distorted through recording techniques.

Note that both the state and federal rules dictate what images the video should show, and you should ensure that the place where the deposition is taken complies with the rules and that the videographer complies with the rules when videoing the deponent and attorneys. The sample state court rule above states, "The area to be used for videotaping testimony shall be suitable in size, have adequate lighting and be reasonably quiet. The physical arrangements shall be fair to all parties."[36] The federal rule states, "The deponent's and attorneys' appearance or demeanor must not be distorted through recording techniques."[37] Therefore, how the videographer frames the image of the deponent matters. If the camera shot is from below the deponent's face, it can portray the person as imposing rather than in a neutral manner. If the camera angle is down on the deponent's face, it can give the impression that witness is weak. The best practice is to have the camera at the deponent's eye-level. Further, the camera shot should be neither too close nor too far away. Rather, the image should show the person's head and upper body down to the tabletop.

Another important practice is pay close attention to what the officer says at the outset of the video deposition. Make sure that the officer covers all the matters that the court rule requires. It is best to have the rule's requirements in front of you and check them off as the officer says them.

2.   Prior Inconsistent Statement

As we discussed in Chapter 6 "Cross-Examination Visuals," confronting a witness with a prior inconsistent statement is one of the most effective methods of impeachment. Seeing a video clip of the witness testifying at a deposition to something contrary to what the witness has just testified to in court can be devastating impeachment. Ordinarily the prior statement is offered to impeach the witness and not offered for the truth of the matter contained in the statement. Therefore, the prior statement is not precluded by the hearsay rule. Because the prior inconsistent statement is admissible for the limited purpose of impeaching the credibility of the witness, it is not substantive proof of what is contained in the prior statement.

However, under Fed. R. Evid. 801(d)(1)(A) and counterpart states' rules, a statement by a witness given at a deposition that is inconsistent with the witness's testimony at trial is defined as being non-hearsay. Because the inconsistent statement made at a deposition is not hearsay, it is admissible as substantive evidence.

To be admissible the prior statement must be inconsistent with the testimony given by the witness at trial. Too often lawyers try to impeach with a prior statement that is not in fact inconsistent. It is not required that the prior statement be literally inconsistent. *McCormick on Evidence* states this test for whether it is inconsistent: "could the jury reasonably find that a witness who believed in the truth of

---

36. Wash. CR 30(8)(F).

37. Fed. R. Civ. P. 30(3)(B).

the facts testified to would be unlikely to make a prior statement of this tenor."[38] The important point is that before you attempt to introduce a prior inconsistent statement, lock the witness into a statement that is inconsistent with the witness's prior statement.

Fed. R. Evid. 613 governs how a witness can be examined about a prior inconsistent statement as follows:

(a)   Showing or Disclosing the Statement During Examination. When examining a witness about the witness's prior statement, a party need not show it or disclose its contents to the witness. But the party must, on request, show it or disclose its contents to an adverse party's attorney.

(b) Extrinsic Evidence of a Prior Inconsistent Statement. Extrinsic evidence of a witness's prior inconsistent statement is admissible only if the witness is given an opportunity to explain or deny the statement and an adverse party is given an opportunity to examine the witness about it, or if justice so requires. This subdivision (b) does not apply to an opposing party's statement under Rule 801(d)(2).

3.   Statement of a Party Opponent

Fed. R. Evid. 801(d)(2) provides that statements of a party offered by an opposing party are defined as not hearsay. This includes not only the party's own statements but also those "made by the party's agent or employee on a matter within the scope of the relationship and while it existed as well as statements made by the party's coconspirator during and in furtherance of the conspiracy." Such statements are admissible as substantive evidence.

Moreover, Fed. R. Civ. P. 32(1) provides that at "a hearing or trial, all or part of a deposition may be used against a party on these conditions: (A) the party was present or represented at the taking of the deposition or had reasonable notice of it; (B) it is used to the extent it would be admissible under the Federal Rules of Evidence if the deponent were present and testifying...."

Further, Fed. R. Civ. P. 32(a)(3) states: "An adverse party may use for any purpose the deposition of a party or anyone who, when deposed, was the party's officer, director, managing agent, or designee under Rule 30(b)(6) or 31(a)(4)." Therefore, normally an adverse party can introduce either all or part of a video deposition of a party opponent at trial or a hearing as substantive evidence for any purpose. For two examples, you can show the video deposition of the party

---

38.   Charles T. McCormick, *McCormick on Evidence*, Section 34 at 63 (6th ed. West Group 2006).

opponent in opening statement, and you can introduce it into evidence and show it during your case in chief.

N. Electronic Communications

Electronic communications have all but replaced traditional communications, such as a letter or memorandum. Electronic communications include electronic information posted on social media websites, emails, text messages, and the like. As with documentary evidence, the proponent must establish the fundamental three requirements (relevancy, authenticity, and not disqualified by Rule 403) and that either it is non-hearsay or admissible under an exception to the hearsay rule.

The most challenging element to satisfy when laying a foundation, at least the most litigated, is authenticating the electronic communication.

1.   Social Media

Postings on social media, such as LinkedIn, YouTube, and Facebook, can be strong evidence. For example, the United States Court of Appeals for the Ninth Circuit reviewed a case in which the defendant, who claimed self-defense but was convicted of involuntary manslaughter, offered photographs of the alleged victim, Keith McCraigie, posted on McCraigie's MySpace page holding a shotgun and wearing what appeared to be gang-associated clothes. The appeals court ruled that the trial court should have admitted the photographs as impeachment evidence when three prosecution witnesses had testified to never having seen McCraigie with a firearm.[39]

United States v. Browne[40] decided that the normal rules for authentication should apply to social media even though social media accounts can be accessed and manipulated, as follows:

> We hold today that it is no less proper to consider a wide range of evidence for the authentication of social media records than it is for more traditional documentary evidence. The authentication of electronically stored information in general requires consideration of the ways in which such data can be manipulated or corrupted, *see generally Lorraine v. Markel Am. Ins. Co.*, 241 F.R.D. 534 (D. Md. 2007), and the authentication of social media evidence in particular presents some special challenges because of the great ease with which a social media account may be falsified or a legitimate account may be accessed by an imposter, *cf.*

---

39. *United States v. Garcia*, 729 F.3d 1171, 1179 (9th Cir. 2013).
40. *United States v. Browne*, 834 F.3d 403, 412 (3d Cir. 2016).

Griffin v. State, 419 Md. 343, 19 A.3d 415, 424 (2011) (analyzing state analogue to Rule 901). But the authentication rules do not lose their logical and legal force as a result. *See Tienda v. State*, 358 S.W.3d 633, 638–39 (Tex. Crim. App. 2012) (describing the legal consensus as to the applicability of traditional evidentiary rules to electronic communications and identifying the many forms of circumstantial evidence that have been used to authenticate email printouts, internet chat room conversations, and cellular text messages); *see also Parker v. State*, 85 A.3d 682, 687 (Del. 2014) (analyzing state evidentiary rules and concluding that "[a]lthough we are mindful of the concern that social media evidence could be falsified, the existing [rules] provide an appropriate framework for determining admissibility."); *Burgess v. State*, 292 Ga. 821, 742 S.E.2d 464, 467 (2013) ("Documents from electronic sources such as the printouts from a web-site like MySpace are subject to the same [state] rules of authentication as other more traditional documentary evidence and may be authenticated through circumstantial evidence."). Depending on the circumstances of the case, a variety of factors could help support or diminish the proponent's claims as to the authenticity of a document allegedly derived from a social media website, and the Rules of Evidence provide the courts with the appropriate framework within which to conduct that analysis.

Although no rules specifically address the authentication of social media, Fed. R. Evid. 901(a) and state counterparts have typically been applied as the required evidentiary predicate to authenticate social media. Fed. R. Evid. 901(a) requires that the proponent of the social media establish sufficient evidence that it is what the proponent claims it to be. Unless the author of the media post were to testify that the post is authentic, the proponent of the social media will need to resort to circumstantial evidence to establish authenticity. Typically, courts have relied upon Fed. R. Evid. 901(b)(4), which is one of the examples of how to satisfy Rule 901(a), in analyzing whether the social media has been authenticated. Rule 901(b)(4) states that the following is an example of evidence that satisfies Rule 901(a): "The appearance, contents, substance, internal patterns, or other distinctive characteristics of the item, taken together with all the circumstances."

A variety of circumstantial evidence can be offered to lay the foundation for social media. It is common for the proponent of the exhibit to call the recipient of the communication to authenticate it. However, the testimony of the recipient standing alone can be insufficient. For example, in *Commonwealth v. Williams*,[41] defendant Dwight Williams was convicted of murder in the first degree. At trial, a witness Noyes testified to the content of messages she received at her MySpace from a person she testified was the defendant's brother. The messages came in

---

41. *Commonwealth v. Williams*, 926 N.E.2d 1162 (Mass. 2010).

without objection and then defense counsel moved to strike them, but the trial judge declined to do so. On appeal, one asserted error was that the messages were not properly authenticated. The Supreme Judicial Court of Massachusetts provided the following analysis of both the necessary foundation for authenticating social media communications and why testimony of the recipient of the message standing alone is insufficient, and specifically required evidence of the identification of the author of the communication:

> The defendant's authentication argument is based on his claim that the Commonwealth did not "prove... that the source of the alleged [MySpace] messages was Jesse Williams [the defendant's brother]." An item offered in evidence must be "what its proponent represents it to be."... Authenticity is usually proved by testimony of a witness either "(1) that the thing is what its proponent represents it to be, or (2) that circumstances exist which imply that the thing is what its proponent represents it to be."...
>
> Noyes testified that Williams was the defendant's brother, that he had a picture of himself on his MySpace account, and that his MySpace name was "doit4it." She testified that she had received the messages at issue from Williams, and the document (which had been marked for identification) indicated that those messages were in fact sent by the user with the screen name "doit4it" and bore a picture of Williams. Noyes testified that she responded to three of the messages, and that he sent communications back to her; she did not respond to the fourth message. The contents of the messages demonstrate that the sender was familiar with Noyes and the pending criminal cases against the defendant and desired to keep her from testifying.
>
> There was insufficient evidence to authenticate the messages and they should not have been admitted. Although it appears that the sender of the messages was using Williams's MySpace Web "page," there is no testimony (from Noyes or another) regarding how secure such a Web page is, who can access a MySpace Web page, whether codes are needed for such access, etc. Analogizing a MySpace Web page to a telephone call, a witness's testimony that he or she has received an in-coming call from a person claiming to be "A," without more, is insufficient evidence to admit the call as a conversation with "A."... Here, while the foundational testimony established that the messages were sent by someone with access to Williams's MySpace Web page, it did not identify the person who actually sent the communication. Nor was there expert testimony that no one other than Williams could communicate from that Web page. Testimony regarding the contents of the messages should not have been admitted.[42] (citations omitted)

---

42. *Id.* at 1172-73.

However, testimony of the recipient of the social media taken together with other circumstantial evidence can prove sufficient. An example of how to lay a foundation by coupling testimony of the recipient with other circumstantial evidence to establish the actual author of the communication is *Campbell v. State*.[43] In *Campbell*, the prosecution at trial called Ana, the recipient of messages purporting to be from defendant Campbell's Facebook account. The Texas Court of Appeals held:

> In analyzing whether the evidence is sufficient to support the trial court's ruling, we start by noting that the content of the messages themselves purport to be messages sent from a Facebook account bearing Campbell's name to an account bearing Ana's name. While this fact alone is insufficient to authenticate Campbell as the author, when combined with other circumstantial evidence, the record may support a finding by a rational jury that the messages were authored and sent by Campbell.[44]

The court ultimately decided that when Ana's testimony was considered with the other circumstantial evidence, the evidentiary foundation was sufficient, stating:

> From the record before us—including (1) the similarities between the speech pattern presented in the messages and Campbell's speech pattern at trial; (2) the fact that the messages reference the incident and were sent just a few days after the incident; (3) testimony establishing that only Campbell and Ana have ever had access to Campbell's Facebook account; and (4) Ana's testimony that she did not have access to Campbell's Facebook account at the time the messages were sent—we conclude that there was prima facie evidence such that a reasonable jury could have found that the Facebook messages were created by Campbell. Accordingly, we cannot conclude that the trial court abused its discretion in admitting the evidence over Campbell's objection to authentication.[45]

United States v. Farrad[46] serves as another illustration of how to authenticate visuals on social media under Fed. R. Evid. 901(a). *Farrad* involved the authentication of photographs posted on Facebook. Malik Farrad, a convicted felon, accepted a friend request on Facebook from an undercover police officer. The officer saw that posted on Facebook was a photograph showing three handguns. The officer got a warrant to search Facebook's records for information under the defendant's name. The officer found another photograph of a person who looked like the

---

43. *Campbell v. State*, 382 S.W.3d 545 (Tex. Ct. App. 2012).

44. *Id*. at 551.

45. *Id*. at 553.

46. *United States v. Farrad*, 895 F.3d 859, 878 (2018).

defendant holding a gun. Farrad was charged and convicted of unlawful possession of a firearm. In *Farrad*, the United States Court of Appeals for the Sixth Circuit discussed authentication of a visual on social media in another case, *United States v. Thomas*, as well as the case before the court, as follows:

> The question, then, is the central one: the authentication of the photos. Although it did not discuss the business-records exception, the closest analogue from our precedents is *United States v. Thomas*, 701 F. App'x 414 (6th Cir. 2017)—a case that itself illustrates that the business-records exception was not necessary to admit the photos here. The defendant in that case, Jabron Thomas, was charged with armed bank robbery, and he was identified at trial in part through photos obtained from Facebook and another social-media platform, Instagram.... He argued that the photos "could not be authenticated and were thus inadmissible in part because [the investigator who obtained them] admitted that he did not know who created the Facebook page or whether the Facebook page itself was authentic."... We turned that argument aside, however, noting that there was simply enough evidence presented "to support a finding that the [photograph] [was] what the proponent claim[ed] it to be."... (quoting FED. R. EVID. 901(A)). The photos "appeared to show Thomas with distinctive tattoos" and clothing, which was enough given that "the government was not seeking to authenticate Jabron Thomas's [or any] Facebook page or Instagram page (nor any of the factual information contained therein, such as Thomas's workplace)[,] and the government was not even necessarily presenting the photographs as 'pictures of Jabron Thomas'—the jury was free to consider the photographs as identifying Thomas or not."... Given that there was sufficient evidence that the photos were what they were claimed to be, in short, we ruled that there was no abuse of discretion in admitting them....
>
> That rationale is all that is needed to resolve the ultimate question here. As already mentioned above, not only did the details of the account match Farrad,... but more importantly, the photos appeared to show Farrad, his tattoos, and (perhaps most probatively) distinctive features of Farrad's apartment, as confirmed by police investigation.... The Government was at most seeking to introduce these photos as evidence uploaded by a particular Facebook account that tended to show Farrad in possession of a real gun; the photos were not, however, offered as definitive and irrebuttable proof.... No specific evidence was shown to suggest that the photographs were not "accurate representation[s] of the scene depicted."... In short, while there were still questions about the photos that merited probing, those questions were not so glaring as to prevent the photos from clearing the relatively lower hurdle of authentication....

The district court was correct to admit them.[47] (citations in the opinion and citations in the opinion to the trial record omitted)

The remaining question is: What is the standard that the judge should apply in determining whether sufficient evidence exists to conclude that the social media visual is admissible? *United States v. Vayner*[48] set forth the standard, which many courts and federal courts have adopted.[49] *Vayner* held:

> "The requirement of authentication is a condition precedent to admitting evidence." *Sliker*, 751 F.2d at 497; *see also United States v. Maldonado-Rivera*, 922 F.2d 934, 957 (2d Cir. 1990) ("In general, a document may not be admitted into evidence unless it is shown to be genuine."). Rule 901 of the Federal Rules of Evidence governs the authentication of evidence and provides, in pertinent part: "To satisfy the requirement of authenticating or identifying an item of evidence, the proponent must produce evidence sufficient to support a finding that the item is what the proponent claims it is." Fed. R. Evid. 901(a). "This requirement is satisfied if sufficient proof has been introduced so that a reasonable juror could find in favor of authenticity or identification." *United States v. Pluta*, 176 F.3d 43, 49 (2d Cir. 1999) (internal quotation marks omitted). The ultimate determination as to whether the evidence is, in fact, what its proponent claims is thereafter a matter for the jury. *See Sliker*, 751 F.2d at 499.[50]

This standard that requires that the proponent of a social media visual need to lay a foundation of facts sufficient to support a reasonable juror's determination that the visual is authentic is not the only one courts have used. The Maryland Court of Appeals in *Griffin v. State*[51] set a higher standard, holding that the proponent of the evidence must produce sufficient evidence to demonstrate that the item of evidence is what the proponent claims it to be.[52]

In 2015, the Maryland Court of Appeals revisited the standard question in *Sublet v. State*,[53] and embraced the holding in *Vayner*, deciding that to authenticate social media evidence the proponent would need to lay a foundation from which a

---

47. *Id.* at 877-78.

48. *United States v. Vayner*, 769 F.3d 125 (2d Cir. 2014).

49. Elizabeth A. Flanagan, #Guilty? Sublet v. State and the Authentication of Social Media Evidence in Criminal Proceedings, 61 Vill. L. Rev. 287, 295 (2016).

50. *United States v. Vayner*, 769 F.3d 125, 129-30 (2d Cir. 2014).

51. *Griffin v. State*, 19 A.3d 418 (Md. 2011).

52. *Id.* at 423.

53. *Sublet v. State*, 113 A.3d 695 (Md. 2015).

reasonable juror could find that the media communication was what the proponent claimed it to be.[54] Also, the court drew upon the *Vayner* decision by conducting an analysis of the distinctive characteristics and circumstantial evidence in reaching its conclusions regarding authentication.

In *Parker v. State*,[55] the Delaware Supreme Court discussed two competing theories of social media authentication, which the Court identified as the "Texas" and the "Maryland" theories, holding:

> Parker claims that the Superior Court erred in admitting statements posted on her Facebook profile. The Superior Court admitted the evidence under Rule 901 of the Delaware Rules of Evidence. Parker argues that we should adopt the rule set forth in *Griffin v. State*, a Maryland Court of Appeals decision, to authenticate social media evidence. Under the *Maryland approach*, social media evidence may only be authenticated through the testimony of the creator, documentation of the internet history or hard drive of the purported creator's computer, or information obtained directly from the social networking site. Unless the proponent can demonstrate the authenticity of the social media post to the trial judge using these exacting requirements, the social media evidence will not be admitted, and the jury cannot use it in their factual determination. Under this approach, social media evidence is only authenticated and admissible where the proponent can convince the trial judge that the social media post was not falsified or created by another user.
>
> Conversely, the State advocates for the *Texas approach*, under which a proponent can authenticate social media evidence using any type of evidence so long as he or she can demonstrate to the trial judge that a jury could reasonably find that the proffered evidence is authentic. The Texas approach involves a lower hurdle than the Maryland approach, because it is for the jury—not the trial judge—to resolve issues of fact, especially where the opposing party wishes to challenge the authenticity of the social media evidence.
>
> The Superior Court adopted the Texas approach and found that Parker's social media post was sufficiently authenticated by circumstantial evidence and by testimony explaining how the post was obtained. On appeal, Parker claims that social media evidence requires greater scrutiny than other evidence and should not be admitted unless the trial judge is convinced that the evidence has not been falsified. We disagree. We conclude that the Texas approach better conforms to the requirements of Rule 104 and Rule 901 of the Delaware Rules of Evidence, under which the jury ultimately must decide the authenticity of social media evidence. *A trial judge may admit a relevant social media post where the*

---

54. *Id.* at 718.

55. *Parker v. State*, 85 A.3d 682 (2014).

proponent provides evidence sufficient to support a finding by a reasonable juror that the proffered evidence is what the proponent claims it to be. We find no abuse of discretion by the trial court in admitting the social media evidence in accordance with the Delaware Rules of Evidence. Accordingly, we affirm.[56] (emphasis added).

Furthermore, in "Authentication of Social Media Evidence," Judge Paul Grimm, serving on the United States District Court for the District of Maryland, writes about the legal theory of conditional admissibility/relevance:

> In the vast majority of cases, when the proponent of documentary or similar evidence—whether digital or hard copy—offers the exhibit into evidence, there either is no authenticity objection at all or a formalistic objection that the foundation offered was inadequate because of an asserted failure to produce evidence that would fit within one of the methods of authentication illustrated in Rule 901(b) or Rule 902. Seldom does the objecting party offer a competing version of facts that would rebut those offered by the proponent to show that the exhibit is what the proponent contends it is. When all that the objecting party offers is speculation or conjecture about who, other than the putative creator, "could" have created the evidence, such questions are properly left to the jury in determining how much weight, if any, to give to the evidence—provided that the trial judge is convinced that the proponent has met the relatively low threshold required by Rule 901(a) of producing facts that would be sufficient for a reasonable jury to conclude that the evidence was created by the putative creator. In these circumstances, it is the trial judge's decision whether the evidence is authentic pursuant to Rule 104(a).
>
> Only in the comparatively less frequent case where the proponent of the evidence proves facts sufficient to justify a jury's conclusion that the evidence is authentic, and the opponent proves facts that also would justify a reasonable jury in reaching the opposite conclusion does the judge not have the final say about the admissibility of the evidence. In such an instance, the court is faced with a conditional relevance issue under Rule 104(b). When a conditional relevance issue arises, the proper action for the trial judge to take is to conditionally admit the evidence and instruct the jurors that if they agree with the proponent, they may consider the evidence, giving it the weight they think it deserves. If they side with the opponent, however, they should not consider the evidence. When there is plausible evidence of both authenticity and inauthenticity,

---

56. *Id.* at 682-83.

the trial judge should not exclude the evidence. *State v. Eleck* illustrates the frequent misunderstanding of this confusing rule.[57]

While you will need to offer extrinsic evidence to authenticate most social media, government websites are an exception. Federal Rule of Evidence 902(5) states that a "publication purporting to be issued by a public authority" is self-authenticating.

2. Emails and Text Messages

Because text messages and email are common modes of communication, they are everyday trial exhibits. As with social media communications, a primary challenge for the proponent is laying the foundation to authenticate the exhibit that is ordinarily a printout of the email or text message. Fed. R. Evid. 1001(d) states, "[f]or electronically stored information, 'original' means any printout—or other output readable by sight—if it accurately reflects the information." Therefore, the printout complies with the best evidence under Fed. R. Evid. 1002.

The proponent of a text message or email should seek to lay an evidentiary predicate with the same sort of extrinsic evidence that was outlined in the prior section concerning social media. A witness could testify that the printout is what the proponent claims because the witness wrote it, and thus, Fed. R. Evid. 901(a) would be satisfied. Or, the proponent would produce sufficient circumstantial evidence to show that the exhibit is what the proponent claims it to be, such as by establishing the exhibit's distinctive characteristics, which is the Fed. R. Evid. 901(b)(4) example of how to satisfy Fed. R. Evid. 901(a).

State v. Thompson[58] provides a valuable discussion of what the proponent of a text message will need to establish as an evidentiary foundation, the standard for admissibility, as well as examples of how foundations for admissibility have been laid in several cases. First, the North Dakota Supreme Court cited the state's counterpart to Fed. R. Evid. 901 as controlling. Next, the court stated that the trial court should adhere to the standard followed in federal cases in deciding whether the exhibit is admissible as follows:

> Under the federal rule, the proponent of offered evidence need not rule out all possibilities inconsistent with authenticity or conclusively prove that evidence is what it purports to be; rather, the proponent must

57. Honorable Paul W. Grimm et al., "Authentication of Social Media Evidence," 36 Am. J. Trial Advoc. 433, 457-459 (2013).

58. *State v. Thompson*, 777 N.W.2d 617 (N.D. 2010).

provide proof sufficient for a reasonable juror to find the evidence is what it purports to be.[59]

Then, the court held that it would follow the lead of other appellate decisions where circumstantial evidence was used to authenticate text messages and provided examples from those cases. Those cases are instructive concerning how to lay a foundation for a text message or an email. The court stated:

> Although this Court has not previously considered an issue about the foundational requirements for the admissibility of text messages, other courts have held that similar electronic messages were authenticated by circumstantial evidence establishing the evidence was what the proponent claimed it to be. *See United States v. Siddiqui*, 235 F.3d 1318, 1322–23 (11th Cir. 2000) (e-mails properly authenticated when they included defendant's e-mail address, the reply function automatically dialed defendant's e-mail address as sender, messages contained factual details known to defendant, messages included defendant's nickname, and messages were followed with phone conversations on same topic); *United States v. Tank*, 200 F.3d 627, 630–31 (9th Cir. 2000) (foundational requirement for chat room conversation established when defendant admitted he used screen name "Cessna" when he participated in recorded conversations, several co-conspirators testified he used that name, and defendant showed up at meeting arranged with person using screen name "Cessna"); *United States v. Simpson*, 152 F.3d 1241, 1249–50 (10th Cir. 1998) (authentication established when chat room printout showed individual using name "Stavron" gave officer defendant's name and address and subsequent e-mail exchanges indicated e-mail address belonged to defendant); *United States v. Safavian*, 435 F.Supp.2d 36, 40 (D.D.C. 2006) (e-mail messages held properly authenticated when the e-mail addresses contain distinctive characteristics including the e-mail addresses and a name of the person connected to the address, the bodies of the messages contain a name of the sender or recipient, and the contents of the e-mails also authenticate them as being from the purported sender to the purported recipient); *Dickens v. State*, 175 Md. App. 231, 927 A.2d 32, 36–38 (2007) (threatening text messages received by victim on cell phone were properly authenticated when circumstantial evidence provided adequate proof message was sent by defendant); *Kearley v. Mississippi*, 843 So.2d 66, 70 (Miss. Ct. App. 2002) (e-mails adequately authenticated when witness vouched for accuracy of e-mail printouts and police officer testified defendant admitted sending e-mails); *State v. Taylor*, 178 N.C. App. 395, 632 S.E.2d 218, 230–31 (2006) (text messages properly authenticated when telephone

---

59. *Id.* at 624.

employees testified about logistics for text messages and about how particular text messages were stored and received and messages contained sufficient circumstantial evidence the victim was the person who sent and received the messages); *In re F.P.*, 878 A.2d 91, 93–95 (Pa. Super. Ct. 2005) (instant messages properly authenticated through circumstantial evidence including screen names and context of messages and surrounding circumstances); *Massimo v. State*, 144 S.W.3d 210, 215–17 (Tex. App. 2004) (e-mails admissible when victim recognized defendant's e-mail address, e-mails discussed things only the victim, defendant, and few others knew, e-mails written in way defendant would communicate, and third-party witnessed defendant sending similar threatening e-mail)....[60]

United States v. Lewisbey[61] is one more example of how to lay an evidentiary predicate for an electronic message. The United States Court of Appeals for the Seventh Circuit described the circumstantial evidence produced to authenticate the text messages as follows:

To authenticate the text messages, the government needed only to "produce evidence sufficient to support a finding" that the messages were actually sent and received by Lewisbey. FED. R. EVID. 901(a). The government clearly did so. The iPhone was confiscated from Lewisbey at the time of his arrest, and in a recorded phone call from the jail, he told his mother that the police took his phone. The Samsung device was recovered from his bedroom at his parents' home, a room that both parents identified as belonging exclusively to him. The "Properties" section of the iPhone described the phone as "Big Dave's," and the contacts directory included information for Lewisbey's mother listed under the heading "Mom," and also the name and number of his former attorney. Both phones listed contact information for the Texas Home Depot stores where Lewisbey used to work. And the confidential informant arranged gun sales with Lewisbey on the Samsung phone. That's more than enough to establish that the two phones were indeed Lewisbey's. *See* FED. R. EVID. 901(b)(4) ("The appearance, contents, substance, internal patterns, or other distinctive characteristics of the item, taken together with all the circumstances," can establish that "the item is what the proponent claims it is.").[62]

---

60. *Id.* at 624-25.

61. *United States v. Lewisbey*, 843 F.3d 653 (7th Cir. 2016).

62. *Id.* at 658.

Checklist—Evidentiary Predicated for Visual Exhibits

Evidentiary Requirements for a Foundation

❑ Three evidentiary requirements for admissibility of a visual exhibit are:
1. The exhibit must meet the relevancy requirement under Fed. R. Evid. 401 and 402;
2. The visual must pass muster under Rule 403—its probative value is not substantially outweighed by unfair prejudice; and
3. The exhibit must be authentic under Rule 901 or 902.

❑ When the exhibit contains words, it must either be non-hearsay or fall under an exception to the hearsay rule.

❑ To be admissible, a duplicate of an original document must satisfy the original writings rules—Rules 1001-1004.

Real Evidence

❑ Is the real visual exhibit relevant?
❑ Is the real evidence visual authentic?
  ✓ Can a witness testify that a readily identifiable exhibit is what the proponent claims it is?
  ✓ If the exhibit is not readily identifiable or fungible, you must prove a chain of custody?
  ✓ Is it authentic under Rule 901 or self-authenticated under Rule 902?
❑ Does it pass Rule 403?

Documentary Evidence

❑ Is it relevant?
❑ Is it authentic under Rule 901 or self-authenticated under Rule 902?
❑ Does it pass Rule 403?
❑ Is it admissible under the original writing rules, Rules 1001-1004?
❑ Is it admissible as non-hearsay or under an exception to the hearsay rule?

Demonstrative Evidence

❑ Is it relevant?
❑ Is it authentic under Rule 901 or self-authenticated under Rule 902?

- ❑ Does it pass Rule 403?
- ❑ Is it admissible under the original writings rules—Rules 1001-1004?
- ❑ Is it admissible as non-hearsay or under an exception to the hearsay rule?
- ❑ Is it otherwise admissible?

Chapter 9

Creating Demonstrative and Video Evidence

> "I strive for two things in design: simplicity and clarity. Great design is born of those two things."
>
> Lindon Leader, strategic design consultant

A. Being Self-Sufficient

In this chapter, we work from the assumptions that either you want to design your litigation visuals or you do not have any desire to do so but lack the budget to hire a professional designer and thus must create it yourself out of necessity. Here we examine software programs that you could take advantage of to design graphics even if you have no artistic talent. Naturally, if you are an artist, you may be fully capable of creating visuals freehand. Also, in this chapter, we explore software that can be employed to record, edit, and create video evidence.

A caveat deserves mentioning here. While an attorney can create the litigation visual, if it will be necessity to call a witness regarding this exhibit, it is advisable for an investigator or support person make the visual or be able to explain the process and any software that was employed because counsel cannot testify.

B. SmartDraw Overview

If your case calls for a diagram of a floor plan, landscape, a crime scene, a timeline, or some other graphic, and you don't have a budget for graphics, SmartDraw[1] is for you. SmartDraw is a software product recognized by the courts.[2]

SmartDraw has a library of over 5,000 clip art graphics that can be used to construct demonstrative evidence. It is relatively inexpensive for a yearly online subscription by comparison with what it usually would cost to have a graphic artist create it, and no artistic skills are required. You could also purchase a download of SmartDraw for Windows, but it will be more expensive. SmartDraw offers an academic discount for law professors and law students for the online subscription and for the download. SmartDraw permits you to try the software for seven days.

With SmartDraw software, you produce a demonstrative that is designed with simplicity, clarity, and accuracy. You can create demonstrative evidence for pretrial negotiations and trial. As was discussed in Chapter 8 "Evidentiary Predicates," for the demonstrative evidence to be admissible, the three prerequisites for admissibility must be satisfied. The exhibit must be shown to be authentic and relevant, and must pass the Evidence Rule 403 tests (its probative value cannot be "substantially outweighed by a danger of one or more of the following: unfair prejudice, confusing the issues, misleading the jury, undue delay, wasting time, or needlessly presenting cumulative evidence"). Therefore, you will need to design the demonstrative evidence with the aid of witness(es) who can at trial testify to the exhibit's relevance and further that it is a fair and accurate depiction of what the witness(es) saw. If the diagram differs in any respect, it must not be a misleading discrepancy, and the witness who is called to establish its accuracy should explain how it differs.

Once you have designed the demonstrative evidence, you have multiple options for displaying it. You can paste it into a PowerPoint slide where it can be shown in a slideshow. Alternatively, it could be printed out, enlarged, and adhered to a poster board. Or, you could place the printout on a document camera so that it will be projected on a screen.

C. Mastering SmartDraw

SmartDraw is easy to master because the templates and tools are clearly defined. When you open SmartDraw, you will see that most of the screen is filled with templates of over 70 categories of diagrams.

---

1. https://www.smartdraw.com.

2. *Timelines, Inc. v. Facebook, Inc.* 938 F. Supp. 2d 781, 787 (N.D. Ill. 2013).

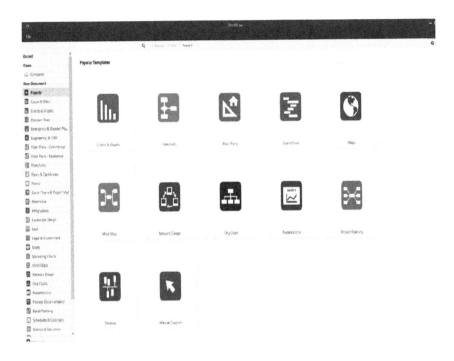

On the left side of the screen you will see a panel with the categories containing over 800 templates. With this panel you can choose the type of diagram with which you wish to work. When you click on the type of diagram, it brings up what is referred to by SmartDraw as a "smart panel" containing shapes that you can apply in constructing your diagram.

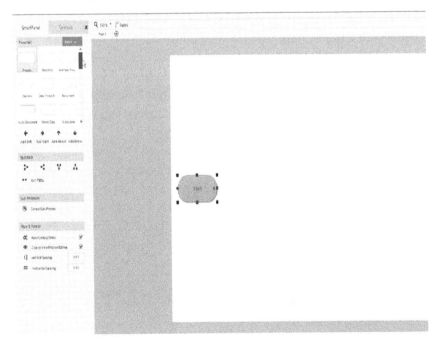

To the right of the smart panel label is a tab labeled "Symbols" that contains the library of over 5,000 pieces of clip art, and it will automatically bring up the symbols that are appropriate for the kind of diagram you intend to develop. To build your diagram, click on the object you want from the library and drag it to where you would like it placed in the diagram.

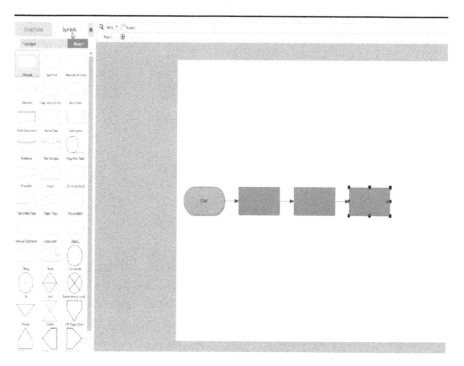

At the top of the screen on the left you will see a tool bar with the customary symbols for things such as undo, save, and print. These tabs are followed on the right by tabs that allow you to share what you have created by email or by exporting it to PDF, Word, or PowerPoint. The ribbon under the tool bar that runs across the top of the screen contains the tools that you will need to create your diagram, such as shape, line, text, and styles.

The main part of the screen is your work area where you create the diagram. As symbols are added to that area, it automatically expands to accommodate them. To add text, just click on a symbol and begin typing. By right-clicking you can access tools to work with such as inserting a picture. To add or change colors, click on the **Theme** tab on the ribbon and select the color you want. There are also tabs for style, effects and so on. The **Design** tab on the ribbon provides tools that enable you to move objects in the diagram.

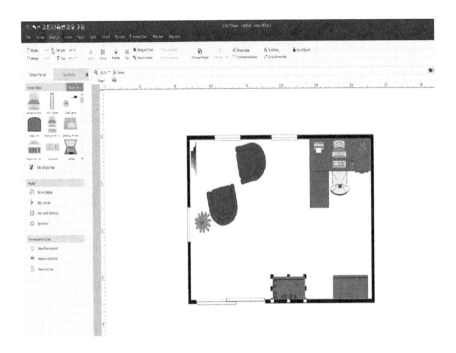

After you have completed the diagram save it by clicking on the **Save** tab on the tool bar at the top of the screen and give the diagram a name. If you wish to close the diagram, click the **X** on the upper left side of the screen.

In the following sections, we examine how SmartDraw can be used to create crime scene diagrams, timelines, floor plans, and landscape diagrams. Excellent video tutorials exist for utilizing SmartDraw to design the different types of demonstratives. As we go through the types, you will find the links to the video tutorials in the footnotes in this chapter. Also, you can watch a video to see how to get started with SmartDraw; its link is in the footnote.[3]

In the last section of this chapter, we examine software alternatives to SmartDraw.

D. Crime Scene Diagram

SmartDraw is for prosecutors and criminal case defense attorneys because it provides a handy, inexpensive way to create a crime scene diagram. As previously mentioned, counsel cannot testify, and therefore, you will need a witness who can authenticate the diagram. To begin, on the home page for SmartDraw choose the **Legal** category of Visuals on the left side of the screen and then select **Crime Scene Diagram**, which provides crime scene templates and examples.

---

3. https://www.youtube.com/watch?v=zKX8zFzuZc8.

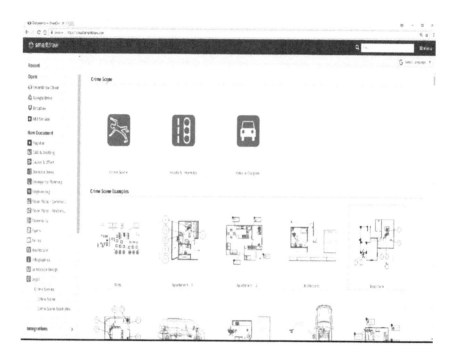

For example, you could click on **Crime Scene** as shown on the upper left of the screen, bringing up a blank screen on which you can begin to create the diagram. And, on the left is a smart panel with the symbols that you can place into the diagram by dragging them from the left side of the screen and dropping them onto the screen.

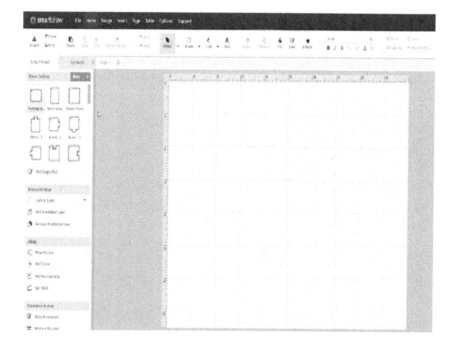

If the crime occurred in a room, you could design the room to the exact dimensions and with the right objects, such as the furniture, in the right places, with the **Floor** plan function explained in section D. Or if the crime scene was outside, the **Landscaping** function can be applied as is explained in section E.

Once the scene of the crime has been designed, you go to the crime scene library on the smart panel on the left. There you can draw upon the objects provided, such as clip art of blood spatter patterns, body outlines, and so on. With a control handle, objects can be rotated and resized. With a click on a shape, you can choose a picture from your computer and insert it. For example, you could insert a picture of the crime victim lying on the bed in the room that you have designed.

Crime scene diagrams are not limited to rooms and outdoors; SmartDraw has a selection of vehicles in the library for case where the scene of the crime is a vehicle. Appropriate Crime Scene Library symbols can be inserted into the vehicle.

You can also label things in the room. Place the cursor on a shape in the room and label it with text. For instance, you could have a text box with the word "Firearm" in it, and then with SmartDraw's arrow tool have the arrow at the end of a line point to where the firearm is lying on the floor.

SmartDraw has a video tutorial showing how easy it is to create a crime scene diagram.[4]

E. Floor Plan Diagram

When the incident in your case happened inside a building, you want to be able to show your audience, whether it is a judge, jury, mediator, or others, what took place. You want to be able to communicate it visually. We have already examined how to construct a crime scene diagram for a criminal case. A floor plan may be needed to show your audience what happened in a criminal or civil case. For instance, you would want to have a floor plan diagram of a grocery store if the negligence case involved a slip and fall in a grocery store.

---

4. https://www.youtube.com/watch?v=V4cFAQ-VUtk.

SmartDraw makes it simple to design a floor plan. Begin by clicking on **Popular** on the left column and then click on **Floor Plan**; this will bring up numerous floor plan templates from which you can pick one. The floor plans are varied, including not only plans for residences but also offices and more. You can also select **Custom Floor Plan**, giving you the opportunity to draw on a blank slate.

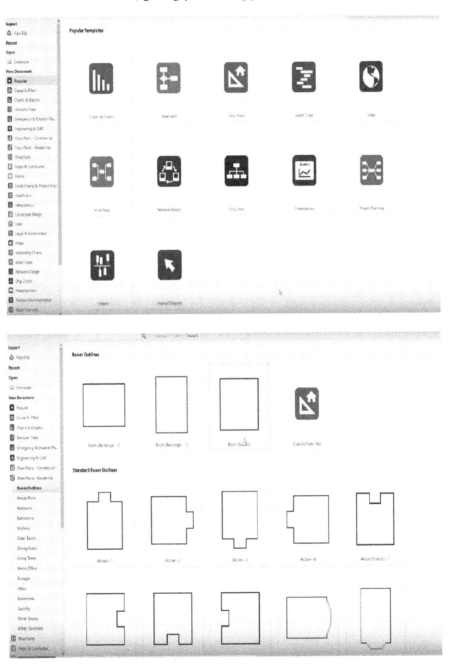

If you were designing a floor plan for a room, you would go to the smart panel on the left that provides you with the tools for drawing the floor plan, such as the Add Wall tool. Just drag the wall to the workspace and click on it when you have the placement you desire. Just keep adding walls until you have completed the room. To size the room to the dimensions you wish, click on the **Design** tab on the ribbon at the top of the screen, and then click on the **Dimensions** tab. Tools on the left enable you to add alcoves and otherwise reshape the room. Add windows and doors by dragging them from the left column onto the diagram where you want them placed.

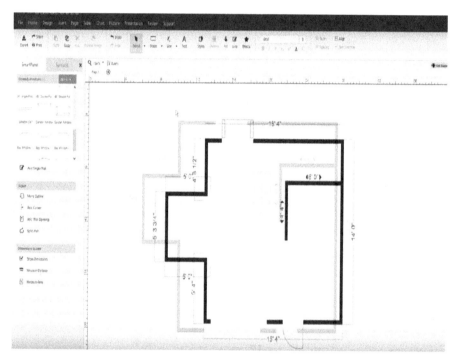

To add furniture, appliances, and so on to the floor plan go to the smart panel on the left and click on **Symbols**. Then, select what you are seeking from the vast library. Then, drag and drop them where you want in the room. Using the **Units** and **Scales** tab on the left column you can draw using any scale selected from the architectural, mechanical engineering, civil engineering, and metric scales.

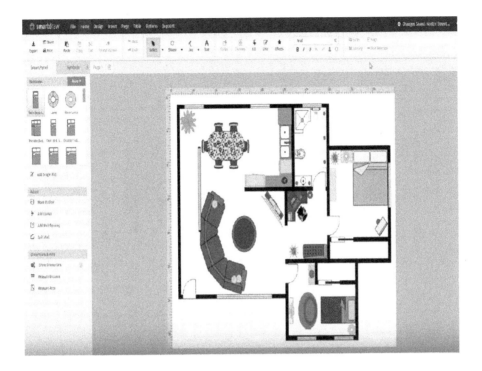

SmartDraw has a video tutorial showing how easy it is to create a floor plan.[5]

F. Landscape Diagram

If the critical events in your case occurred outdoors, a landscape diagram will allow you to show your audience where things happened. The approach to creating a landscape diagram runs along the same lines as that for drawing a floor plan. You can find templates for a wide array of landscapes from back yards to parks by clicking on landscapes in the left side column.

---

5. https://www.youtube.com/watch?v=VDz5WhDQtWU.

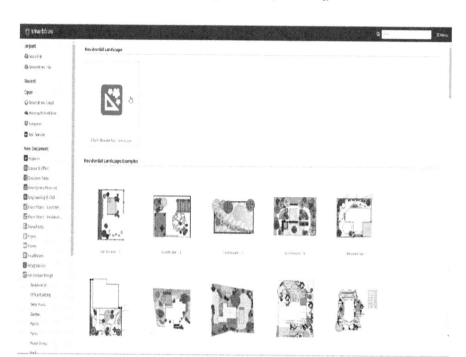

As an illustration, you can begin with a blank residential landscape by clicking on the block at the top. This will bring up the tools in the left-side smart panel that you will need to draw the landscape.

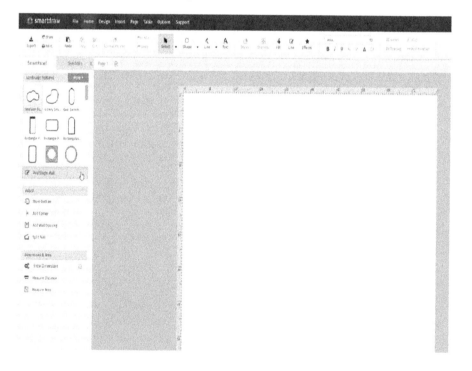

To create the boundaries for the landscape, click on the **Add Wall** feature, which will allow you to develop them. You can either use the cursor to stretch or shrink the boundaries or click on the dimension tab to pick the dimensions you want.

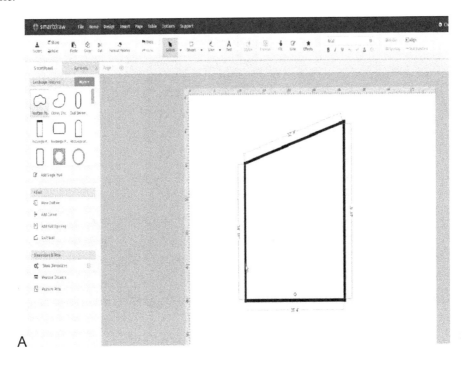

A

You can add texture, such as brick, by clicking on the ribbon at the top and then add it to your landscape. For instance, you could add the brick texture to the boundaries. In the symbols area in the smart panel on the left, you will find **Landscape Features** with another library of things that could be found in the landscape, such as lawn furniture. Just drag and drop them onto your drawing.

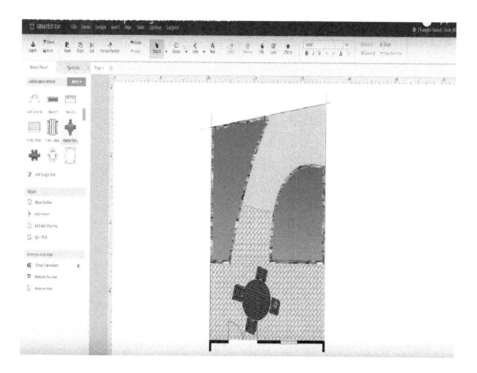

SmartDraw has a video tutorial showing how easy it is to create a landscape diagram.[6]

G. Timeline

Timelines are invaluable litigation visuals. For example, when you are explaining the chronology of events to the jurors during your opening statement, a timeline provides a way to communicate it visually. That timeline will make the chronology clearer to them, and they will retain the information better than if counsel described the sequence of events with mere words.

As usual, begin in the left column and select **Timelines** from the alphabetical list. This will bring up a number of timeline templates. Pick the one you would like to use, and it will appear on the screen.

---

6. https://www.youtube.com/watch?v=5jECN43a3Bs.

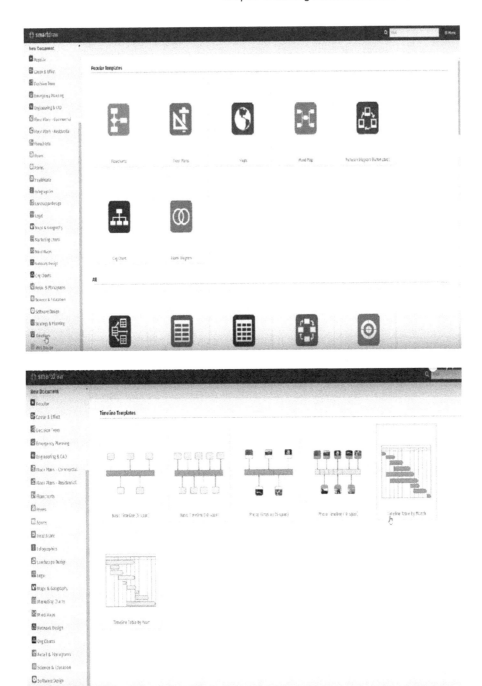

The following timeline template is a basic timeline. It has markers (boxes into which you can type in the event you want on the timeline) already on the timeline and is ready to be manipulated by you. Just click on the marker to add text inside the marker. In the box on the line below the marker you type in the time increment that you want whether it is minutes, days, months, years, or whatever. Then move to the next marker to enter the next event with the time unit in the box on the line. On the left in the smart panel you can find a variety of symbols, such as arrows pointing up and down and differently shaped markers. You can drag a symbol and attach it to the timeline. You can slide the markers to where you want them placed on the timeline.

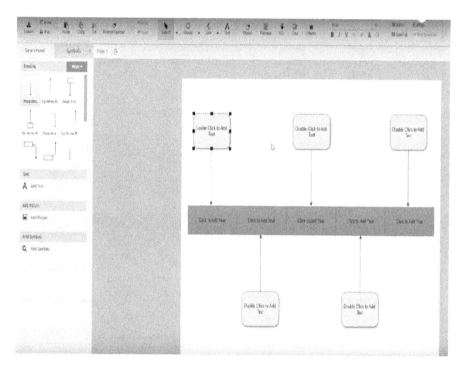

If you want to alter the shape of the marker, click on the **Change Shape** above in the **Design** tab.

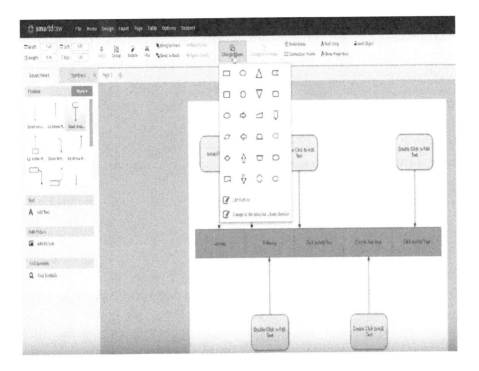

Also, if you want to add photographs to the timeline, you can do that by selecting the **Add Picture** in the smart panel and pick the photograph you want shown on the timeline from pictures on your computer.

SmartDraw has a video tutorial showing how easy it is to create a timeline.[7]

H. Alternatives

Of course, there is alternative software for creating diagrams and timelines. TimeMap,[8] which is part of LexisNexis CaseMap suite, is another option for creating timelines. You could also use PowerPoint. To use PowerPoint, click on **SmartArt** on the ribbon on the tool bar at the top, and then on the drop-down, click on **Process**, which will give you timeline templates.

---

7. https://www.youtube.com/watch?v=LAEXlKhBk-E.

8. https://www.lexisnexis.com/trial/nars183756.asp?access=1-4704320228&treatcd =1-5186766511&keyword=timemap%20software&gclid=Cj0KCQiA8f_eBRDcARIsAEKwRGf wBXhL0BRm2HKLivLedE8rKYS4TUk4iNyHJz3GsiFpy1I7tSgUvrEaAuDWEALw_wcB.

Lucidchart[9] is yet another diagramming application and touts 11 million users. Comparisons of SmartDraw and Lucidchart can be found online.[10] Two other alternatives to SmartDraw are Visio[11] and Creately.[12]

I. Video Evidence

Video evidence can come from crime scenes, depositions, surveillance cameras, body cameras, social media, personal computers, day-in-the-life videos, and so on.

TechSmith Camtasia®[13] has been used for decades by national and local law enforcement to record and edit videos. In addition to importing lots of different video files, Camtasia records videos from hard-to-get places like surveillance systems, Facebook, and more.

TechSmith Camtasia® is a software program that works on both Windows and Mac. With TechSmith Camtasia® you can make a video and capture any video or other images shown on your computer screen. Further, with TechSmith Camtasia® you can do advanced video editing with ease, including annotating the video and making video clips. TechSmith Camtasia® offers a free trial.

When you open Camtasia, we recommend watching the first three tutorials to familiarize yourself with the basics of recording, editing, and sharing videos.

---

9. https://www.lucidchart.com.

10. https://www.smartdraw.com/software/smartdraw-vs-lucidchart.htm; https://www.g2crowd.com/compare/lucidchart-vs-smartdraw.

11. https://www.microsoft.com/en-us/store/collections/visio?cat0=devices.

12. https://creately.com.

13. https://www.techsmith.com/video-editor.html.

Camtasia can slow down a video and spotlight to your evidence. Let's see how. Import video by clicking the plus sign (+). The imported video will show up in the media bin. Click and drag that video (also known as a clip) down on the timeline.

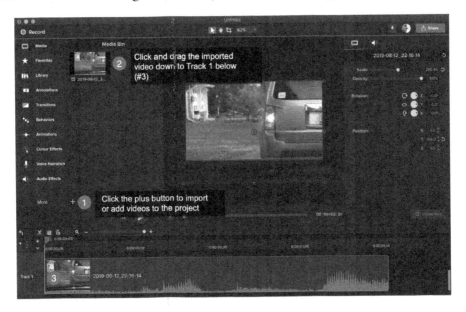

To focus the viewer's attention, we need to get to the important part of the action. To do so, click on the **playhead** (pictured below), specifically the gray portion of the object above the timeline:

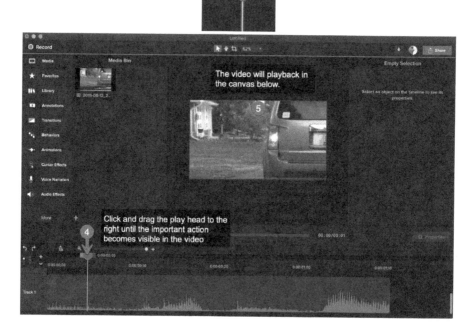

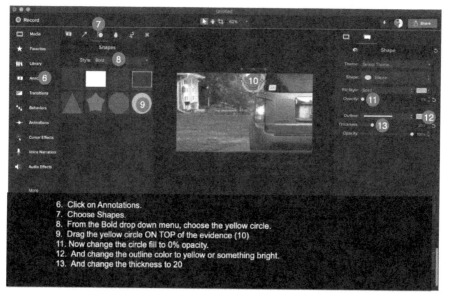

6. Click on Annotations.
7. Choose Shapes.
8. From the Bold drop down menu, choose the yellow circle.
9. Drag the yellow circle ON TOP of the evidence (10)
11. Now change the circle fill to 0% opacity.
12. And change the outline color to yellow or something bright.
13. And change the thickness to 20

Camtasia can be used to silence or change the volume of the audio. In 2019, Camtasia introduced some improvements, which included adding a sound normalizer that can convert the recorded volume, which could be low because the source was a distance from the microphone, to a level at which it can be clearly heard.

Snagit[14] is a less expensive alternative software to Camtasia. With Snagit you can capture video and do some editing. Yet another software program for capturing and editing video is iSkysoft iMedia Converter Deluxe.[15] TechSmith Camtasia®, iSkysoft iMedia Converter Deluxe, or Snagit should be part of your tool kit for creating video evidence.

Checklist—Creating Demonstrative and Video Evidence

Software for Designing Demonstrative Evidence

❑ Consider SmartDraw software that can be used to design demonstrative evidence.
❑ SmartDraw can design the following demonstratives, among others:
  ✓ Crime scene diagrams
  ✓ Floor plan diagrams
  ✓ Landscape diagrams
  ✓ Timelines
❑ Consider these alternatives to SmartDraw:
  ✓ TimeMap
  ✓ PowerPoint
  ✓ Lucidchart
  ✓ Visio
  ✓ Creately

Video Evidence

❑ Consider these software programs that can capture and edit video:
  ✓ Camtasia
  ✓ Snagit
  ✓ iMedia Converter Deluxe

---

14. https://www.techsmith.com/snagit-pricing.html.

15. https://videoconverter.iskysoft.com/.

Chapter 10

Ethical and Legal Issues

> "At bottom, a visual demonstration during summation is evaluated in the same manner as an oral statement. If an attorney can point to an exhibit in the courtroom and verbally make an argument, that exhibit and argument may also be displayed to the jury, so long as there is a clear delineation between argument and evidence, either on the face of the visual demonstration, in counsel's argument, or in the court's admonitions."
>
> *People v. Anderson*, 74 N.E.3d 639, 641 (N.Y. 2017)

A. The Benefits and Risks of Technology

This chapter covers the improper use of visuals during trial, such as displaying a visual in closing argument that either expresses a personal opinion, comments on a defendant's right to remain silent, or misstates the law. We also examine preservation and discovery issues as they relate to conventional and electronic visuals.

Lawyers are aware of the requirement that they must provide competent representation. But what does that mean with regard to technology? Competency means counsel is knowledgeable concerning the benefits and risks of technology. Model Rule of Professional Conduct 1.1 Competence provides:

A lawyer shall provide competent representation to a client. Competent representation requires the legal knowledge, skill, thoroughness and preparation reasonably necessary for the representation.[1]

Comment 8 to Rule 1.1 on Competence specifically addresses the need for lawyers to keep current about the benefits and risks of technology as follows:

To maintain the requisite knowledge and skill, a lawyer should keep abreast of changes in the law and its practice, *including the benefits and risks associated with relevant technology,* engage in continuing study and education and comply with all continuing legal education requirements to which the lawyer is subject. (emphasis added)

This professional responsibility mandate that a lawyer be knowledgeable and skilled regarding the benefits and risks of relevant technology is an incentive to pursue continuing legal education on the subject and to stay informed about pertinent technology.

B.   Challenges: It's the Content That Counts

When analyzing any challenge to a trial visual, it is important to keep in mind that it is the content of the visual, rather than the medium, that is important. For example, in *State v. Rivera*,[2] the defendant appealed his conviction claiming that the trial court erred in allowing the prosecutor to show a PowerPoint slide declaring the defendant's guilt because it is improper for a prosecutor to express a personal opinion regarding the defendant's guilt. The Appellate Division of the Superior Court of New Jersey decided that, based upon the PowerPoint slide and other prosecutorial conduct, the conviction should be overturned. The court held:

Our courts have not yet addressed the use of PowerPoint presentations during opening statements or summations in criminal trials in a published opinion. Other courts have, however, considered the matter.

The Nevada Supreme Court has concluded that a PowerPoint, "as an advocate's tool, is not inherently good or bad" and that "its propriety depends on content and application." *Watters v. State*, __ Nev. __, 313 P.3d 243, 247 (2013). The Court further determined that a PowerPoint accompanying an opening is permissible if "the content is consistent with the scope and purpose of opening statements and does not put inadmissible evidence or improper argument before the jury." . . . .

---

1. https://www.americanbar.org/groups/professional_responsibility/publications/model_rules_of_professional_conduct/rule_1_1_competence/.

2. *State v. Rivera*, 99 A.3d 847 (N.J. Super. Ct. App. Div. 2014).

We fully agree that the content, not the medium, is important. That view is consistent with the approach our Supreme Court has taken with respect to other technological advances used in connection with trial court proceedings.[3]

In and of themselves, visuals are just another means of communication. If you can say it, you should be able to show it. Only the content of the communication should be at issue. In *Arizona v. Sucharew*,[4] the Arizona Court of Appeals (Div. 1) found no error where the PowerPoint shown during opening statement did no more than show the exhibits that would later be admitted in the course of the trial and tracked what the prosecutor said in opening statement. The court stated:

> Defendant argues that the trial court abused its discretion in permit- ting the prosecutor to use the "PowerPoint" presentation in his open- ing statement because the presentation involved a "computer generated exhibit." Although a computer was used in the presentation, the actual presentation did not include any computer simulation or other similar evidence; rather, it was essentially a slide show of photographic exhib- its. The photographs included in the presentation were the same ones disclosed to defendant during pretrial discovery and later admitted into evidence at trial. Moreover, even though the photographs included superimposed descriptive words and labels, the words and labels simply tracked the subject matter of the prosecutor's opening statement to the jury, and defendant made no objection to any of the content or substance of the actual opening statement. We conclude, therefore, that there was no abuse of discretion by the trial court in permitting the State's use of the "PowerPoint" presentation. See *People v. Green*, 47 Cal. 2d 209, 302 P.2d 307, 312 (1956) (holding trial court had discretion to permit use of motion picture and photographs later admitted into evidence during opening statement), disapproved on other grounds in People v. Morse, 60 Cal. 2d 631, 36 Cal. Rptr. 201, 388 P.2d 33 (1964).[5]

The antithetical proposition to "if you can say it, you can show it" is "if you can't say it, you can't show it." In *United States v. Burns*,[6] the trial court permitted the prosecution to present a PowerPoint during opening statement. The slideshow contained images of items that did not become evidence, specifically a fistful of cash and a large quantity of crack cocaine. The United States Court of Appeals for the Sixth Circuit reviewed the PowerPoint presentation and held that those

---

3. *Id.* at 855.

4. *Arizona v. Sucharew*, 66 P.3d 59 (Ariz. Ct. App. 2003).

5. *Id.* at 64.

6. *United States v. Burns*, 298 F.3d 523 (6th Cir. 2002).

photographs might have confused the jury and should not have been shown, but the court presumed that the trial court's instructions against viewing the opening statements as evidence cured any harm that might have been caused. The appeals court went on to hold that the "potential prejudicial effect of the slides was not so great as to overwhelm the jury's ability to follow the court's instructions not to consider the opening statements as evidence."[7]

The prior examples involve situations in which counsel addressed the jury. The principle that "it is the content that counts, not the medium" applies also to visuals displayed during the taking of testimony. In *State v. Vance*,[8] the defendant argued on appeal that trial court abused its discretion by allowing a witness to testify with the aid of a PowerPoint presentation describing the manufacture of methamphetamine. The court ruled that the PowerPoint presentation was demonstrative evidence and that the trial court properly allowed it to be shown as follows:

> The PowerPoint presentation was used as context for Gibson's subsequent testimony regarding photographs of the actual items found in Defendant's residence. It would have been confusing to the jury if the depiction of the manufacturing process cut off before the final steps, which would have included the use of anhydrous ammonia. We see no abuse of discretion in the district court's permitting the entire manufacturing process to be described as context for the items found.[9]

The following sections cover discovery issues and specific challenges to the use of visuals on legal and/or ethical grounds. In each instance, it is important to note that the focus of trial and appellate court decisions have concentrated on the content of the visual.

C. Unadmitted Evidence

If the content of a visual is inadmissible, displaying it to the jury ordinarily will result in a mistrial or reversal unless the appellate court finds that the error was harmless and was cured by an instruction as it did in *United States. v. Burns*.[10] In *In re Pers. Restraint of Glasmann*,[11] the Washington Supreme Court reversed a conviction and criticized the prosecutor's use of visuals in a PowerPoint presentation, stating:

---

7. *Id.* at 543.

8. *State v. Vance*, 204 P.3d 31 (N.M. Ct. App. 2008).

9. *Id.* at 36 (2008).

10. *Supra* note 5.

11. *In re Pers. Restraint of Glasmann*, 286 P.3d 673, 678 (Wash. 2012).

Here, the prosecutor intentionally presented the jury with copies of Glasmann's booking photograph altered by the addition of phrases calculated to influence the jury's assessment of Glasmann's guilt and veracity. In the photograph, Glasmann is unkempt and bloody, a condition likely to have resulted in even greater impact because of captions that challenged the jury to question the truthfulness of his testimony. While the State argues that it merely combined the booking photograph, admitted as exhibit 89, with the court's instructions and argument of the law and facts, the prosecutor's conduct went well beyond this. Indeed, here the prosecutor's modification of photographs by adding captions was the equivalent of unadmitted evidence. There certainly was no photograph in evidence that asked "DO YOU BELIEVE HIM?" *See* State's Resp. to PRP, App. G at 5. There was nothing that said, "WHY SHOULD YOU BELIEVE ANYTHING HE SAYS ABOUT THE ASSAULT?"... And there were no sequence of photographs in evidence with "GUILTY" on the face or "GUILTY, GUILTY, GUILTY." *See id.* Yet this "evidence" was made a part of the trial by the prosecutor.

The concurring opinion in *Glasmann* provides this advice regarding litigation technology:

Certainly, lawyers may add and should use technology to advance advocacy and judges should permit and even encourage new techniques. But we must all remember the only purpose of visual aids of any kind is to enhance and assist the jury's understanding of the evidence. Technology should never be permitted to dazzle, confuse, or obfuscate the truth. The jury's deliberations must be based solely upon the evidence admitted and the court's instructions, not upon whose lawyer does the best job of manipulating, altering, shuffling, or distorting the evidence into some persuasive visual kaleidoscope experience for the jury.[12]

In contrast, the New York Court of Appeals in *People v. Anderson*[13] concluded that trial exhibits may be shown to the jury in an altered form, holding:

We reject defendant's position that trial exhibits in a PowerPoint presentation may only be displayed to the jury in unaltered, pristine form, and that any written comment or argument superimposed on the slides is improper. Rather, PowerPoint slides may properly be used in summation where, as here, the added captions or markings are consistent with the trial evidence and the fair inferences to be drawn from that evidence. When the superimposed text is clearly not part of the trial exhibits, and

---

12. *Id.* at 715.

13. *People v. Anderson*, 74 N.E. 3d 639 (N.Y. 2017).

thus could not confuse the jury about what is an exhibit and what is argument or commentary, the added text is not objectionable. The slides, in contrast to the exhibits, are not evidence. The court properly instructed the jury that what the lawyers say during summations is not evidence, and that in finding the facts, the jury must consider only the evidence. In this case, as was appropriate, the jury was told that the physical exhibits admitted into evidence would be made available to them, while the slides were not supplied to the jury during deliberations.[14]

If your jurisdiction follows the *Glasmann* approach or might be inclined to do so, and you wish to display a visual that alters a trial exhibit, you will need to ensure that it cannot be interpreted by the trial or an appellate court as unadmitted evidence.

D. Personal Opinion

It is unethical for an attorney to state certain personal opinions during trial. Model Rules of Professional Conduct 3.4: "Fairness to Opposing Party and Counsel" states:

> A lawyer shall not: …(e) in trial,… state a personal opinion as to the justness of a cause, the credibility of a witness, the culpability of a civil litigant or the guilt or innocence of an accused.[15]

In *Berger v. United States*,[16] the United States Supreme Court discussed the prosecutor's role and the impact that a prosecutor's improper assertions of opinion could have upon a jury:

> [I]t is fair to say that the average jury, in a greater or less degree, has confidence that (the obligations to produce proper convictions and prevent wrongful ones), which so plainly rest upon the prosecuting attorney, will be faithfully observed. Consequently, improper suggestion, insinuations, and, especially, assertions of personal knowledge are apt to carry much weight against the accused when they should carry none.

---

14. *Id.* at 641.

15. https://www.americanbar.org/groups/professional_responsibility/publications/ model_rules_of_professional_conduct/rule_3_4_fairness_to_opposing_party_counsel/.

16. *Berger v. United States*, 295 U.S. 78, 88, 55 S. Ct. 629, 633, 79 L. Ed. 1314 (1935).

In *In the Matter of Personal Restraint of Edward Michael Glasmann*,[17] the Washington Supreme Court denounced the prosecutor's expression of a personal opinion in a closing argument PowerPoint presentation as follows:

> A prosecutor could never shout in closing argument that "Glasmann is guilty, guilty, guilty!" and it would be highly prejudicial to do so. Doing this visually through use of slides showing Glasmann's battered face and superimposing red capital letters (red, the color of blood and the color used to denote losses) is even more prejudicial. *See Gregory*, 158 Wash.2d at 866–67, 147 P.3d 1201. "[V]isual arguments manipulate audiences by harnessing rapid unconscious or emotional reasoning processes and by exploiting the fact that we do not generally question the rapid conclusions we reach based on visually presented information." Lucille A. Jewel, *Through a Glass Darkly: Using Brain and Visual Rhetoric to Gain a Professional Perspective on Visual Advocacy*, 19 S. Cal. Interdisc. L.J. 237, 289 (2010). Further, [w]ith visual information, people believe what they see and will not step back and critically examine the conclusions they reach, unless they are explicitly motivated to do so. Thus, the alacrity by which we process and make decisions based on visual information conflicts with a bedrock principle of our legal system—that reasoned deliberation is necessary for a fair justice system.[18]

The Washington Supreme Court had another opportunity to revisit the issue of the propriety of visuals containing expressions of the prosecutor's personal opinion in *State v. Walker*.[19] A prosecutor from the same office that prosecuted Glasmann had a PowerPoint presentation of approximately 250 slides with over

---

17. *In re Glasmann*, 175 Wash.2d 696, 286 P.3d 673 (2012).

18. *Id.* at 680.

19. *State v. Walker*, 341 P.3d 976 (Wash. 2015).

100 headed "DEFENDANT WALKER GUILTY OF ASSAULT IN THE FIRST DEGREE." The court's opinion included ten of the computer slides.

Slides in *State v. Walker* opinion

The Washington State Supreme Court in *State v. Walker*[20] held:

> We have no difficulty holding the prosecutor's conduct in this case was improper. Closing argument provides an opportunity to draw the jury's attention to the evidence presented, but it does not give a prosecutor the right to present altered versions of admitted evidence to support the State's theory of the case, to present derogatory depictions of the defendant, or to express personal opinions on the defendant's guilt. *Glasmann*, 175 Wash.2d at 706–07, 712, 286 P.3d 673. Furthermore, RPC 3.4(e) expressly prohibits a lawyer from vouching for any witness's credibility or stating a personal opinion "on the guilt or innocence of an accused." The prosecution committed serious misconduct here in the portions of its PowerPoint presentation discussed above—it included multiple exhibits that were altered with inflammatory captions and superimposed text; it suggested to the jury that Walker should be convicted because he is a callous and greedy person who spent the robbery proceeds on video games and lobster; it plainly juxtaposed photographs of

---

20. *Id.* at 985.

the victim with photographs of Walker and his family, some altered with racially inflammatory text; and it repeatedly and emphatically expressed a personal opinion on Walker's guilt.

Although a lawyer may not express a personal opinion "as to the justness of a cause, the credibility of a witness, the culpability of a civil litigant or the guilt or innocence of an accused,"[21] counsel is not precluded from arguing that the evidence proves the guilt of the accused or that the lack of evidence establishes that the defendant is not guilty. In *State v. Michaels*,[22] the Superior Court of New Jersey Appellate Division reviewed a prosecutor's closing argument involving the use of a puzzle that when it was assembled spelled "guilty" and the court found no error, as follows:

> Defendant next contends that the State's display of the word "guilty" on a board during summation was prejudicial misconduct. The prosecutor referred to the jury's task of sorting through nine months of trial evidence as "difficult to assimilate, to collate, to grasp all the elements of evidence in this case as overwhelming as that evidence was." It was "[s]ort of like a puzzle. The pieces of a puzzle." The prosecutors, therefore, illustrated the solution by assembling magnetic letters on the board to spell "guilty," just as the evidence would spell guilty when properly assembled by the jury. Defense counsel objected and stated: "I would appreciate his removing the word guilty because, I think, it implies more than he's entitled to have implied, especially over a prolonged period of time." The court allowed the word to remain on the board.
>
> A prosecutor may comment on the evidence in a vigorous and forceful presentation during summation and draw any reasonable inferences supported by the proofs.... It is for the jury to accept or reject those inferences and conclusions drawn therefrom.... It was not improper to use a puzzle analogy to argue that defendant was guilty. There is no basis on which to conclude that placing the word "guilty" on a board had either an immediate impact upon the jurors, or a "subliminal" influence as suggested by defendant. The State was free to contend that the evidence proved defendant guilty as charged. Defendant's contention is clearly without merit.[23] (citations omitted)

---

21. Model Rules of Prof'l Conduct r. 3.4(e) (Am. Bar Ass'n 1983).

22. *State v. Michaels*, 625 A.2d 489 (N.J. Super. Ct. App. Div. 1993).

23. *Id*. at 522.

E. Improper Argument

Again, if you cannot say it, you cannot show it. In *State v. Reineke*,[24] the Oregon Court of Appeals reversed the defendant's conviction because the prosecutor's PowerPoint presentation infringed upon the defendant's right to remain silent. The presentation argued that the defendant's refusal to speak to the police was one of four reasons he should be convicted of murder. The court held:

> We have no trouble concluding that the jury in this case was likely to draw a prejudicial inference from the prosecutor's references to defendant's invocation in her PowerPoint presentation. The prosecutor's PowerPoint presentation expressly urged the jury to decide that defendant's refusal to speak to the police was one of the four reasons that he was guilty of murdering the victim. The state argues that we should not conclude that defendant was prejudiced because we cannot determine how long the "GUILTY" PowerPoint slides were in front of the jury. The record, however, demonstrates that the prosecutor used the PowerPoint presentation in conjunction with her oral argument, which tracked what was on the slides, and that at least three slides implied that defendant was guilty because he "refus[ed] to speak at the police station." Those repeated references to defendant's silence and guilt during closing argument were not subtle, isolated, or fleeting. For the same reason, we reject the state's argument that the prosecutor's oral statements to the jury somehow detracted from the direct implication in the PowerPoint slides that defendant's refusal to speak indicated that he was guilty. We conclude that it is highly likely that the jury drew an adverse inference that defendant's refusal to speak to the detectives was evidence of his guilt.[25]

F. Misstate the Law

A visual that misstates the law can result in a mistrial or a reversal of the verdict. In *California v. Otero*,[26] the California Appellate Court described how the prosecutor used a PowerPoint diagram to explain the meaning of the reasonable-doubt burden as follows:

> During argument, the prosecutor told the jury she wanted to give them an example of reasonable doubt. She used a PowerPoint diagram. At

---

24. *State v. Reineke*, 337 P.3d 941 (Or. App. 2014).

25. *Id.* at 947-48.

26. *California v. Otero*, 210 Cal. App. 4th 865, 148 Cal. Rptr. 3d 812 (2012).

the top of the diagram in large bold print were the words "No Reasonable Doubt." The diagram consisted of the outlines of California and Nevada. In southern Nevada was a dollar sign. "Ocean" was printed to the left of California. San Diego was printed inside California, but it was printed in the northern part of the state. Below San Diego was a star and the word Sac. Below that was San Francisco. In Southern California was Los Angeles. The following statement was at the bottom of the diagram: "Even with incomplete and incorrect information, no reasonable doubt that this is California."

Using the diagram, the prosecutor argued to the jury: "I'm thinking of a state and it's shaped like this. And there's an ocean to the left of it, and I know that there's another state that abuts this state where there's gambling. Okay. And this state that I'm thinking about, right in the center of the state is a city called San Francisco, and in the southern portion of the state is a city called Los Angeles. And I think the capital is Sac-something. And up at the northern part of the state there's a city called San Diego. I'm just trying to figure out what state this might be."

"Is there any doubt in your mind, ladies and gentlemen, that that state is California? Okay. Yes, there's inaccurate information. I know San Diego is not at the northern part of California, and I know Los Angeles isn't at the southern. Okay. But my point to you in this—"[27]

The California Appellate Court, in *Otero*, concluded that "[i]t is misconduct for a prosecutor to misstate the law during argument.... This is particularly so when misstatement attempts 'to absolve the prosecution from its prima facie obligation to overcome reasonable doubt on all elements.'"[28] Then, the court discussed an "analogous situation" in *People v. Katzenberger*[29] where the prosecutor in closing argument utilized a puzzle of the Statue of Liberty to make a similar argument regarding a reasonable doubt. The court in *Otero* observed:

In *Katzenberger*, the puzzle was identifiable when six of eight puzzle pieces were in place and "the prosecutor told the jury, 'this picture is beyond a reasonable doubt,' inappropriately suggesting a specific quantitative measure of reasonable doubt, i.e., 75 percent." (*People v. Katzenberger, supra*, 178 Cal. App. 4th at p. 1268, 101 Cal. Rptr. 3d 122.) The use of a diagram such as the one used in this case is simply not an accurate analogy to a prosecutor's burden to prove beyond a reasonable doubt each and every element of a charged offense. Here the diagram was identifiable using but one of eight pieces of information supplied by the diagram (12.5 percent of the information supplied) and unlike the

27. *Id.* at 869-70 (2012).

28. *Ibid.*

29. *People v. Katzenberger*, 178 Cal. App. 4th 1260, 101 Cal. Rptr. 3d 122 (2009).

puzzle in *Katzenberger*, where all pieces contained accurate information, here the diagram contained inaccurate information, making the error more egregious. Not only is the standard of proof reduced to substantially below the condemned percentage in *Katzenberger*, but the jury was informed that reasonable doubt may be reached on such slight proof even when some of the evidence is demonstrably false.[30]

Although the court in *Otero* held that the misstatement of law was error, it decided that the error was harmless because the trial judge ordered that it be taken down as soon as the defense objected, and the judge admonished the jurors to disregard it.[31]

G. Preservation and Discovery

With regard to visuals, two other topics deserve attention here because of the special legal and ethical issues they present as follows: (1) preservation of information in civil cases, particularly electronically stored information, and (2) the prosecutor's special responsibilities to preserve evidence and to disclose exculpatory evidence to the defense.

I. Preservation in a Civil Case

As counsel, you will need to inform your client when to preserve evidence, what evidence to preserve, and who should be told to preserve it. American Bar Association Civil Discovery Standard 10 states:

> When a lawyer who has been retained to handle a matter learns that litigation is probable or has been commenced, the lawyer should inform the client of its duty to preserve potentially relevant documents in the client's custody or control and of the possible consequences of failing to do so.[32]

The obligation to preserve usually commences when litigation can be reasonably anticipated. At that juncture, counsel has a duty to notify those in possession of the information to put a litigation hold on the information, to safely store it, and to not destroy it, which would constitute spoliation. Naturally, the information to be preserved includes relevant visuals.

---

30. *California v. Otero*, 210 Cal. App. 4th 865, 873 (2012).

31. *Ibid.*

32. American Bar Association Civil Discovery Standard 10, American Law Institute (2004)

Preservation of electronically stored information (ESI) is particularly important because most information is stored electronically. ESI includes: emails; social media (such as Facebook, Twitter, and Instagram); instant messages; photographs; videos, and so on. Much of this digitally stored information includes visuals. If the client is a corporation that regularly destroys ESI, counsel should instruct the company to suspend those procedures.

Federal Rule of Civil Procedure 37(e) provides potential sanctions for failing to preserve ESI, as follows:

> If electronically stored information that should have been preserved in the anticipation or conduct of litigation is lost because a party failed to take reasonable steps to preserve it, and it cannot be restored or replaced through additional discovery, the court:
>
> (1)   upon finding prejudice to another party from loss of the information, may order measures no greater than necessary to cure the prejudice; or
>
> (2)   only upon finding that the party acted with the intent to deprive another party of the information's use in the litigation may:
>
> (A)   presume that the lost information was unfavorable to the party;
>
> (B)   instruct the jury that it may or must presume the information was unfavorable to the party; or
>
> (C)   dismiss the action or enter a default judgment.

2.   Prosecutor's Special Responsibilities

The prosecutor in a criminal case is obligated to turn over exculpatory information to the defense. The landmark case was *Brady v. Maryland*, which involved a prosecution for murder where the defendant requested records of extrajudicial statements of the defendant's accomplice in which the accomplice admitted committing the murder. The United States Supreme Court held:

> We now hold that the suppression by the prosecution of evidence favorable to an accused upon request violates due process where the evidence is material either to guilt or to punishment, irrespective of the good faith or bad faith of the prosecution.
>
> [This principle] is not punishment of society for misdeeds of a prosecutor but avoidance of an unfair trial to the accused. Society wins not only when the guilty are convicted but when criminal trials are fair; our system of the administration of justice suffers when any accused is treated unfairly. An inscription on the walls of the Department of Justice states

the proposition candidly for the federal domain: "The United States wins its point whenever justice is done its citizens in the court." A prosecution that withholds evidence on demand of an accused which, if made available, would tend to exculpate him or reduce the penalty helps shape a trial that bears heavily on the defendant. That casts the prosecutor in the role of an architect of a proceeding that does not comport with standards of justice, even though, as in the present case, his action is not "the result of guile," to use the words of the Court of Appeals.[33]

This prosecutorial obligation extends not just to the prosecutor but also members of the prosecution team. In *Kyles v. Whitley*,[34] the United States Supreme Court held that "This in turn means that the individual prosecutor has a duty to learn of any favorable evidence known to others acting on the government's behalf in the case, including the police..."

A prosecutor is also under an ethical obligation to disclose exculpatory evidence negating guilt or mitigating punishment to the defense. Model Rule of Professional Conduct 3.8(d) states:

> The prosecutor in a criminal case shall: ...(d) make timely disclosure to the defense of all evidence or information known to the prosecutor that tends to negate the guilt of the accused or mitigates the offense, and, in connection with sentencing, disclose to the defense and to the tribunal all unprivileged mitigating information known to the prosecutor, except when the prosecutor is relieved of this responsibility by a protective order of the tribunal...[35]

The obligation to turn over exculpatory evidence clearly includes visual evidence. For example, in *People v. Springer*,[36] the New York Appellate Division reversed a conviction and dismissed an indictment where the prosecutor intentionally destroyed surveillance videos relevant to the central issue even though the prosecutor claimed that he believed "the photographs showed nothing that would be of value in an identification procedure."[37]

---

33. *Brady v. Maryland*, 373 U.S. 83, 87-88 (1963).

34. *Kyles v. Whitley*, 514 U.S. 419, 437 (1995).

35. https://www.americanbar.org/groups/professional_responsibility/publications/model_rules_of_professional_conduct/rule_3_8_special_responsibilities_of_a_prosecutor/.

36. *People v. Springer*, 122 A.D.2d 87 (N.Y. App. Div. 1986).

37. *Id.* at 88. *See also State v. Wittenbarger*, 880 P.2d 517, 521 (Wash. 1994) ("To comport with due process, the prosecution has a duty to disclose material exculpatory evidence to the defense and a related duty to preserve such evidence for use by the defense.").

Further, the prosecutor must provide exculpatory evidence to the defense in a timely manner. In *State v. Draper-Roberts*,[38] the prosecutor provided a body-cam video to the defense after defense counsel had delivered an opening statement. When defense counsel moved for mistrial, the trial court denied the motion, granting defense counsel a short continuance to review the video and prepare cross-examination of the officer. The Utah Court of Appeals reversed the conviction, holding that the trial court abused its discretion in denying the mistrial motion. Specifically, the court held that defense counsel was deprived of opportunity to prepare for trial with the video in mind.[39] The court also observed that defense counsel likely lost credibility with the jury because defense did not discuss the video during opening statement. Further, the video was admitted into evidence, and it not only contained hearsay statements but also showed the defendant being advised of her rights and invoking her right to remain silent.[40]

Checklist—Ethical and Legal Issues

Benefits and Risks of Technology

❏ Ask yourself: "Am I cognizant of the benefits and risks of technology, as required by Model Rule of Professional Conduct 1.1 on lawyer competency?"

Ethical and Legal Boundaries

❏ Ask yourself: "Is the content of the visual admissible in evidence?"
❏ Unadmitted visual evidence should never be shown to the fact finder.
❏ Under Model Rule of Professional Conduct 3.4, a visual should that express the lawyer's personal opinion regarding the justness of the cause, the credibility of a witness, or the culpability of a civil litigant or the guilt or innocence of an accused.
❏ Counsel cannot show the jurors anything that counsel would be prohibited by law or the Rules of Professional Conduct from saying to them.
❏ A visual cannot misstate the law.
❏ In accordance with the law, counsel should preserve visuals, including electronically stored information.
❏ A prosecutor has special responsibilities to preserve exculpatory evidence and to provide it to the defense.

---

38. *State v. Draper-Roberts*, 378 P.3d 1261, 1267 (Utah Ct. App. 2016).

39. *Id.* at 1267.

40. *Id.* at 1268.

Chapter 11

Professional Technicians and Visuals Designers

> "Good design is clear thinking made visible, bad design is stupidity made visible."
>
> Edward Tufte, American educator and
> statistician

A. Professionals

You may decide to employ professional trial technicians to handle the hardware and software tasks and/or designers to create litigation visuals. This chapter discusses the circumstances under which parties may decide to enlist the services of these professionals. It covers what experienced trial technicians can offer as well as those offered by companies that create litigation visuals and how much those services can cost. Further, in addition to those already provided throughout the book, this chapter provides examples of graphics that professional designers can provide and websites that you can visit in order to examine other examples of litigation graphics. Finally, we explain how the legal team can coordinate with these professionals, and in doing so, build an effective litigation team.

B. Professional Technicians

I. Decision to Employ

An experienced trial technician can provide the following services, among others: store and organize data with software, and sit in during pretrial alternative dispute resolution sessions or trial to operate the technology that will retrieve and display the visuals.

The trial team's decision to employ a professional trial technician may be driven by a lack of confidence in its ability to operate the technology, or a simple recognition that hiring a trial technician allows it to place greater focus on the trial itself without having to worry about the potential for technical glitches, or other similar issues. In cases that involve many exhibits, it is much easier to leave it in the hands of a professional. Additionally, if the trial attorney has a technical problem when running his or her own presentation and attempts to try to fix the problem while continuing to talk, the result can be problematic: the lawyer can lose a train of thought; his or her confidence; and a strong presence before the jury. There is simply too much for the trial team to worry about, and many lawyers decide they do not want to add technology to the list.

The decision whether to employ an outside professional for trial services support (strategy, graphics, or technology) typically revolves around the size and complexity of the case as well as the potential risk or exposure (or demand). Careful evaluation of the cost/benefit ratio should be taken into consideration when looking to employ outside service professionals. Adding a trial support person is analogous to adding another staff member, such as a senior paralegal or an associate, to the team. Costs for such professionals vary greatly mostly due to experience, but other factors such as geographic location, client-driven budget concerns, and out-of-pocket costs (whether passed on to the end client or absorbed by the service professional). For a qualified consultant, you should expect to pay around $200 per hour, although there can be flexibility around the dollars charged per hour, the amount of hours charged per day (not-to-exceed), fixed-fee scenarios, absorption of out-of-pocket hard costs, and so on. A good technical presentation consultant is well worth the cost as trial is not where you should be looking to cut corners and shave a few dollars off per hour as the smooth and seamless presentation of evidence is paramount to making a good case and maximizing time and efficiency for the jury.[1]

The costs of hiring a trial technician are not always a barrier. For example, in some cases, the parties on each side agree to share the costs of a trial technician, who can publish exhibits and create callouts and highlights. If the trial technician is simply handling the in-court technology and not serving in any kind of advocacy role, such as creating persuasive visuals for one side, there is no downside to such an approach.

2. Teamwork

It is critical that the legal team and the technicians be coordinated with one another to form an effective trial team. Teamwork begins with the legal team's dedication to and respect for today's technology and the technicians who operate it. This is a truism whether the legal team is relying on in-house technicians or professional technicians. The trial lawyer should bear in mind that if anything goes wrong with the technology, it will not be the technician that the judge and jury will blame and hold accountable. It will be the lawyer. Consequently, it is in the lawyer's best interest that the technician has what is needed to do the job.

A legal team that lacks respect for technology and the technicians is heading for disastrous results. If the in-house equipment is outdated, it is more likely to crash or malfunction. If technology is not seen as an important and integral part of trial preparation, it can be left to the last minute, leading to a mad rush to get it into place on time and be ready for trial. Lawyers should gain an understanding of the amount of time that it can take a technician to perform the assigned work, such as redacting documents or creating video clips. If the technician is not given the necessary time to professionally accomplish assigned tasks, the work product can be substandard, and the exhausted technician can be less effective in court. To instill in the legal team an understanding of the potential and limitations of litigation technology, the law office should provide in-house training on basic litigation visuals.

Lawyers should work with the technician who will be in trial and be thoroughly familiar with the data and how it is organized and called up. Specifically, the lawyer, like a quarterback on a football team calling plays, should have a stock language for describing what the lawyer wants the technician to show on the screen. For example, the lawyer routinely should refer to the item of evidence by its exhibit number. If the exhibit is a multiple page document, counsel refers to the exhibit number and the desired page number. The lawyer and the technician

---

1. Conversation with Chris Tiedemann, COO, Prolumina Litigation Communications, Sept. 4, 2019.

should practice the routine. Further, when preparing for direct examination, the lawyer can provide the technician with an outline that indicates what exhibits will be called for and when during the examination. Ideally, the technician would be present during witness preparation for the direct.

Additionally, the lawyer and technician should have agreed upon terms for annotations (see page 246 for standard annotations), such as "On exhibit 47, please call out the second sentence in the second paragraph." Also, the lawyer can add an agreed upon descriptor for the exhibit, such as "Exhibit 47, the email dated January 5, 2019."

In trial, communication between the trial lawyer and the technician must be clear and convivial. The technician should be treated with respect in front of the jury, referred to by surname and never belittled. The lawyers on the trial team should make the technician part of the team in every respect. The technician should be involved at the earliest possible time in the case and be given adequate time to prepare for trial. The technician should have a full comprehension of the trial plan and participate in the planning. The technician should go to the trial court and meet with the court staff to discuss technology. Lawyers should provide the technician with the equipment and support needed for trial, and this includes backup equipment.

As a member of the trial team, the technician's demeanor, behavior, comportment, and appearance matter. The technician should wear courtroom attire and abide by customary and ethical standards. For examples, the technician should not fraternize with the other side (unless both sides are sharing the costs of the trial technician), and, as with any lawyer or witness, never talk about the case except as called for in court. Also, the technician should not speak to counsel in court except at times agreed to before trial—when counsel is about to complete direct examination and turns to the trial team before concluding it for an input, and so on.

To achieve smooth communication between the lawyer and technician requires pretrial preparation. Further, if a problem arises during the trial either with the technology or with how the lawyer is communicating with the technician, the team should deal with it in a calm manner because the judge and jury are watching.

C. Professional Visuals Designers

I. Decision to Employ

Lawyers or the legal assistants can create simple graphics. Chapter 9 "Creating Demonstrative and Video Evidence" explains that even with a small budget you can acquire SmartDraw[2] software that will give you access to over 5,000 pieces

---

2. https://www.smartdraw.com.

of clipart and templates that even a person with no artistic skills can use to create dynamic graphics for a case, such as a diagram of a floor plan or landscape or a crime scene or for a timeline or for some other graphic.

Your law office may establish its own unit to create visuals and provide digital evidence for lawyers in the office. For example, more than 15 years ago the Los Angeles District Attorney's Office, under the supervision of Ronald Bowers, had a separate unit in which he, as an experienced deputy district attorney, and his paralegal staff prepared visual aids for cases handled by other prosecutors in the office.[3] As another example, the Wayne County Prosecutor's Office in 2017, under the leadership of prosecutor Kym L. Worthy, established a Litigation Technology Unit to assist assistant prosecuting attorneys in creating and presenting digital evidence and ensure that it is provided to defense counsel.[4]

On the other hand, if your case calls for a more complex visual, such as a computer-animated plane crash, medical illustration, or an automobile collision, you likely will need to employ a computer graphics vendor, and in most cases, an appropriate expert witness. With computer animation it is possible to show motion and a series of events. An animation can turn the jurors into eyewitnesses to the crucial events, such as the malfunctions of a piece of machinery. Or, the jury can see how the driver of a vehicle was negligent.

Some vendors specialize in medical visuals[5] that include medical illustrations, medical animations, 3D models, and other medical demonstrative evidence. A model can be a valuable visual aid when counsel explains what occurred in the case, such as a customized model of skull to explain the skull fractures, during opening statement or closing argument. And an expert can use a model to explain the expert's findings, such as describing the locations of the fractures with the aid of the model of a skull.

Another reason may drive the lawyer and/or the lawyer's staff to hire professionals. The lawyer and/or the lawyer's staff may have created visuals but the visuals lack professional polish and persuasive power. When this occurs, counsel would be wise to get professional help in enhancing the visuals for trial, provided the budget allows it.

When professional vendors create the visuals, the costs can vary depending on the scope of the work. For example, the cost of hiring professional vendors to create trial graphics can range anywhere from $500 to $50,000.

---

3. https://ronaldbowers.com/about-ronald-e-bowers.

4. https://www.waynecounty.com/elected/prosecutor/litigation-technology-unit.aspx.

5. https://www.legalartworks.com; https://medivisuals.com.

2. The Designers

Now, let's view samples of the work of some graphics designers to see what designers can provide.

a. *Sound Jury Consulting Graphics*

Sound Jury Consulting (SJC) Graphics, a subdivision of Sound Jury Consulting, prides itself in "providing high-impact, high-value graphics for reasonable prices."[6] This company maintains offices in Seattle, Washington, and Portland, Oregon, and it provides litigation support services around the nation. SJC can either construct a PowerPoint presentation from scratch or provide graphics for an existing slideshow. SJC Graphics also can provide display boards and other graphics for trial or arbitration hearings. SJC has provided many of the timelines and other persuasive graphics examples throughout this book. The following is an example of an argument visual on damages.

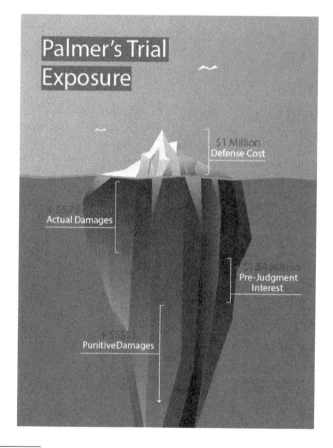

---

6. http://www.soundjuryconsulting.com.

b.   *High Impact Visual Litigation Strategies*

High Impact Visual Litigation Strategies[7] is based outside Denver, Colorado, and has a clientele across America as well as in Canada, Australia, and Western Europe. High Impact describes itself as "a full-service litigation support firm that blends scientific accuracy with Hollywood-level graphics to deliver custom legal exhibits that educate and engage audiences in trial and mediation."[8]

High Impact develops animation videos that bring the event to life, such as an airplane crash, product failure, structural collapse, and so on. Next is a screenshot of a video showing the explosion of a West Virginia metal processing plant.

Narration from U.S. Chemical Safety Board PSA

c.   *MediVisuals®*

MediVisuals®[9] employs 15 full-time medical illustrators and medical animators with master's degrees from accredited graduate programs enabling them to communicate effectively with treating physicians and medical experts. Since 1984, MediVisuals® has worked on over 33,000 medical-legal cases throughout the United States and internationally. MediVisuals'® goal is "to create accurate, realistic, easily understood medical illustrations, graphs, timelines, interactive products, and animations." Their illustrations and animations are also used by medical doctors, researchers, and publishers. Offices are in Richmond, Virginia; Dallas, Texas; and New Orleans, Louisiana.

---

7. https://highimpact.com/.

8. https://highimpact.com/about.

9. https://www.medivisuals.com.

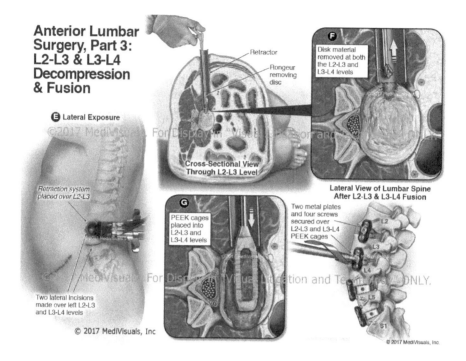

d. SKE Forensic Consultants Inc.

SKE Forensic Consultants Inc.,[10] located in Oakland, New Jersey, specializes in accident reconstruction, also creates demonstrative evidence. It developed the following visual that reconstructs a pedestrian accident.

---

e. *Courtroom Visuals*

Courtroom Visuals,[11] based in Atlanta, Georgia, provides a variety of services to trial lawyers, including trial support with experienced technicians. It also creates trial visuals, including graphics, models, medical illustrations, and animations. The following is Courtroom Visual's model of a chicken processing plant where a fire erupted, as displayed in the courtroom.

f. *Prolumina Litigation Communications*

Prolumina is a boutique litigation strategy consultancy located in the Pacific Northwest that provides services across the United States. Prolumina's services include case strategy and jury services, visual consulting and graphic design, and in-court trial presentation technical consultants.[12]

---

11. https://www.courtroomvisuals.com.

12. http://www.prolumina.net/.

The visual that follows shows a frame shot from an animated video created for a motorboat product liability case.

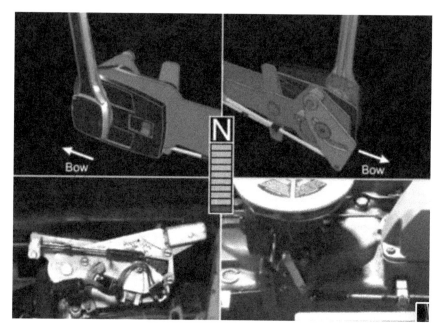

Checklist—Professional Technicians and Visual Designers

Professional Technicians

❏ Consider the services that a professional technician can provide, such as:
   ✓ Assisting in case analysis and theme development;
   ✓ Storing and organizing case material with software; and
   ✓ Operating the hardware and software during litigation.
❏ Factors to consider in deciding whether to employ a professional technician:
   ✓ The legal team lacks the competency to perform the tasks; and/or
   ✓ The case and the budget allow for employing of a professional.
❏ To be effective, the legal team and the technician must work as a team, and to achieve teamwork, the following is required:
   ✓ The legal team must respect the technician and what the technology provides;
   ✓ The technology must be up-to-date and properly maintained;
   ✓ The trial lawyer should be familiar with how the data is organized in the software and how it will be called up;
   ✓ The trial lawyer and technician should practice what they will do in trial;

✓ The trial lawyer and technician should agree upon the terminology to be used in court for working with visual evidence;
✓ In trial, the lawyer should treat the technician with courtesy and respect;
✓ The technician should be involved in the planning for trial;
✓ The trial lawyer and technician should agree upon the terminology to be used in court for working with visual evidence; and
✓ In trial, the lawyer should treat the technician with courtesy and respect.

Professional Visual Designers

❑ Factors to consider in deciding whether to employ a professional designer:
   ✓ The legal team lacks the competency to design the visual; and/or
   ✓ The case and the budget will allow for employing the professional designer.
❑ A catalog of professional designer vendors includes:
   ✓ Sound Jury Consulting Graphics
   ✓ High Impact Visual Litigation Strategies
   ✓ MediVisuals®
   ✓ SKE Forensic Consultants Inc.
   ✓ Courtroom Visuals
   ✓ Prolumina Litigation Communications

Chapter 12

Nonlinear Software

A. Nonlinear Software
B. Functions
C. Mac Users
D. Hands-on
E. CaseMap
F. Mastering Sanction
   1. Creating and Opening a Case File in Sanction
   2. Importing Transcripts, Media, and Exhibits into Sanction
      a. Importing with Wizard
      b. Importing by Drag and Drop
   3. A Presentation
      a. Creating a Presentation
      b. Showing a Presentation
      c. Adding Annotations with the Annotation Tool Gallery
      d. Alternative Ways to Access Annotation Tools
      e. Deleting Annotations
      f. Exhibit Stamps
      g. Redaction
   4. Searching in Sanction
      a. Searching a Case
      b. Word Searching a Transcript
   5. Text Clips
   6. Video Clips
   7. Keyboard Shortcuts
G. ExhibitView
   1. A Presentation
   2. PDF+
H. TrialDirector
I. OnCue
J. PowerPoint

"In almost every job now, people use software and work with information to enable their organization to operate more effectively."

Bill Gates, Microsoft Corporation co-founder and
philanthropist

A. Nonlinear Software

In Chapter 2 we described the two types of computer software as linear (PowerPoint and Keynote) versus nonlinear (TrialDirector,[1] Sanction, Exhibit-View, OnCue, and TrialPad). We have recommended that linear software is well suited to situations where you, during opening statement or summation, or your expert, during testimony, address the jury like an instructor teaching a class. You can practice the presentation in advance and deliver it by moving slide-by-slide in a well-organized manner. However, linear software is less suitable than nonlinear software for direct and cross-examination.

Clearly nonlinear software is the best tool for direct and cross-examination because nonlinear software allows you to store, easily retrieve, and show visuals when you need them, rather than in a linear fashion. For example, with nonlinear software you can create a callout on a document on the fly, while you would need to design a slide with a callout if you were using linear software. You can readily load all of the exhibits into nonlinear software and be able to retrieve them with ease; with linear software, you would need to prepare a slide for every visual. Nevertheless, in Chapter 13 on linear software, we discuss how to make linear software perform many of the tasks that nonlinear software is designed to do. Therefore, those who cannot afford the higher cost of nonlinear software but want the ability to display visuals in a nonlinear way can do so at least to a degree.

While this chapter examines nonlinear software, Chapter 13 is devoted to linear software, and Chapter 14 examines tablets and litigation applications, such as TrialPad. We will describe how these presentation software programs work so that you can effectively use them in pretrial and trial. Fundamentals for these software programs are explained in terms that non-technologically savvy lawyers, legal assistants, and law students can understand. With plain terms and simple instructions, we explain how to not only operate Sanction, PowerPoint, and other software but also how to get the most out of them. We explain how nonlinear software can be a valuable tool to facilitate pretrial preparation.

Ultimately, the decision as to what nonlinear software to adopt is yours to make. We do recommend that you take advantage of the trial periods that the different vendors offer to familiarize yourself with different nonlinear software products so that you can make an informed decision. Because budgeting for nonlinear

---

1. https://iprotech.com/software/trial-director-360/.

software is a factor to consider in deciding which software to purchase, we include how much each software costs.

We devote a substantial part of this chapter to Sanction for a couple reasons. First, it has proven to be tried and true. Sanction is the software used by the Office of the United States Attorney, the Office of the Prosecutor of the International Criminal Tribunal at the Hague, and prosecutors' offices across America. Second, by covering Sanction in some depth in this chapter, you will become familiar with how to run nonlinear software, and consequently, you will be able to readily try out and test the other nonlinear software we discuss here—TrialDirector, OnCue, and ExhibitView.

B. Functions

Sanction and similar nonlinear software can perform multiple functions for a litigator, and the following are some of the major ones:

- Organize and store the case: Drag and drop documents, images, and transcripts from your computer into the presentation software.
- Retrieve and display exhibits: Type in an exhibit number and the exhibit is projected onto a screen in the courtroom or a pretrial venue.
- Retrieve and display a video: Type in the label given the video and the designation of the desired clip, such as a page of a video deposition, and it will play on the screen.
- Retrieve and display a PowerPoint or Keynote presentation: Type in the identification of the presentation and it is available on the screen.
- Show a deposition transcript synchronized with a video deposition: This feature allows the jurors to see the video deposition on a split screen with the transcript.
- Layering: The software allows the trial lawyer to remove layers of a visual, such as layers in anatomical illustrations.
- Edit videos: Sanction enables counsel to edit a video when needed, such as to comply with a judge's ruling during trial that a part of the video must be redacted.
- Annotating an exhibit: With the software, for instance, you can highlight portions of an exhibit shown on a screen or monitor, such as a sentence in a document, in order to emphasize it for the jury.

C. Mac Users

The nonlinear software programs we will explore here are designed for Microsoft Windows, and therefore, if you are a Mac user, you will need to install

Windows on your Mac. You will be able to download software on your Mac by installing Windows with Windows Boot Camp.[2] Once you have installed Windows, you can restart your computer and press down on the **Option** key as it restarts, and you will be given the choice between the Mac operating system or Windows.

Before you set out to partition your disk for Boot Camp make sure you have at least 64 GB of space available (128 GB is recommended for the best performance). If you do not have that much free space, you will need to free up space.

To install Windows, go to the Applications folder and click on **Utilities** and under Utilities, open Boot Camp Assistant. The on-screen instructions will guide you to partition the startup disk and then download install Windows. Apple Support[3] provides further useful information regarding Boot Camp.

D. Hands-on

In this chapter, we will walk you through how to organize and store a case in Sanction as well as how to retrieve and present with Sanction. Sanction was originally designed for large-scale civil litigation.

The best way to understand how to operate Sanction, or any other presentation software for that matter, is to download it and work with it. You can get a 30-day free trial of Sanction software, which is part of the CaseMap Suite of products.[4]

To get the most out this chapter and learn how to operate Sanction, you should download Sanction and use it in conjunction with instructions provided here. Our instructions on operating this software do not purport to be complete, but they will get you comfortable with Sanction and ready for trial. Other resources are the manual for Sanction, as well as a help section within the program. Finally, as with most technical and do-it-yourself tasks, YouTube has several instructional videos for Sanction[5] as it does for TrialDirector.[6]

E. CaseMap

Before we dive into how to create and open a case in Sanction, CaseMap,[7] also a LexisNexis product, deserves discussion. CaseMap is a software program that can

---

2. https://support.apple.com/en-us/HT201468.

3. https://support.apple.com/boot-camp.

4. Conversation with Courtney E. Gregor, Research Attorney, LexisNexis, Jan. 28, 2019.

5. https://www.youtube.com/watch?v=pa31ANHB8ys.

6. https://www.youtube.com/watch?v=txGKY0nfTc8.

7. https://www.lexisnexis.com/en-us/products/casemap.page.

be used to organize and manage case information. It is employed by United States Attorneys' offices as well as Federal Public Defender offices across the country. Simply put, CaseMap organizes case information into five tables: facts, persons, issues, questions, and documents. The CaseMap program can be utilized to produce discovery, create an exhibits' list, Bates stamp documents, produce a privilege log, and with TimeMap (another LexisNexis product)[8] create a timeline for a case. Important here is that Sanction works seamlessly with CaseMap. Sanction can import the case that has been organized and managed in CaseMap. Of course, a case can also be imported from a computer that does not manage case information in CaseMap.

These products provide trial periods so that you can test the products to see if you wish to purchase them. The CaseMap Suite of products is available under the Lexis subscriptions for accredited law schools.[9]

F. Mastering Sanction

I. Creating and Opening a Case File in Sanction

In the beginning you will want to create a case file in Sanction. To do so for a case that is already open, click on the **File** tab at the top of the left column. Then, click **Open**, followed by clicking **New Case**.

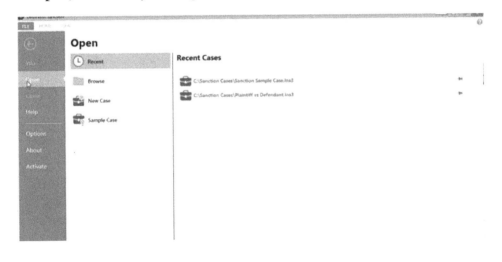

---

8. https://www.lexisnexis.com/en-us/products/timemap.page?access=1-2177364800 &treatcd=1-2177364868&keyword=timemap&gclid=CjwKCAjwhbHlBRAMEiwAoDA34_rS3M K925LbD9HtX59fodFUpL9FM365selUyqSuWVXFMA2sYwZw-xoCHVcQAvD_BwE.

9. Communication with Tyler Bell, Sales Engineer, CaseMap Specialist, Large Law and Federal Government, June 3, 2019.

Next, browse to the folder where you wish to save the case, type in its case name and click **Save**. The case has been created.

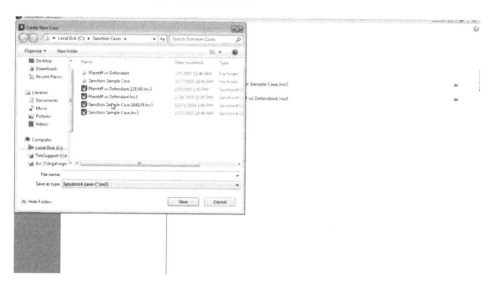

When you wish to open and work on a case, click on the **File** tab at the top of the left case-file column. Then, click on **Open** on the left column. Now you have four choices. First, to access a recent case, click on **Recent**. You can place one of your cases in Recent Cases by clicking on Recent and clicking again on the pin next to the case you wish to place in Recent Cases. Second, you can browse for a Sanction case file, by clicking on **Browse** and then clicking on the file and then clicking **Open**. Third, you can open the Sample Case file.

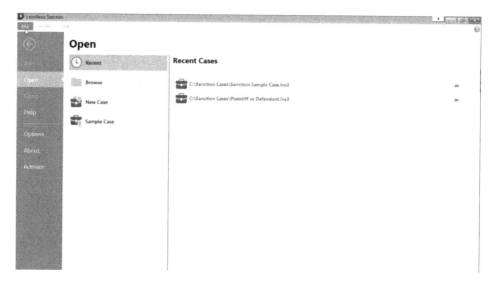

Now, you can browse to the folder where you want to place the case file, and then you click **Save**. The next time you wish to access your file in Sanction, just click **File** then click **Open** and browse for your case file.

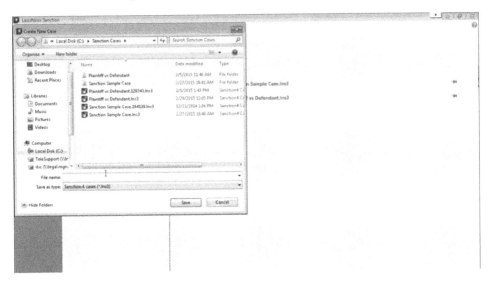

2. Importing Transcripts, Media, and Exhibits into Sanction

Before you can begin working with Sanction, you will need to import the items stored on your computer, including exhibits (images, text clips, and timeline images), media (audio, video, media clips), or transcripts (plain text and transcripts synchronized with video) into Sanction. This can be accomplished in two ways: with Wizard or by dragging and dropping them.

a. Importing with Wizard

The methodology for importing items into Sanction with Wizard is pretty much the same for exhibits, media, and transcripts, and we use how to import a transcript as an example of how to import the other types of items.

On the left column, click **Import** under File, and this will bring up a pop-up box labeled Transcript File Import Wizard.

Click **Next** to bring you to Select Transcript Files, and then you click **Add Files**. Browse through your files and select the one that you want. Click **Open** and you will be able to select transcript from the list of transcripts that will appear. When you click **Next**, the Ready to Import box opens. Finally, to import the transcript into Sanction, just click **Next**.

Another approach to importing transcripts is to click **Info** on the left File column and then click **Import**, and in the drop-down box, click **Transcript** and follow the steps like the ones you would have taken if you used the Transcript File Import Wizard.

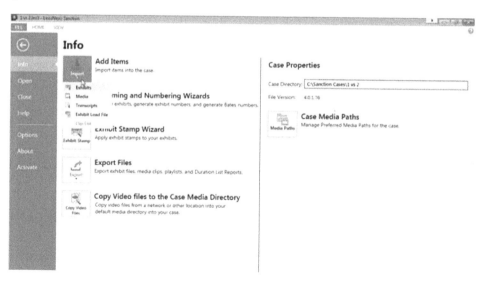

By following these steps, with some variations, you can import exhibits and media with Wizard.

b. *Importing by Drag and Drop*

Instead of using Wizard to import transcripts, media, and exhibits, you can drag and drop them to import them. It is a simple method. When you are in your case, click **Transcripts** at the bottom of the left column. Browse to where you have saved the desired transcript in your computer, select it and then drag it and drop it into the left Transcript column. A confirmation box will appear, and when you click **Close**, your transcript will have been imported to where you want it.

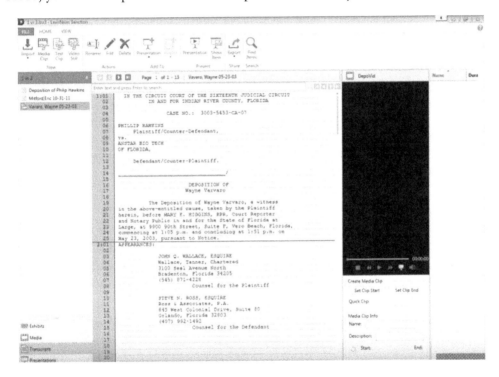

Utilizing these drag-and-drop steps you can import media and exhibits too.

3. **A Presentation**

a. *Creating a Presentation*

When you want to create a new presentation, click on the movie screen image labeled **New Presentation** on the navigation bar at the top of the page. Then, in the pop-up box type in the name of the new presentation and click **OK**. In the future when you want to pull up the presentation, it will be locatable in the lower left column under Presentation.

When you want to create a presentation with an item listed in Sanction, go to the left column, and, on the bottom of that column, click on either **Exhibits** (containing exhibits, images, text clips, and timeline images), **Media** (containing audio, video, and media clips), or **Transcripts** (containing plain text and transcripts synchronized with video) depending upon what you are seeking to include in your new presentation. After you have pulled up the desired item by clicking on it, right-click on it and on a drop-down box, click on **Add to Presentation**. Click on **New Presentation**, type in the presentation's name, and click **OK**. If you want to add an item to a presentation, go to that item, which is either found in Exhibits, Media, or Transcripts, and right-click on it. After you do this, click on **Add to Presentation** in the drop-down box and then on the presentation to which you wish to attach the item. When you go to the presentation in the future the item will be there.

If you want to rename or delete your presentation, select that presentation. To rename or delete the presentation, right-click the presentation and then click **Rename**, type in a new name and click **OK** or click **Delete**.

b. *Showing a Presentation*

Sanction provides you with three options for displaying items. First, you can present items linearly; present items one after another in sequence by clicking on the presentation advance arrow tool located on the far right on the presentation tool bar. Second, if you want to pick an item from a list, click on the item selection window in the presentation window. Then, select the item and then **Go To Item**, and the item will appear. Third, you can show the item by typing in an item identifier. Click on the item selector button in the presentation window and select the **Show** Item image and then type in either the exhibit number, Bates number, or name followed by clicking **Enter**.

c. *Adding Annotations with the Annotation Tool Gallery*

You can annotate an exhibit during a presentation with Sanction's annotation tools. When you have an exhibit in the Presentation view, you can find the Annotation Tool Gallery button in the lower right corner of your screen.

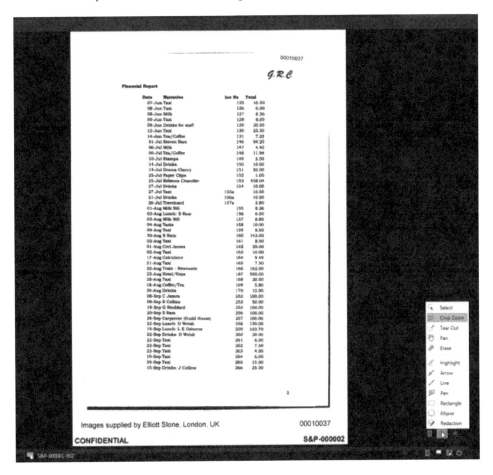

These tools are available to you in the Sanction Annotation Tool Gallery, and their applications are as follows:

Select—Select annotations by dragging the cursor across them and then you can move, delete or resize them.

Crop Zoom—Click **Crop Zoom** in the Gallery, and then drag your cursor across the rectangular portion of the visual you wish zoom in on and it will be magnified.

Tear Out—Also referred to as "callout," allows you to magnify a rectangle portion of an exhibit. To accomplish this, when you have the exhibit in presentation, click **Tear Out**, and you will be given the option of clicking on **Standard** or **Ripped Edge**. Then drag the cursor across the part of the visual you want to annotate and then apply the annotation. Double click to remove the annotation.

Pan—Click on this tool and you can move the exhibit in the presentation screen.

Erase—Use this tool to erase annotations.

Highlight—Just as you would use a highlighter pen to highlight text on a page of paper, you can highlight a chosen rectangular portion of the visual. While yellow is the default color, you can select another color by clicking on **Fill Color**.

Arrow, Line, Pen, Rectangle, or Ellipse—You can apply these shapes to an exhibit to draw the audience's attention to what you want them focus on in the exhibit.

Redaction—Drag the cursor across that portion of the exhibit that should be redacted.

d.   *Alternative Ways to Access Annotation Tools*

A second way to access these annotation tools is to employ the Image Tools Tab that will appear when you have selected an exhibit page. It offers the same annotation tools and looks like this:

A third approach to applying the annotation tools is to use Sanction's Keyboard Shortcuts. Handy Keyboard Shortcuts are as follows:

Select—Ctrl+Shift+S
Tear Out—Ctrl+O
Pan—Ctrl+ Alt+P
Erase—Ctrl+Alt+S
Highlight—Ctrl+H
Arrow—Ctrl+W
Line—Ctrl+L
Pen—Ctrl+N
Rectangle—Ctrl+G
Ellipse—Ctrl+E
Redaction—Ctrl+R

e.   *Deleting Annotations*

What do you do if you wish to remove annotations from an exhibit? Select the page or pages on which the unwanted annotations appear and then removing them can be done in three ways. Just right-click on the exhibit page and a drop-down with **Delete All Exhibit Page Annotations** will appear. Click on that to get the job done.

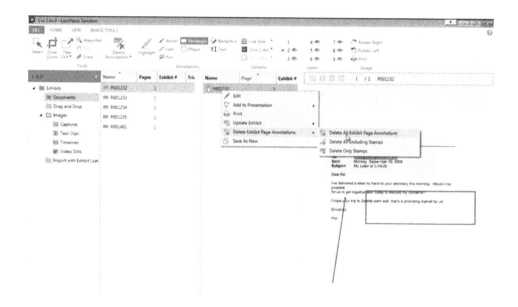

A second way to accomplish the same task is to go to the tool bar at the top of the screen, click on **Delete Annotations**, and then when the drop-down appears, click on **Delete All Exhibit Page Annotations**.

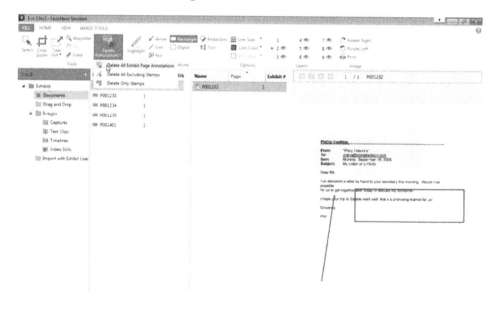

A third way to delete all annotations is to use the Keyboard Shortcut Ctrl+Delete.

f.   *Exhibit Stamps*

How you stamp an exhibit depends upon your court's practices and procedures. Courts often post their practices and procedures online. Some courts will direct counsel to deliver the exhibits to the court's clerk who will pre-mark exhibits while other judges will have counsel submit the documents in a binder with tabs but without exhibit stamps. Other courts will allow counsel to pre-mark the exhibits. For example, a federal court judge's instruction regarding electronic evidence and pre-marking exhibits are as follows:

Jury Electronic Evidence—Instructions for Attorneys

The IT Department for the US District Court will provide a laptop computer that has been prepared specifically for presentation of electronic exhibits to Jurors. This laptop will not have any network access, internet browsing capability, nor tools for opening files that are not specific to viewing or hearing evidence. A wired mouse and AC power adaptor will also be provided with the computer.

The IT Department will also provide a portable 42" flat screen monitor, and a pair of computer speakers, in a location in the Jury room that will allow all Jurors to have a clear view of the content on the screen.

The laptop, loaded with all admitted exhibits, will be brought into the courtroom and hooked into the courtroom display system. This will allow the attorneys, and court staff, to confirm inclusion of the proper Admitted Exhibits. Once Counsel has agreed to the content, the laptop will be presented to the Jurors and a brief tutorial will be given.

Copies of the Admitted Exhibits Portfolio will be provided to counsel at the conclusion of the trial.

Submitting Electronic Evidence

Exhibits must be delivered to... [the] Courtroom Deputy Clerk, the Thursday prior to trial or upon other arrangements made with the clerk. Exhibits are to be delivered in the following format:

- Exhibits must be on a CD in PDF format
- Each exhibit must be a single PDF Document
- PDF documents should be scanned using Optical Character Recognition if possible & encoded as a searchable PDF
- Exhibits that contain audio or video must be playable in Windows Media Player
- Exhibits must be numbered and named. The naming convention for each exhibit must include the exhibit number and a brief description.

For example, plaintiff's exhibit one would be named: 001contract.pdf. Defendant's exhibit 100 would be named: 100email.pdf.
- An exhibit list in Microsoft Word format must be emailed to … Courtroom Deputy Clerk[10]

With Sanction's Exhibit Stamp Wizard, you can apply exhibit stamps to the electronic exhibits. Click the **File** tab on the navigation ribbon at the top of the page followed by clicking **Info** and then clicking **Exhibit Stamp Wizard**. Click **Next** in the Exhibit Stamp Wizard box.

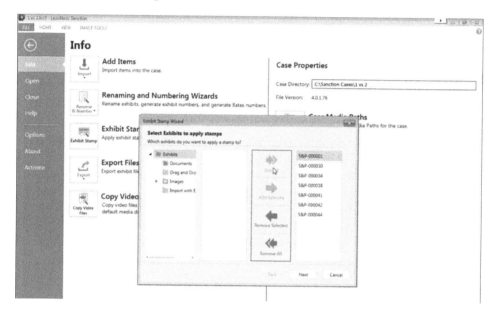

The exhibits to be stamped are listed in the right column. Select the exhibit that you wish to stamp from the list. After you click **Next**, an exhibit stamp will appear in a box on the right side of the screen. Now, you can determine what color the stamp should be, the number, and the placement of the stamp on the exhibit.

10. Judge Marsha J. Pechman Chamber Procedures, U.S. District Court, Western District of Washington, https://www.wawd.uscourts.gov/judges/pechman-procedures.

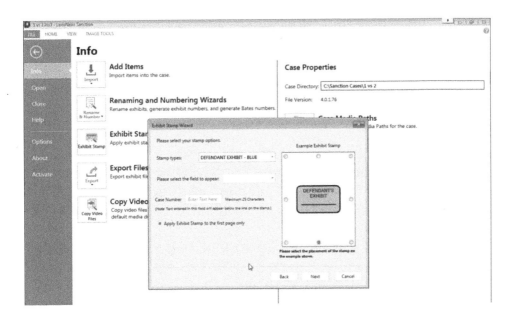

When you click on the **Options as Needed** tab, you will be given the following options to pick one by one: title, such as Plaintiff's Exhibit; and color of the stamp. When you click on **Please Select Field to Appear**, you can select among the following to be applied to the stamp: Page Number; Exhibit Number; Trial Exhibit Number; and Bates Number. You can also type in a Case Number to be applied. Next, you place the stamp on the exhibit. Click **Next** and the Ready to Apply Exhibit Stamp box appears, and you can click **Next** to apply the exhibit stamp and then click **Close**.

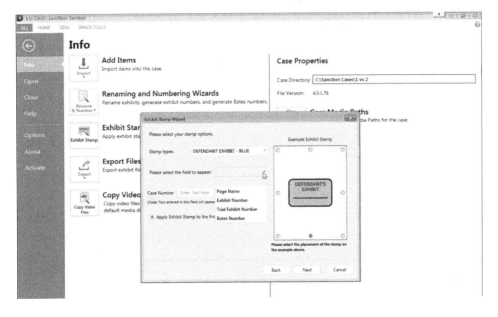

Although Sanction offers different types of numbering types, such as Bates Number and Trial Exhibit Number, communication at trial should be confined to referring to the exhibit only by trial exhibit number because that is what the court record should reflect.

g. *Redaction*

Some exhibits require redaction before they can be displayed in court. For instance, in *Michigan v. Musser*,[11] the Michigan Supreme Court reversed a conviction due to a failure to redact some of the officer's statements made during the interview of the suspect.

Redaction, in general, is time-consuming and requires meticulousness. Redacting a document can be hard work, and redacting video evidence is even worse. Plan to expend plenty of pretrial time reviewing, preparing, redacting, and rendering your video exhibits. Be prepared to make several versions if necessary. Also, be prepared to show opposing counsel and the court the redactions that were made and have legal justification for those redactions in order to ensure credibility, transparency, and admissibility.

4. Searching in Sanction

a. *Searching a Case*

To search for an item in one of your cases, click on the Home tab, and then in the drop box you have the choice to Search for Text by Name, Exhibit Number, Trial Number, Bates Number, or Description. Another option is to Search for Date, which includes either a specific date or "on or before" or "on or after." Enter what you are seeking and click **OK**, and then the results will appear in the box. Double click the item to open it.

b. *Word Searching a Transcript*

If you want to word search a transcript in Sanction, click on the **Home** tab at the top of the screen, followed by clicking the **Transcript** navigation bar at the bottom of the left column. Next, select the transcript you want from the list of transcripts. The transcript will come up, and you can type the word you are seeking into the search bar to bring up the places in the transcript where the word appears.

---

11. *Michigan v. Musser*, 494 Mich. 337, 835 N.W. 2d 319 (2013).

Use the navigation button to the right of the search button to scroll through the transcript to locations where the word appears.

5.   Text Clips

Sanction makes it easy to save a portion of a document as a text clip, such as a text clip from a deposition transcript. In the left column, click on **Exhibits** at the bottom of the left column, then **Images** and next click **Text Clips**. Locate the part of the transcript that you wish clipped and select it. Once you have done that, right-click the selected text and click **New Text Clip** and name the clip for later retrieval.

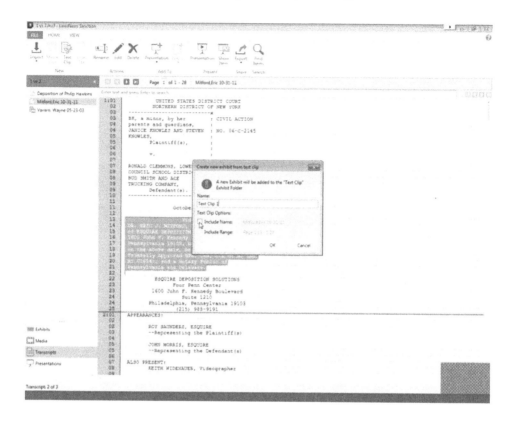

When you want to retrieve and show the text clip, go to Exhibits, then Images, and Text Clips and click on the name that you gave the text clip.

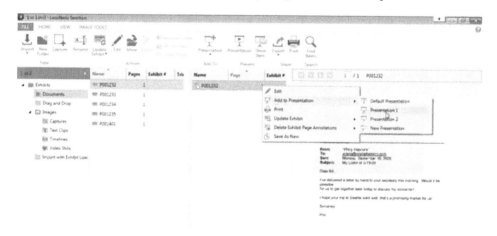

6. Video Clips

With Sanction you can make a clip from a video file or video deposition and then store it in either a presentation or a playlist or both. Click on the **Media** bar on the Home tab and select the desired video file. When the video comes up, go to the place on the video where you want the clip to begin and click **Set Clip Start**.

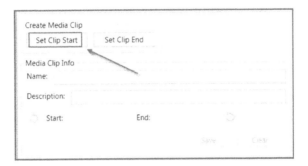

Next, use the play button to go to where you wish to end the video clip and click on **Set Clip End**. Give the clip a name and click **Save**. The clip is now saved in the media clip list.

For the video deposition to have the most impact on the viewer, you will want to have the video synchronized with the transcript, allowing the transcript to scroll on the screen side by side with the video of the deponent being questioned. Either before or after the deposition, ask the reporter or videographer for a synchronized video transcript.

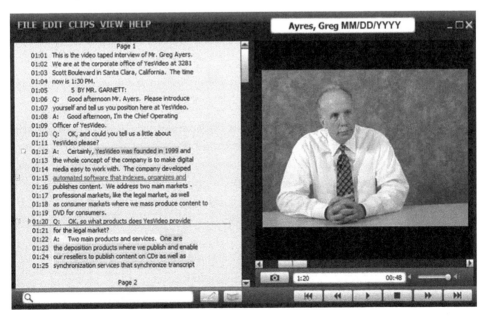

When the video is synchronized with the transcript, you can easily create video clips. With the cursor, highlight the portion of the video that you wish to clip, and then right-click and click on **Add** selection to **Clip List**. A box will pop up and you can give the clip a name. Click **OK**. In the future when you want the clip that you just named, click **List Manager** and you will see the list of clips.

In order to play a video with synced text in the newest version of Sanction, you will need to have the video and transcript synchronized and put into an .mdb file. Once this is done, you can simply load the .mdb file and the video into Sanction, and it will play with the scrolling transcript.

There are many ways to create an .mdb file. You can pay either a court reporter who has the right equipment to do it or an online service, such as Yes Video.[12] Alternatively, you can do it yourself with Sanction 2, which is an older version of the Sanction software, or with a stand-alone product such as TimeCoder Pro.[13] All you need is the video in a standard format and a digital transcript file, such as PTX digital transcript file.

You can also use video editing software, such as Camtasia or AVS video editor,[14] to add subtitles to video files. This may be time consuming but can be done at low cost. Also, online services are available that provide this service.

7.   Keyboard Shortcuts

As we mentioned when discussing annotations, Sanction allows you to utilize Keyboard Shortcuts to perform most tasks that the software can perform. The Sanction 4.0 User Guide provides a full eight-page list of these Keyboard Shortcuts.[15] This list is divided into major functions as follows: Exhibits, Media, Transcripts, Presentations, Presentation window, View tab, Image Tools tab.

G. ExhibitView

Sanction can be compared to other nonlinear software on the market that perform many of the same functions. As an example of how other nonlinear software has similar and dissimilar features, we have chosen to discuss ExhibitView (a product of Solutions LLC) in some depth. In this section, we will also cover other functions that nonlinear software can perform, such as redacting a document, which we did not explore in the discussion of Sanction.

---

12. http://www.yesvideo.com/; https://advancedrep.com/advanced-viewer/.

13. https://iprotech.com/trialdirector-360/#timecoder-pro.

14. https://www.avs4you.com/.

15. http://help.lexisnexis.com/litigation/ac/sanction_docs/Sanction4_KBSC_QRC.pdf.

ExhibitView has several commendable features, including ease of use and its presentation focus. Rather than having dual-screen operation, it has a single screen user interface and an extended screen for the judge and jury to view the presentation.

ExhibitView will work on a Surface tablet and has an iPad application called iTrial. iTrial's focus is on presentations and not on preparing exhibits. ExhibitView has a product manual built into its Help menu. The software also comes with video tutorials.[16]

I. A Presentation

After you have opened ExhibitView, you can click on **Create New Case**[17] in the box on the right on the home screen and give it your case's name. Then, click the **Browse** tab to move to where you would like to save the case. Follow this by clicking the **Create** tab.

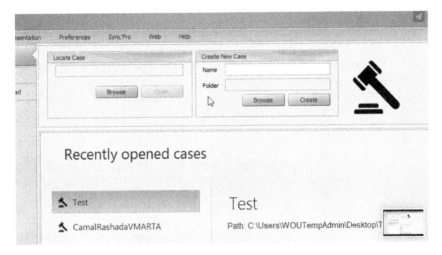

---

16. http://www.exhibitview.net/tutorials/.

17. The step-by-step instructions here mirror the Quick Start Video tutorial of Exhibit-View at http://www.exhibitview.net/tutorials/ and are published here with the permission of ExhibitView.

On your screen you will see three areas as follows: (1) presentation area on the right; (2) exhibit library on the left; and (3) annotation and screen control tools at the top of the screen.

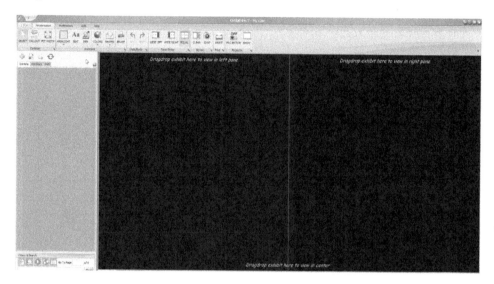

Click on the + sign (indicating that you are to add exhibits) on the left in the exhibit column and then browse to a folder containing exhibits.

When you arrive at the exhibits you want, select one or more or all the exhibits and click **Open**.

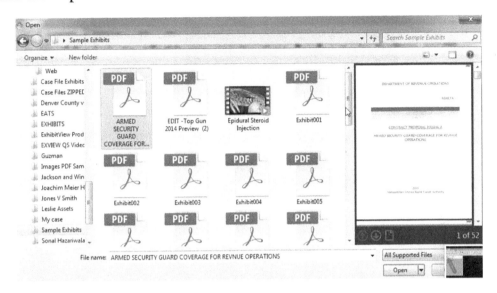

Your exhibits will be shown in the left exhibit library column. Click on the exhibit that you want and drag it to the right onto the screen and drop it there. If you drag only one exhibit it will show on one screen. If you wish to move two exhibits over, you can place one on one screen and the other on the other screen.

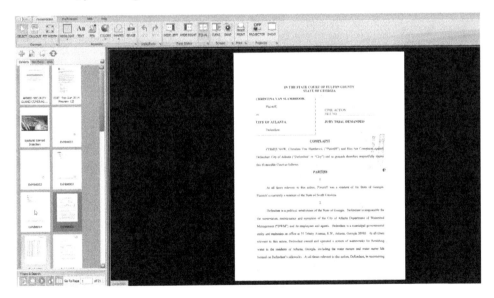

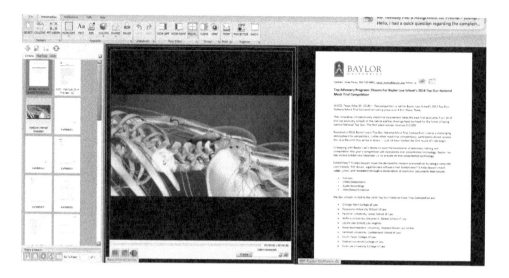

If you have a multi-page document exhibit and want to show a particular page, ExhibitView allows you to use a keyboard shift. Hold down Control+G and then type the page number in the Go To Page space to move to the desired page.

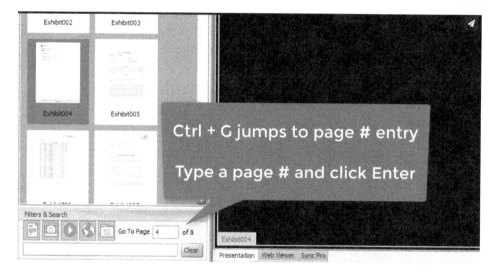

The tool bar at the top of the screen has many of the annotation tools that we discussed when reviewing Sanction. They include the popular ones: creating a callout, highlighting, and marking with a pen. To delete the annotations, you can swipe them with the eraser, double click on them, or type the delete key.

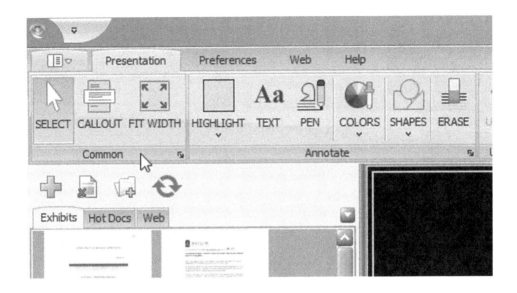

Snap is a nice tool found on the tool bar at the top of the screen. Click on it, and it will take a snapshot of the image on your screen and save it as an image file. For example, this tool will allow you to have a copy of the annotated image that may be able to be used as an exhibit.

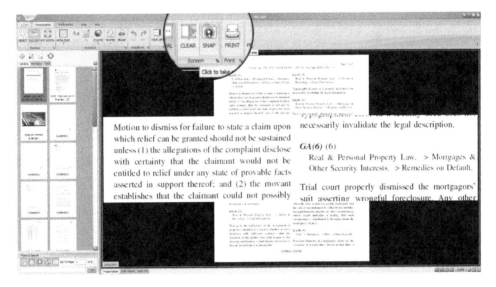

If you wish to print out your entire case or selected documents, just click on the **Print** icon and you will be given those options.

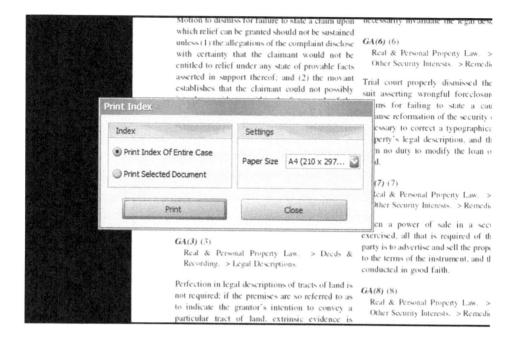

When you want to show what is on your screen, click on the **Projector** button on the tool bar at the top of the page.

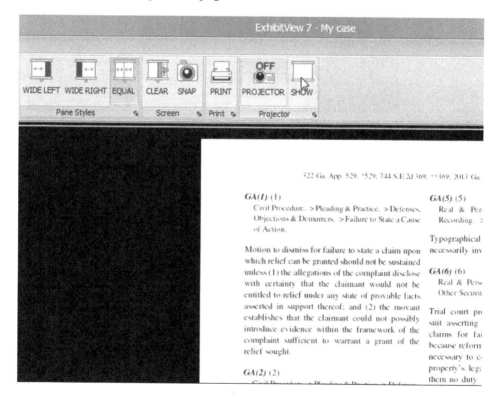

2.   PDF+

ExhibitView has a feature called PDF+ that enables the user to do the following tasks, among others, when working with exhibits: redact documents; attach exhibit stickers and Bates stamps; and search documents. PDF+ comes with a video tutorial.[18]

To familiarize you with PDF+ features and enable you to compare Exhibit-View with Sanction's operating system and features, we will explore how Exhibit-View's PDF+ navigates documents and can be used to label exhibits and redact documents.

Begin by going to the left column on the screen where Windows Explorer can be used to navigate to the exhibits with which you want to work. When you click on that exhibits' folder, it fills the next column to the right with the exhibits. Click on the exhibit in that column and it will appear on the screen.

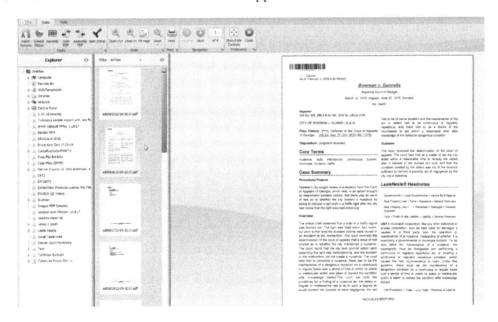

Let's see how you can apply exhibit stickers with PDF+. Go to the tool bar at the top of the screen where you will find the tools that you can use to mark or stamp the exhibit. You have six options: (1) name or rename a batch of exhibits; (2) apply exhibit stickers; (3) apply a bar code; (4) split a PDF; (5) assemble a PDF; or (6) apply a Bates Stamp.

---

18. *Ibid.*

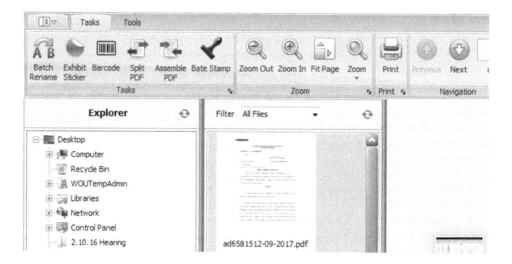

To illustrate how these tools work, assume you wish to apply an exhibit stamp. When you click on **Exhibit Sticker**, a box appears, and you will see that it allows you three lines of text that you can type on the sticker. Then, you can click **Add Sticker** to apply the sticker to one of four locations on the exhibit.

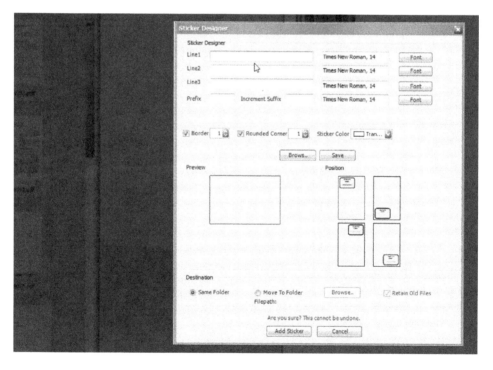

ExhibitView's tool bar provides the following tools: (1) Find; (2) Zoom Out; (3) Zoom In; (4) Fit Page; (5) Zoom; (6) Redact; (7) Undo; (8) True Redact;

(9) Split PDF; (10) Assemble PDF; (11) Rotate Document Clockwise; (12) Rotate Document Anticlockwise; (13) Rotate Page Clockwise; (14) Rotate Page Anticlockwise; (15) Insert Page; (16) Delete Page; (17) Next; and (18) Previous with a box to type in the page.

With the Search and Redact tools as examples we can see how to use the ExhibitView tools.[19] When you redact a document, obviously you need to keep an un-redacted copy of it. When naming the redacted exhibit, it is a good practice to label it in a way that shows it has been redacted. You want to make sure that the un-redacted document is not inadvertently displayed to the jury.

Assume you want to redact the word "bulb" from a document. With the Search tool you locate the various places in the document where the word is located. Then, click on **Redaction** and select either black or white to blot out the word "bulb."

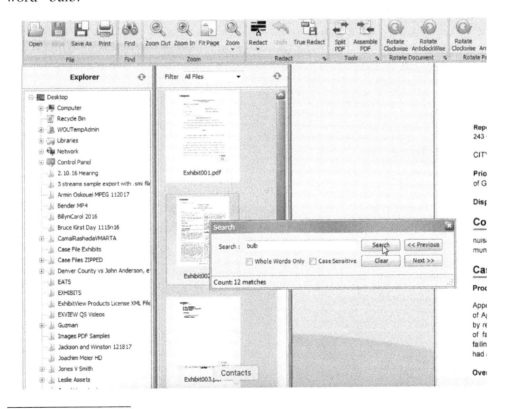

---

19. Once again the step-by-step instructions here mirror the Quick Start Video tutorial of ExhibitView at http://www.exhibitview.net/tutorials/ and are published here with the permission of ExhibitView.

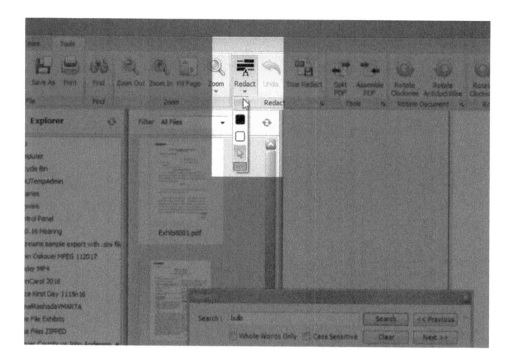

Next, go to each of the places where the word "bulb" appears and white it out using your cursor. When you have completed the redaction, go to the True Redact tab in the tool bar and click on it. All references to the word "bulb" will have been redacted.

H. TrialDirector

TrialDirector provides many of the same functions as Sanction and Exhibit-View. TrialDirector is a software product of Ipro Tech LLC. As we previously discussed, the best way to learn how to operate the software is to work with it. YouTube provides numerous videos on how to operate TrialDirector; indeed, there are 29 video tutorials covering the various aspects of the TrialDirector software's operation.[20] Also, TrialDirector 6 came with a 38-page Quick Start Guide.[21]

---

20. https://www.youtube.com/playlist?list=PL3t4gOo3XT-dWTO0vFxT9HiFvRlK1zh0F.

21. http://static.indatacorp.com/docs/user-guides/TrialDirector-6.3-Quick-Start-Guide .pdf.

The most recent version of this software is TrialDirector 360,[22] and the features of the old and new versions are discussed in a half-hour YouTube video.[23] TrialDirector works with Windows OS only.

I.   OnCue

OnCue,[24] which is a product of Core Legal Concepts LLC, is a relatively new litigation software, having become available in 2014. The software was created by technology consultants for technology consultants. However, it is powerful, flexible, and not confusing, and, consequently, it is suitable for trial lawyers to operate as well. OnCue is nonlinear software, and it offers many of the same functions offered by Sanction and TrialDirector. This litigation software is available on Windows, and therefore on a PC, or on a Surface. Also, as we discussed on pages 237-38, you can partition a Mac so that you can also run Windows and OnCue on a Mac.

As OnCue declares that it is not "[s]imple enough for anyone to learn in 15 minutes: Should any professional tool be described like that? OnCue is not difficult, but it's not a one-trick pony either."[25] Also, the vendor stresses that the software is designed for professional technicians who will be operating it in a courtroom as follows: "Engineered by pros for other pros. The most powerful features will be appreciated by those using it day in and day out. The core features are easy to learn and use with just a little training."[26]

The usual educational tools for learning how to run OnCue are available to you. A great number of them can be found in OnCue's Help Center.[27] There you can find a ten-page Quick Start Guide, video tutorials lasting over five hours on topics (such as activating OnCue, creating a new case, and adding documents), and short written descriptions along with illustrations explaining how to operate different functions of OnCue. Additionally, Mike Ko, a technology consultant, not affiliated with OnCue, has created a YouTube video reviewing OnCue.[28]

By now you should have a good feel for what nonlinear software has to offer. It is now up to you to give the products trial runs and pick the one that works best for you.

---

22. https://iprotech.com/software/trial-director-360/.

23. https://www.youtube.com/watch?v=P3LrMhPpdBA&t=378s.

24. http://www.oncuetech.com/.

25. http://www.oncuetech.com/.

26. *Ibid.*

27. https://support.oncuetech.com/hc/en-us.

28. https://www.youtube.com/watch?v=QeVNinpDMYA&t=249s.

J.   PowerPoint

What is PowerPoint doing in a chapter about nonlinear software? The answer is that if you do not have nonlinear software, you can, to a degree, substitute PowerPoint for nonlinear software. PowerPoint allows users to build hyperlinks into a slide, and programs those hyperlink buttons to jump to specific slides. Thus, the user could be on slide 1, click on the hyperlink, and jump to slide 23. This allows the user to create a menu on one slide and use that menu to jump wherever the user wants in the presentation. For example, slide 1 could be a menu slide that contains 20 hyperlink buttons, each of which will allow the user to jump to whichever slide the user assigned to that button. This hyperlink function allows the user to jump around as needed. Not only can you create hyperlinks from one slide to another but also you can create hyperlinks to images and documents in your case file on your computer.

Creating a hyperlinks menu is easy to do. On a blank PowerPoint slide that will serve as your menu, type the title of the item in your computer that you wish to access. For instance, if you want to link to the complaint in the Ride The Ducks case,[29] type "Complaint—Ride The Ducks" in a text box on the slide. Next, highlight the phrase and right-click, and that will bring down the menu, and then click **Hyperlink** at the bottom of the screen.

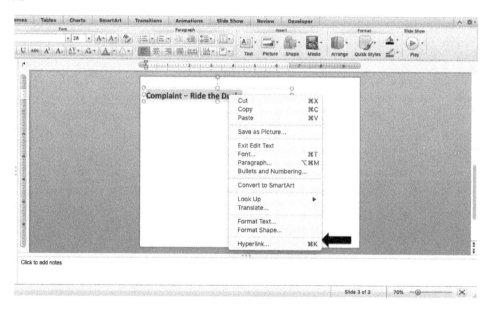

When you click **Hyperlink**, it will bring up the Insert Hyperlink menu and you can click on either **Web Page**, **Document**, or **E-mail Address**. Because the

---

29. *Dinh v. Ride The Ducks Int'l*, No. 16-2-19995-0 SEA.

complaint is a document, you click on **Document**, and this takes you to your usual computer menu where you can browse for the complaint.

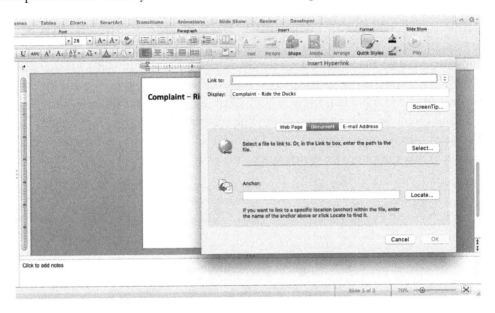

Once you have located the document, here the complaint, just click **Open** and a hyperlink will appear on the Insert Hyperlink page.

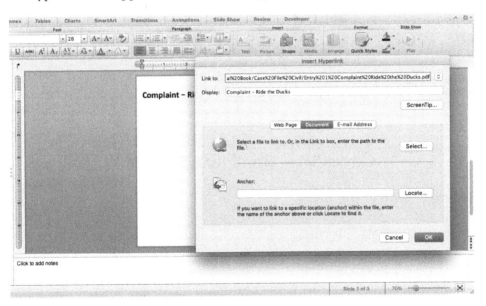

When you click on the **OK** button at the bottom right side of the page, it will create the hyperlink on your menu slide. Now, when you are in slideshow mode with your menu slide on the screen, all you need to do is click on the phrase "Complaint—Ride The Ducks" and the complaint will appear on the screen.

In the Appendix to this book, which is at http://www.fastcase.com/visual litigation, is Appendix 12.1—a pre-made PowerPoint template (pictured next). The template allows you to paste the visuals you want in the blank slides that are already hyperlinked to the slide with the 35 exhibit labels on it. With a touch screen device or iPad, you only need to click on the exhibit number and up pops the image you want to show. This is nonlinear and flexible, and, therefore, it is suitable for use during direct or cross-examination. The template is designed for those who do not wish to purchase more expensive nonlinear software, such as Sanction or Trial Director. While the template is not fancy, it is free.

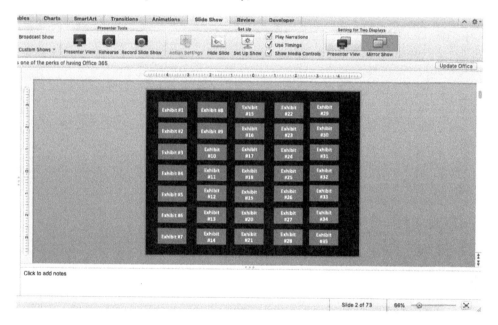

Checklist—Nonlinear Software

Nonlinear Software Uses

- ❑ Store and organize case files;
- ❑ At will, retrieve and display exhibits during direct examination and cross-examination;
- ❑ Show a deposition video with a synchronized transcript;
- ❑ Edit videos; and
- ❑ Annotate visual exhibits.

CaseMap for Storing and Organizing

❏ Consider CaseMap software for storing and organizing case files.
❏ CaseMap works smoothly with Sanction—they are both LexisNexis products.

Sanction Software

❏ Consider Sanction, which is a nonlinear software, because you can retrieve and show visual evidence when you need it rather than in a linear fashion.
❏ Sanction can perform the following functions, among others:
  ✓ Create a presentation
  ✓ Show the presentation
  ✓ Annotate exhibits
  ✓ Create text clips
  ✓ Create video clips
  ✓ Stamp exhibits

Alternative Nonlinear Software

❏ Consider these nonlinear software programs that serve many of the same functions as Sanction:
  ✓ ExhibitView
  ✓ TrialDirector
  ✓ PowerPoint

Linear Software

"Software makes the world go 'round."

Thomas Peterfly, businessman

A. Linear Software

In this chapter we focus on PowerPoint and Keynote, which are linear software programs. This chapter, like Chapter 12, which concentrated on nonlinear software, explains how to operate linear software in easily understandable terms. Linear software programs are ideal for opening statement and closing argument when counsel is addressing the jury. They are also valuable visual aids for when an expert witness, very much in a lecture manner, explains the expert's field of expertise, findings, and opinions to a judge or jury.

B.   The Basics of a Persuasive Computer Slideshow

We have all suffered "death by PowerPoint." In this section, we cover how to design a persuasive computer slideshow with linear software, the most prominent being PowerPoint and Keynote. As we cover the basics of how to create a persuasive and well-designed slideshow, we will simultaneously explain how to avoid the pitfalls that can cause "death by PowerPoint." While these basic principles for constructing a good PowerPoint presentation may seem too basic, sadly, too often they are not followed to the detriment of the subject matter of the presentation, the presenter, and the audience.

I.   Informative

What is wrong with this slide?

DEPOSITION
INSTRUCTION NOT TO ANSWER

Fed. R. Civ. P. 30(c)(2) states that ". . . A person may instruct a deponent not to answer only when necessary to preserve a privilege, to enforce a limitation ordered by the court, or to present a motion under Rule 30(d)(3).

" Rule 30(d)(3) provides that "(a)t any time during the deposition the deponent or a party may move to terminate or limit it on the ground that it is being conducted in bad faith or in a manner that unreasonably annoys, embarrasses, or oppresses the deponent or party. . . If the objecting deponent or party so demands, the deposition must be suspended for the time necessary to obtain an order."

Each slide should be informative but not overloaded. The consequence of putting too much information on the slide is that the slide upstages the speaker. Viewers are trying to read while the speaker is trying to keep their attention.

How can we communicate the core information without overloading the slide with information? One way to get the information across without using one slide crammed with information is to break the information into smaller bits and present it on multiple slides. Also, ask yourself whether you have an image that communicates the same concept. For instance, a timeline could be used to communicate the chronology of events rather than a slide with text describing them.

PowerPoint should never be used to simply project the outline of opening or closing onto a screen. An opening or closing where the attorney is constantly looking at the screen to find out what he is going to say next is difficult to follow and often boring. PowerPoint is not meant to be a crutch. The purpose of visual communication is to add something to the presentation that is not captured by words alone. Simply projecting words onto a screen does not constitute visual communication, so it is important for attorneys to look beyond the crutch.

2. Knowing Your Message

The most important starting point for developing any effective visual is knowing the message that you want to convey. Every graphic should have a clear purpose and message. If the message or purpose is not obvious, the graphic should not be shown. You should never display a visual simply for the sake of having a visual. If the visual does not enhance the overall presentation, it should not be used. Consequently, attorneys should identify what the visual adds to the presentation that words alone cannot add. The added value may enhance the educational or persuasive value of the message. A simple exercise is to articulate, in a single sentence, what the visual conveys to the intended audience. This exercise will help clarify not only the goal of the visual but also the overall design of it. When you know what you want to convey, it is much easier to design a visual that conveys that message.

3. Color

There are entire books about color theory that provide insights into how different colors affect the psychological and emotional responses of jurors. The colors that you select to design your slides are important and should be consistent with the message that you are trying to convey with your visual.

The most common background colors are white, black, blue, and gray. White backgrounds create a sense of simplicity and can prevent the visual from appearing too busy. Black backgrounds make the content appear bolder, but the dark background may convey negative emotions about the content. Gray backgrounds are ideal for slides intended to convey confusion or ambiguity. Blue backgrounds are soothing to the eye and create a sense of comfort and ease.

Once the background color is determined, you should consider your accent colors. Red and orange convey warnings, alarms, or moments of poor decisions. Yellow conveys caution. Green conveys positive actions or forward movements.

The impact of color varies, but it is important to use colors sparingly. Excessive use of color can make a visual difficult to understand or follow, or simply unattractive. With any visual, the audience should immediately understand the message when they look at it. If the colors make it difficult to understand or follow, you have undermined the overall effectiveness of the visual.

One proven reliable combination is a dark blue background of either black or blue with light colored text of either yellow or white. These colors work well in both brightly lit and darker rooms. Whatever colors you select, always test the slideshow in the room in which it will be shown because colors change based upon the setting.

4. Font

Like the colors you choose, the font that you select for the text on your slides should be easy on the viewers' eyes. While Times New Roman is fine for a document, it does not come across well on a slide. Fancy fonts make it even more difficult for your audience. We prefer to use Arial Narrow, Calibri, or Helvetica because they are easy to read at a distance.

5. Viewable

What good is your slideshow if your audience cannot read it. Is the font too small to be viewable? The best way to determine whether the slideshow is viewable is to sit in your audience's seats. Can they read the text on the screen across the courtroom from their seats in the jury box? You may need to enlarge the fonts, or you may need to use callouts of part of the text so the audience can read it.

6. Varied

Research shows the average attention span a person is about eight seconds, down from twelve seconds a decade ago, and twenty seconds a couple of decades ago. Notably, the attention span of a goldfish is about nine seconds. Shortened attention spans are the natural product of the technological changes that have defined that last couple of decades. We live in a culture that is constantly changing. We consume information faster than ever and get bored quicker than ever. This places a great burden on attorneys to introduce greater variety into their presentations.

This means that you should explore a variety of presentation techniques. For example, attorneys should not rely only on PowerPoint slides. They may want to print some graphics on foam boards, which creates variety by allowing them to go back and forth between the electronic presentation and the physical boards in the courtroom.

To maintain interest, a slideshow should have slides with varied content. If every slide is filled with text, it can be boring and difficult to follow. Death by bullet point is very real, and jurors will make conscious or unconscious decisions very early in the presentation as to whether the presentation is going to be interesting or boring, and consequently, worth listening to. Jurors routinely complain about text-heavy slides particularly when what the attorney says varies from the text on the slide. This creates competing language, meaning the jurors try to reconcile what is on the slide with what the attorney is saying. In this situation, the core message can get lost, undermining the overall value of the visual.

Instead, slides should be truly visual, meaning they have imagery. This will draw jurors' interest and provide entertainment value, which is critical. After all, trial, in many respects, is a battle for jurors' attention. The more you can do to retain that attention, the greater your chances are of a successful outcome.

7. Enhance the Presentation

Last and most important, the PowerPoint medium should not outshine the messenger and the message. Edward Tufte, author, statistician, and artist, has expressed his low regard for PowerPoint as follows:

> PowerPoint's convenience for some presenters is costly to the content and the audience. These costs arise from the cognitive style characteristic of the standard default PP presentation: foreshortening of evidence and thought, low spatial resolution, an intensely hierarchical single-path structure as the model for organizing every type of content, breaking up narratives and data into slides and minimal fragments, rapid temporal sequencing of thin information rather than focused spatial analysis, conspicuous chartjunk and PP Phluff, branding of slides with logotypes, a preoccupation with format not content, incompetent designs for data graphics and tables, and a smirky commercialism that turns information into a sales pitch and presenters into marketeers. This cognitive style harms the quality of thought for the producers and the consumers of presentations.[1]

The slideshow should enhance your presentation; it should not be a distraction or a substitute for it. To avoid reliance upon the slideshow, counsel should prepare the presentation independent of PowerPoint—free of the hierarchical format that PowerPoint offers. A presentation of one bullet point after another can cause death by PowerPoint. Prepare your presentation as though PowerPoint would not be utilized. Only after you have developed your talk should you create a Power-Point to enrich your presentation with visuals.

---

1. Edward Tufte, *Beautiful Evidence*, 158, Graphic Press LLC (2006).

As you plan your presentation, you will be thinking of visuals that can enrich your talk. If you can use images and videos instead of words on the screen—a picture is worth a thousand of them—do so. PowerPoint images and videos enrich the presentation and are indeed essential. Even Edward Tufte, who has a low opinion of PowerPoint, has stated, "Of course full-screen projected images and videos are necessary; that is the one harmless use of PP . . . ."[2]

Do not read the slides when communicating with your pretrial audience at an alternative dispute resolution venue or in a courtroom. While slides provide convenient cues to you when you are addressing an audience, they are no substitute for your personal direct communication. Practice the presentation and know the material to be delivered by heart. To turn the focus from the slideshow to you, press the B button on the computer or the blank-screen button on your remote because that will turn the screen blank, shifting the audience's attention back to you.

C. Beyond Basics

PowerPoint is an extremely versatile software program. You can go beyond slides with text and bullet points that can lead to stupefaction. For instance, as we discussed in the preceding chapter at pages 268-70, PowerPoint with its hyperlink feature can serve as a substitute for nonlinear software.

Because PowerPoint comes with a multitude of tools that empower you to do such things as animate and insert pictures, shapes, and media (videos and sounds), you can create a vast array of visuals. For example, while you could purchase Time-Map, which allows you to easily create a timeline, with PowerPoint you can also build a timeline. Or, with PowerPoint, you can paste a map onto a slide and then paste labels onto that map to indicate the locations of places that are pertinent to the case. Using the PowerPoint Text Box feature, you can place text on a slide and then with the Shapes feature insert a callout with the important part of the text.

These are just a few examples of what you can do with PowerPoint. Many of the other visuals in the following section on mastering PowerPoint and elsewhere in this book were created with PowerPoint. In sum, PowerPoint is like an artist's palette and paints; it enables you to design a wide variety of litigation visuals.

D. Mastering PowerPoint

PowerPoint is a presentation software that is readily accessible because it is part of Microsoft's Office suite. PowerPoint is available for both a PC and a Mac. Keynote is part of Apple iWork and is solely for Mac.

---

2. *Id.* at 168.

To get started with PowerPoint, click on the **P** on the Dock at the bottom of the screen as seen on the next page (or wherever you position the Dock on your computer) and then click on **New** on the upper left side of your screen and that will open PowerPoint with a new slide on your workspace. The first slide to pop up will be the title page slide, which you may decide to use.

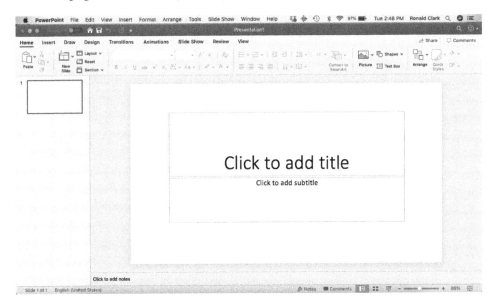

Should you wish a different slide template to work on, click on **New Slide** on the ribbon on the left side of the screen and this will produce a drop-down of several other templates to choose from.

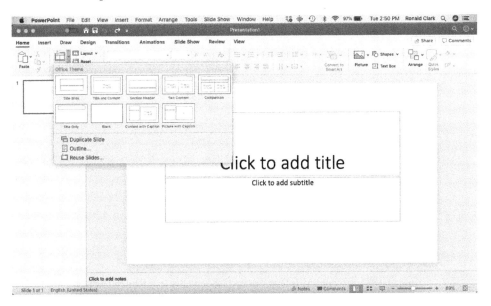

Next, you will likely wish to pick the background color for all your slides. To accomplish this, first click on **Format** on the ribbon at the top of the screen and then click on **Slide Background** on the drop-down menu.

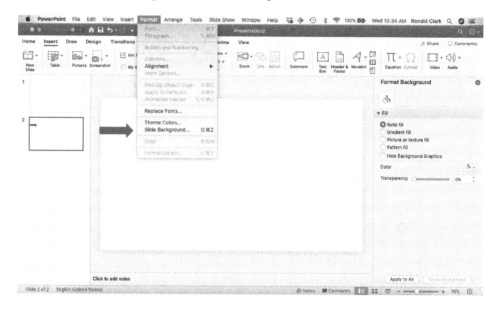

The next drop-down on the right side of the screen is entitled Format Background showing a small paint icon and a default of Solid fill for the slide (you can pick another fill).

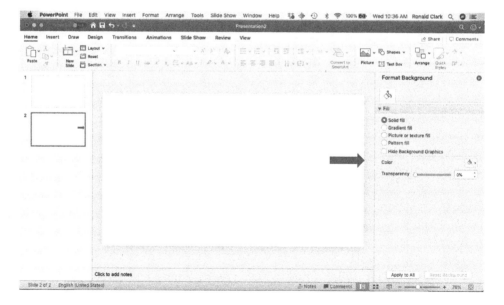

The arrow in the screenshot below is pointing at an even tinier paint can, and if you click on that, it will produce a drop-down palate of colors from which you can choose for the background for your slides (here we use black as an example). Once you have chosen the background color and format, click on the **Apply to All** tab at the bottom right, and the background will be applied to all your slides.

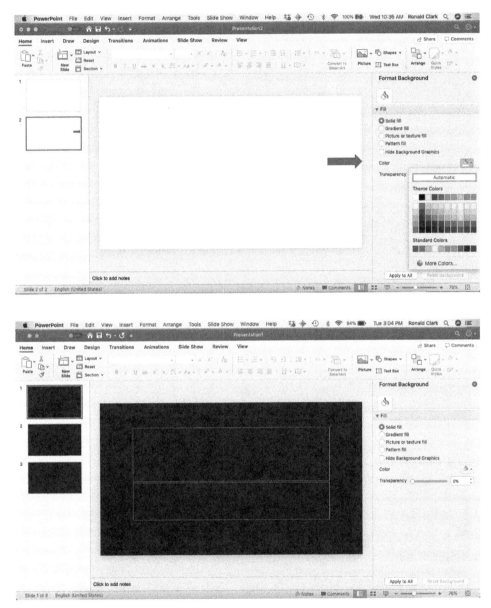

You can also create your own custom backgrounds, which is a great way to set yourself apart from others. For example, here is a custom template that Sound Jury Consulting created for a case that was tried in Anchorage, Alaska.

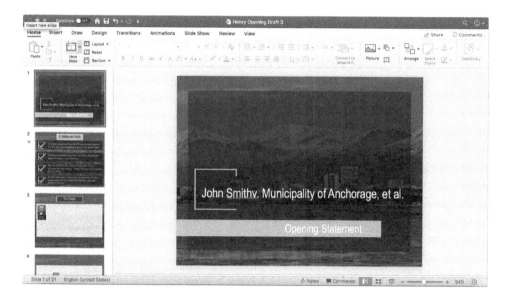

SJC used the skyline of Anchorage to create a custom background. However, it was not as simple as just inserting a picture into the background. SJC had to modify the picture to make it easy to place text and images over it as they created content for the slides.

In order to accomplish this, SJC selected the View option on the top ribbon and then selected Slide Master.

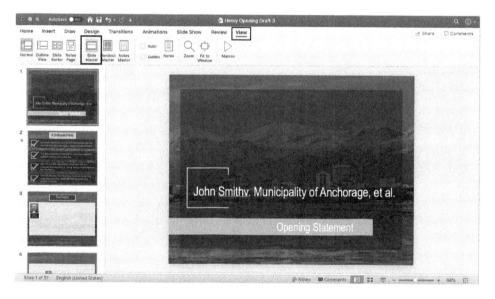

This will take you to a screen that looks like the following:

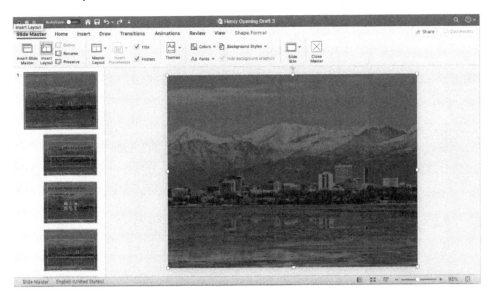

You should select the top slide in the selection pane on the left side of the workspace. Once you select this, anything you put on the slide that appears in the screen will constitute your custom background. To create this background, SJC inserted a picture of the Anchorage background, and then changed it to a black and white picture by double-clicking the picture. This opened formatting options on the right side of the screen. We selected Picture Color and Presets and chose the black and white option.

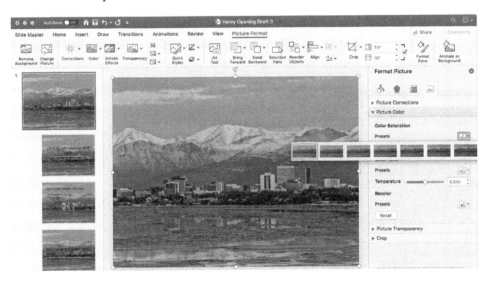

Once SJC changed the picture to be black and white, they inserted a square shape over this picture and selected blue as the color for the square shape. Then, SJC increased the transparency of the blue square so that you could see through it to see the background picture, creating the following background.

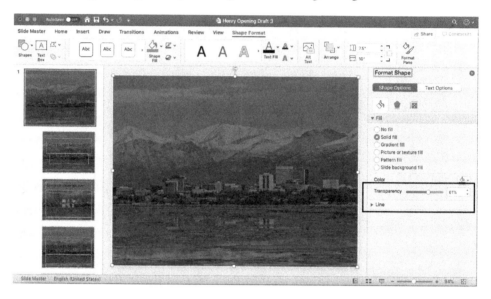

Once SJC had a background, they selected Close Slide Master to return to the screen where content could be added to the slides. Because SJC used the blue as a background, they selected complimentary colors for the content on the slide, which were yellow, white, and navy blue. SJC used these same colors throughout the entire slideshow as you can see below.

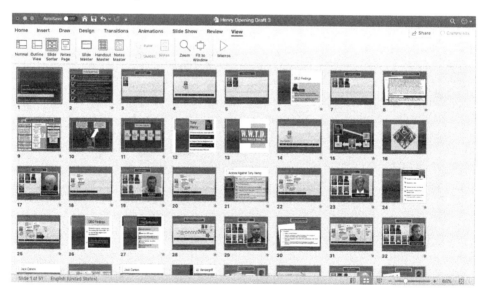

You will want to insert something—text, picture, video, and so on—onto your slide. For this you click on the **Insert** tab on the ribbon. This will bring up the treasure trove of visuals, text, and audio that you can put on slides. You are given these tabs to choose from: **Table** (insert a table—you decide how many columns and rows); **Pictures** (from your browser, file, or online); **Screenshots** (snapshot of any window open on your desktop); **Add-ins** (everything from licensed photos for PowerPoint presentations to comic characters for presentations); **Shapes** (arrows, circles, callouts, and more); **Icons** (visually communicate using symbols); **3D Models** (three-dimensional object that can be rotated to see all angles); **Smart-Art** (lists, hierarchies, relationship charts, and so on); **Chart** (bars, areas, lines, and so on); **Text Box** (perhaps the most important—click on it and you get a box on your slide into which you type your text); and **Video** and **Audio** (clips from your browser, file, or online).

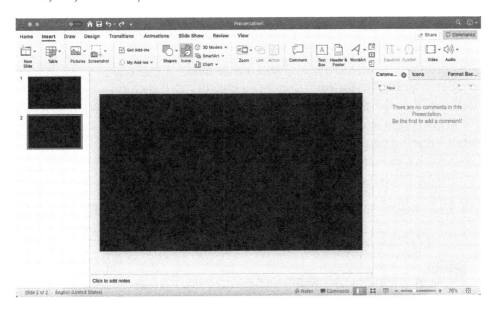

If you wish to insert text on the slide, click **Text** on the ribbon at the top of the screen (indicated by the arrow), and a text box appears on the screen where you can type in your text. Using the cursor, you can move and alter the text box. You can enlarge the font and the text box will automatically enlarge so it fits.

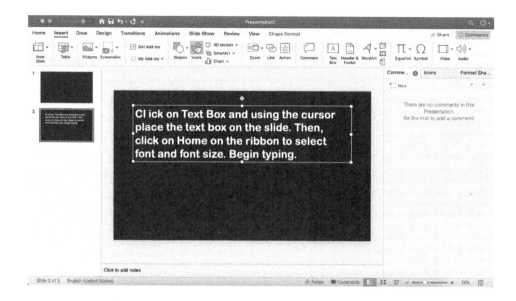

Inserting pictures, videos, and audio clips into your slides is easy with Power-Point. For example, if you wish to insert a photograph, click on the word **Picture** on the ribbon at the top of the screen (indicated with arrow). A drop-down window will give you a selection of where on your computer you can locate the wanted picture, including your browser, picture file, or online. Select the picture you wish inserted in the slide. PowerPoint provides a variety of ways in which the photograph may be displayed.

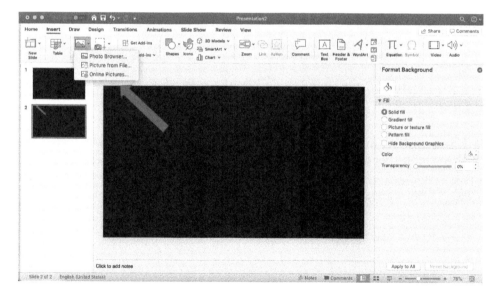

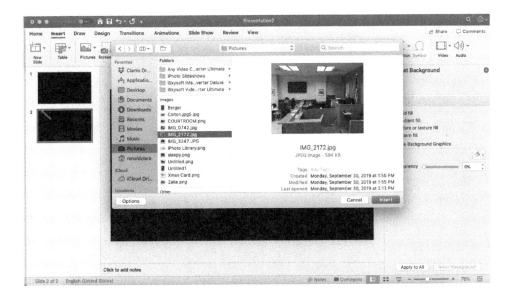

In the example of the PowerPoint created for the Alaska trial, SJC used shapes and text boxes to create a visually appealing title slide.

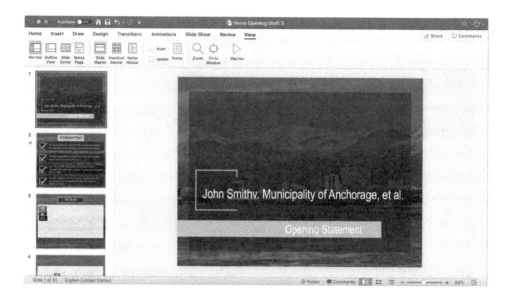

In this example, SJC started by adding a square shape and selecting blue for the color. They then modified the transparency of that blue shape to make it transparent. This is the darker, but transparent blue box centered in the slide. SJC then inserted a yellow square shape to create the appearance of a ribbon. Finally, they added a text box over that yellow square, where they wrote "Opening Statement." The color slides can be viewed on the book's website: http://www.fastcase.com/visuallitigation.

SJC added a second text box above the yellow ribbon where they entered the name of the case. You will notice that there is a yellow box shape to the left of the case name that has an opening on the right side of it. For this, SJC actually created four yellow lines and moved them around to create the appearance of the box with the opening on the right side of it. Once SJC had all the yellow lines in place, they grouped them. Grouping shapes in PowerPoint means you selected multiple shapes and merge them into a single shape. The benefit of grouping is that you can move and copy the new shape without moving each individual shape that went into making the overall shape.

To group multiple shapes, you need to make sure each shape is selected. The best way to do this is to hold the **Shift** key while you select each shape that you want to include in the group. Once you have selected all the shapes that you want in the group, you should right-click, which will produce a drop-down box that has the grouping option. Select **Group** and your shapes will all be merged into a single shape.

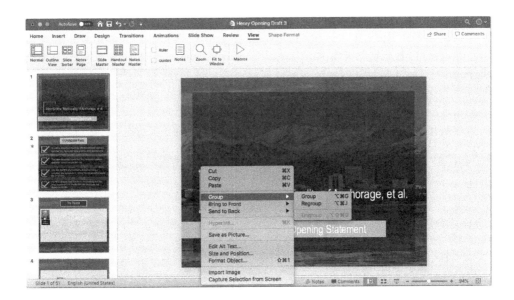

Notably, you can still modify individual shapes in a group. Just double-click on that particular shape, and you can modify that shape without affecting the other shapes in the group.

Once you get comfortable with working with shapes and colors to create visually pleasing slides, you can create different designs within the same PowerPoint presentation that maintain the background and accent colors but provide different visual appearances that are more interesting and pleasing to view. For example, here is one slide from the same SJC slide set.

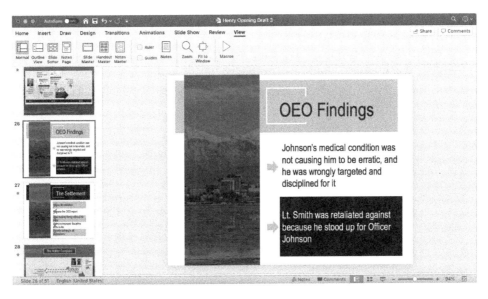

On this slide, all SJC did was create two white squares the height of the slide. SJC placed one on the left side of the screen and a much wider one on the right side of the screen. This created the appearance of only showing a sliver of the original background. They did the same with two yellow squares at the top of the screen, to create a ribbon that contained their title for this slide ("OEO Findings"). Then they added additional content on top of those squares.

You can also create document callouts, such as the following:

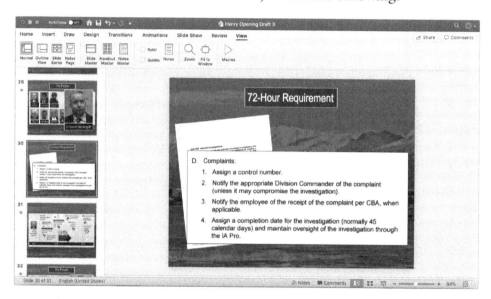

To create a document, callout, open the PDF document and took screenshots. Then insert those screenshots into the slide using the same method you would use to insert any kind of picture into a slide.

Using these techniques, SJC tried to create visual variety in the presentation, while still relying on their custom background and accent colors. This variety makes the presentation more interesting and engaging for jurors. Following are some examples of the variety SJC incorporated.

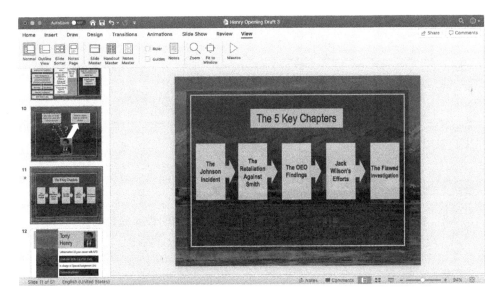

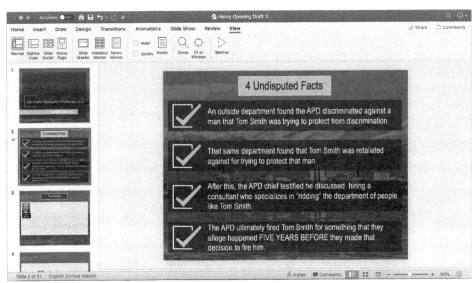

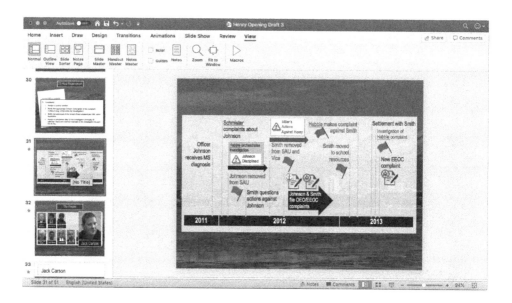

PowerPoint also allows you to draw on a slide. Just click **Draw** on the ribbon at the top of the screen and you will be provided with a pen, pencil, and eraser.

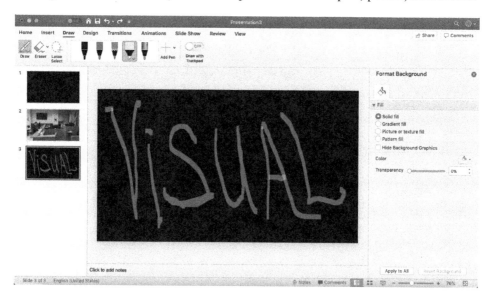

Although we have not covered all of PowerPoint's functions and features, by following these simple directions you should be able to construct a PowerPoint presentation that is professional and persuasive.

E. Alternatives

Apple's Keynote is a comparable presentation software to PowerPoint, but it is exclusive to a Mac. Another computer slideshow presentation software is Prezi. Prezi allows for nonlinear storytelling.

Checklist—Linear Software

Linear Software

❑ PowerPoint
❑ Keynote
❑ Prezi

Elements of a Persuasive Computer Slideshow

❑ Each slide is informative but not overloaded with information;
❑ The colors in the slides are a dark background with light-colored text;
❑ Text font is easy on the viewer's eyes;
❑ The audience can read the slide;
❑ The slides do not contain sound effects; and
❑ The slideshow is subordinate to the speaker.

Chapter 14

Tablets and Litigation Applications

> "The reason that Apple is able to create products like the iPad is because we've always tried to be at the intersection of technology and the liberal arts."
>
> Steve Jobs, co-founder Apple Computer

A. iPad for Litigation

An iPad tablet is an ideal tool for a trial lawyer. With nothing more than a tablet in your hands, you can move about the courtroom or pretrial venue and pull up any item in your case file and show it on a monitor or project it onto a screen. Once the image is on the screen, you can annotate it with a callout or highlighting. You can show your PowerPoints for opening statement and closing argument with your tablet. When you wish to have the screen go blank, allowing you to directly communicate with your audience, you can do that with your tablet.

With an iPad, you are in control. You do not need to employ a communications expert. Indeed, because you are not relying on another person to operate the equipment, you do not need to give that other person directions, which inevitably interrupts the flow of the trial. Beyond these considerations, you save money. Your jurors expect you to use technology. They are comfortable with it, and your use of it will help you make a connection with them.

Alternatives to the iPad exist; Microsoft's Surface Pro is one. Using the touch screen feature on a detached Surface Pro along with either a Microsoft Wireless Adapter and/or a nonlinear PowerPoint slides template found on this book's companion supplement website http://www.fastcase.com/visuallitigation. Appendix 14.1, the user can be a very effective with this Microsoft product.

B.   TrialPad

TrialPad by LIT SOFTWARE, LLC came on the market in 2010, the same year that the iPad was introduced. TrialPad has been updated several times since then, and it is now an outstanding tool for storing, retrieving, and presenting visuals in a courtroom and elsewhere. TrialPad is an application with most of the functionality of Sanction and TrialDirector. Other advantages of TrialPad include cost and accessibility. TrialPad is relatively inexpensive, compared to some alternatives. TrialPad also can be learned in short order. Ease of use in the courtroom or a pretrial venue is a major benefit.

1.   Functions

TrialPad's functions include most of those we described for nonlinear software, such as Sanction, and some of them are that TrialPad can:

- Organize and store the case—Store documents, images, and so on from your computer into a case file in TrialPad.
- Retrieve and display exhibits—On the left side of the screen, your evidentiary items are listed, and when you touch to select the desired one, and press the present button, the image is projected onto a screen in the courtroom or a pretrial venue.
- Callout a portion of the image—Select a portion of the image and use the callout tool to blow up that portion to give the audience a better view.
- Annotate the image—TrialPad has multiple tools that allow you to annotate the image by highlighting, redacting, or writing on it with the pen tool.
- Work with exhibits—TrialPad tools allow you to create exhibit labels and notations regarding the admission of the exhibit into evidence.

2.   Hands-on

The axiom that there is no substitute for experience when comes to learning how to do something, like learning how to operate TrialDirector or Sanction, applies equally well to TrialPad. TrialPad's user manual is available online.[1] Also, you can watch a tutorial for TrialPad on YouTube.[2]

3.   Mastering TrialPad

The beauty of TrialPad is that it is easy to learn how to operate. When you open TrialPad, it takes you to a landing page, which is the Cases screen where on the left you can find your cases in folders.

Your first step will be to create a Case Folder by selecting the **New Case** tab (with + on it) on the left side of the screen at the top. A dialog box will appear, and you can name the file. When you select the **View** button, your Case Folder will be shown.

Next, you will want to import your case file into TrialPad. This can be accomplished in multiple ways. You can import the file by selecting the **Cloud Storage** button on the left column; this will bring up the options for importing from the cloud.

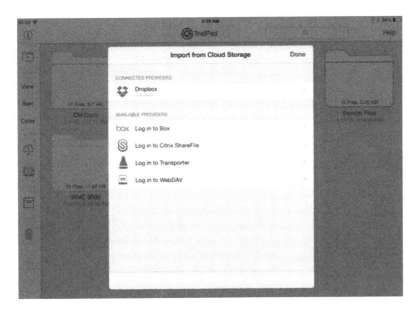

1. https://static1.squarespace.com/static/54908c62e4b057b61056af60/t/5971f8171e5 b6c828a936c01/1500641343687/User+Guide+-+TrialPad+4.6.pdf.

2. https://www.youtube.com/watch?v=oZNdNF2-23s.

Another way to import your case file is to use the iTunes share function. Connect your computer to the iPad with a USB cable and open iTunes. Then, select the **iPad** tab at the top of the screen, followed by **Apps** (with + sign) in the left column. Scroll down the right side of the screen to File Sharing in the Apps list, where you find the TrialPad Documents window. Next, drag and drop files from your computer to the TrialPad Documents window. When you next open TrialPad, there will be a New Files (X) indicator. Select the **New Files (X)** indicator to put the imported file into a case.

When you open a Case Folder, the Case Screen is shown on the right while the left column shows the Document List containing the contents of your case file, such as witness statements and photographs. At the top of the column on the left are four tabs that will enable you to organize your files, as follows:

1. **Name**—Give the case file a name.
2. **Custom**—This tab allows you to sort the files as you wish. Press the select tab and drag the file to a new place to change the order of the items, and then press Done.
3. **Admitted**—This tab reveals only the admitted exhibits.
4. **Exhibit #**—This tab reveals only those items that have been assigned an Exhibit Sticker by TrialPad.

Once you are connected to either a projector or monitor and are ready to display your visuals, you can slide the **Output** switch, which is at the bottom of the screen, to On. When you switch on the display, the screen will show a blank. At the bottom of the screen are three buttons that allow you to manipulate what is shown on the screen in the courtroom as follows:

1. **Blank**—Select this button whenever you want the screen to be blank.
2. **Present**—The Present button is what you press when you want to have what you see on your iPad displayed on the screen in the courtroom.
3. **Freeze**—When you have something on the screen and want to find other evidence to display, the Freeze button will freeze what is on the screen while you locate and work with the items in your case folder. For example, while exhibit 3 is on the screen, you could select a new document, exhibit 8, from the left column and create a callout of text on that exhibit 8. Meanwhile, the audience only sees the frozen one—exhibit 3. When you want to replace the frozen item (exhibit 3) with what you want to replace it (exhibit 8), press the **Present** button.

Three other important tools are at the bottom of the screen to the right side:

1. **Spit Screen**—Select this button to divide the screen in half, allowing you to show two different documents at the same time.
2. **Undo**—When you have annotated an evidence item, such as a document, you can undo the annotations one at a time.
3. **Clear**—Press this button and it clears all annotations.

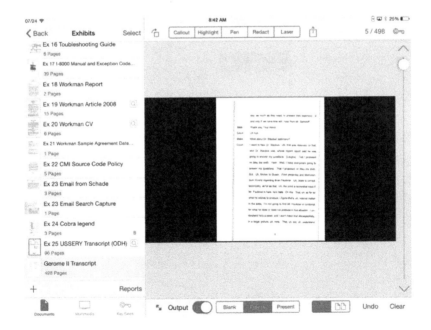

Four buttons across at the top of the screen provide you with tools to emphasize portions of the evidence that the audience is seeing on the screen in the courtroom: Callout, Highlight, Pen, and Laser. For the greatest effect, you can use more than one of these tools. For instance, you could call out a sentence in a document and then circle a key word in the sentence with the pen tool.

The Callout tool enables you to magnify a portion of a document. Merely select the **Callout** button and then go to the document with your finger and drag from the top left of the portion of the area you wish enlarged to the lower right. Once the callout is up, you can move it up or down with your finger.

To highlight a portion of text, use the Highlight tool. Hold down the **Highlight** tool and highlighter colors will appear, and you can select the color you would like. Then, use your finger in the same fashion that the Callout tool is used to highlight the text.

The Pen tool can be used to write or draw on a document or a photograph. When you press on the **Pen** tool, you will be given color options for your pen, four different stroke widths, and the ability to draw a straight line or free style.

The fourth tool for adding emphasis to an item on the screen is a laser pointer. This tool makes your finger into a laser pointer. Select **Laser** and point to whatever you wish on a document or photograph. Press down and hold the tool to get a choice of colors.

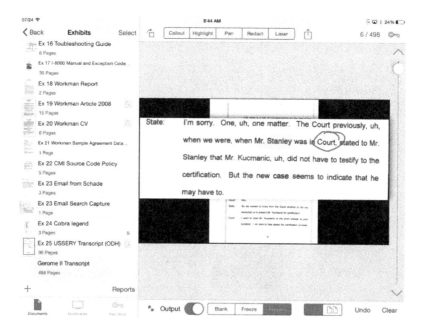

If you need to rotate the item on the screen, just select the Rotation symbol at the top of the page.

Redaction of an exhibit is easy with TrialPad, and can be done while things are in progress. The Redact tab is found at the top of the page. Select the portion of the exhibit you wish to redact with the same method used to call out or highlight, dragging from top left to lower right. Hold down the Redact button and black or white color options will come up.

You can print out or email any item, including an entire document. Thus, printouts of any annotated or redacted documents can be admitted into evidence as exhibits. Just select the symbol at the top of the page.

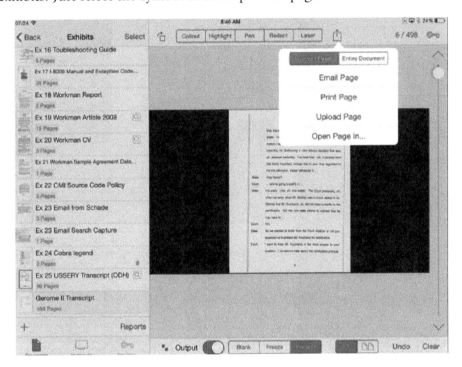

If you press your finger down on an item on the screen, it will give you these four options: Mark Admitted, Rename Document, Assign Exhibit Sticker, and Close Document.

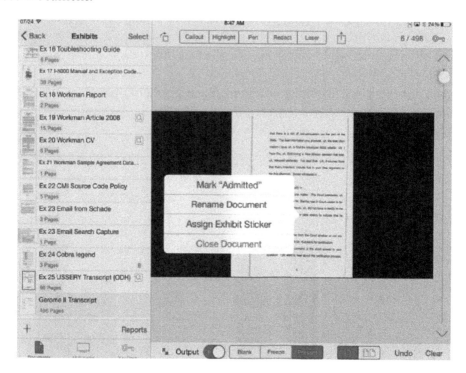

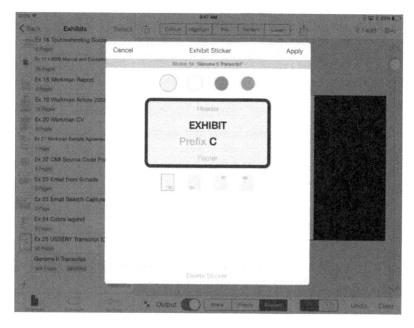

When you mark an exhibit admitted, it is recorded in the Reports Folder that keeps track of admitted exhibits, exhibit numbers, and other legal documents.

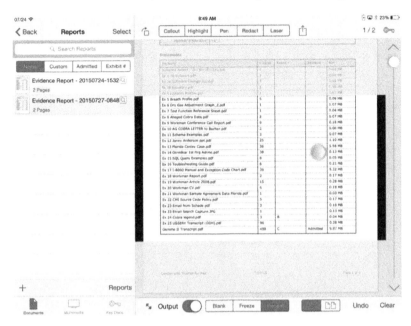

Key Docs is a very useful tool. The button for Key Docs is in the top right of the screen, and the symbol for it is a key. Press this button and with the drop-down showing Current Page or Entire Document, you tap and save a page or the whole document on the screen. With this tool, you can organize documents by issue or witness and with annotations, such as callouts or highlighting.

You can organize Key Docs by creating a folder for witnesses and inserting Key Docs into it. Press the + icon on the lower left side, create a folder in the Key Docs section and give the folder a name. Place the Key Docs into that folder. To quickly navigate to any key document, such as a page in a deposition, select the **Key Doc** tab at the bottom left side of the page and that will guide you to it.

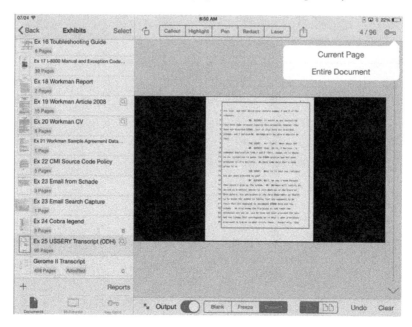

The Key Docs button is one of three at the bottom of the column on the left. A second tab is Documents, which is the location for all your images and documents. The third tab is Multimedia, where your video clips are kept. Once you select the tab, you will have your videos on the left column. To edit one of your videos, select the **Clip Media** tab at the top of the page, and you will move to Apple's video editing tools.

C. Hardware

In Chapter 15, we discuss in greater depth the hardware needed to display images in the courtroom. If you are going to work with a tablet, Apple's iPad Mini is perfect for the tasks because it is small enough to be easily handled but has a large enough screen that it is very readable. You may prefer a larger tablet such as Apple's iPad Pro. Also, you will need a large flat-screen monitor. Or, rather than using a monitor, a projector and screen.

The simplest way to present with an iPad is to directly connect it to a monitor or projector with a cable. But, if you want mobility in a courtroom, you will want to wirelessly use the tablet. To accomplish this, you will need an Apple TV, which is a digital media player that is shown in the following picture.

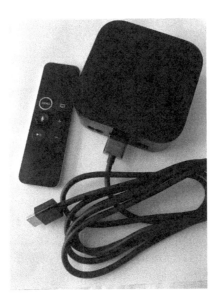

For Apple TV to work in the room where you are presenting, it must have active Wi-Fi, and you must activate AirPlay on your iPad. To connect the Apple TV with your iPad and the monitor or projector, use an HDMI cable from Apple TV to the HDMI port on the projector or monitor. If it is an old model projector with a VGA port, you will need an adapter. Once connected, turn on the monitor or projector, power up the Apple TV, and enable AirPlay on your iPad. To activate AirPlay, swipe up from the bottom of the iPad screen and when the AirPlay symbol comes up, turn it on. Then, you will be able to wirelessly work with your iPad in the courtroom.

An alternative is to use a Microsoft wireless adapter[3] with Microsoft Surface. The adapter plugs into your monitor or projector. A word of caution about going wireless: you may well run into gaps and resets. You should be prepared with cords for a hardwire backup.

D. TrialDirector and ExhibitView for iPad

TrialDirector, by inData, offers its TrialDirector software as an app for iPads. Likewise, ExhibitView offers an iTrial app for iPads. This app works with the PC-based ExhibitView Trial Presenter software.

---

3. https://www.microsoft.com/accessories/en-us/products/adapters/wireless-display-adapter-2/p3q-00001.

E. Other Litigation Tools

The marvelous thing about a computer tablet is that this hand-held device gives you access to several litigation tools, and some of them, such as PowerPoint and Notes, come free with your software suite. Other applications, such as iJuror can be added to your iPad at a relatively low cost.

I. Notability App and the Apple Pencil

The Notability application combined with the Apple Pencil and an iPad are far superior tools for taking pretrial and trial notes than the yellow pad and pen. You can see tutorials for this application on YouTube.[4] In addition, on the home page for Notability at the bottom of the left column you will find a question mark; when you select that a Help Center drop-down appears.

After you open Notability, you can customize your settings with the Settings button at the bottom of the left column. Here from the drop-down menu you can manage your account with different options, such as Dropbox and Google Drive. To set the look of your note-taking screen, select **Documents** and give the note a title; slide on **Include Date** and your note will automatically be stored with a date. Also, in the Documents drop-down you can select lined or unlined paper and the paper's color. You will also find other options for Typing, such as checking spelling, and for Handwriting, such as a left-hand option.

To bring up a new page, tap on the pen and paper symbol on the upper right corner. Across the top of the page are your tools from left to right as follows:

- T for text box—This allows you put text anywhere on the page.
- Pen symbol—This button activates the pen feature. Tap on this pen symbol and you can set the color of the ink and the size of the pen point.
- Highlighter symbol—This button activates the highlighter and you tap on the symbol and options for color and width.
- Eraser symbol.
- Scissors symbol—This symbol brings up wraparounds that you can use to surround text, drawings, or whatever is on your note pad and then move it on the page.
- Hand symbol—Select this and you move your page around.

---

4. https://www.youtube.com/watch?v=BnNpuaAp_QQ; https://www.youtube.com/watch?v=aGX33DNL0oo; https://www.youtube.com/watch?v=SRgg8l8nAWo.

- Microphone—With this button you can start and stop recording sound with the same button. After you have finished recording, tap on the down arrow next to the microphone, and it will reveal where you can tap to listen to the recording and manage it.

Your note-taking method may vary from setting to setting. For instance, at a mediation, you may decide to type rather than handwrite and thus use Notability. However, if you are in front of a jury you may decide to handwrite your notes with the Apple Pencil on the tablet.

After you have finished taking notes, you can export it with the Share symbol on the left side of the page, which when selected brings up options including, among others, Email, Dropbox, and Print.

Notability has other handy features. You can search your writing by typing the key word in the search symbol on the upper right side of the page. Pictures can be imported into the page. Also, you can convert your handwriting into text.

Alternatives to Notability, iPad, and Apple Pencil are Microsoft Surface and a Windows pen, which serve the same purposes.

Keep the yellow pad and pen; they could come in handy if you lose your Apple Pencil.

2. PowerPoint or Keynote

Right there on your iPad you have Keynote as part of the Apple suite. Keynote, which is linear software, can create and show computer slideshows. Also, Microsoft's PowerPoint can be added to the iPad. These computer slideshows can provide visuals for both opening statement and closing argument and can be used by an expert when explaining the field of expertise as well as findings and opinions. Slideshows can also be shown in pretrial settings.

To operate a PowerPoint slideshow select **Slide Show** in the tool bar at the top of the page and then on **Presenter View**. In Presenter View, the main screen shows the slide being projected on the screen.

To run the slideshow in Presenter View merely use your finger to swipe to the left to move between slides and to move the text and photographs on a slide. You can annotate the slide on the screen by selecting the pencil symbol on the top right side of the page. You also can select the type of writing instrument you would like to use. Finally, if at any time you want to make the screen go blank so that the audience's attention returns to you, just select on the blank screen symbol that is up on the right side of your iPad.

Checklist—Tablets and Litigation Applications

A Tablet for Litigation

❑ Consider using litigation applications on an iPad.
❑ Alternatively, consider using them on Microsoft's Surface Pro.
❑ Factors to consider are:
    ✓ Litigation applications, such as TrialPad, are relatively inexpensive compared to, for instance, Sanction or TrialDirector.
    ✓ With a tablet, the trial lawyer can control the retrieval and display of visual evidence.

TrialPad Application

❑ The TrialPad application on an iPad can perform the following functions:
    ✓ Organize and store the case file;
    ✓ Retrieve and display electronic visuals;
    ✓ Call out portions of an image;
    ✓ Annotate the electronic visuals; and
    ✓ Stamp exhibits.
❑ Alternatives to TrialPad are TrialDirector for iPad and ExhibitView's iTrial.

Other Litigation Tools

❑ Consider these other litigation applications:
    ✓ Notability and the Apple Pencil for taking pretrial and trial notes; and
    ✓ PowerPoint and Keynote on an iPad to create and present computer slideshows.

Chapter 15

Hardware and Effective Courtroom Presentations

A. Six Prerequisites for an Effective Courtroom Presentation
   1. The Hardware
      a. The Necessary Hardware
      b. Comprehensive Hardware Checklist
      c. Operating the Hardware Checklist
   2. Court Rules and Procedures
   3. Backup and the Document Camera
      a. Backup
      b. Document Camera
   4. Preparation and Testing
   5. Staging the Courtroom
   6. Courtroom Communication
B. Whose Hardware?

> "There are tremendous benefits for all parties to facilitate a generous amount of time to setup, test, and remedy any issues that occur throughout the trial. Anecdotally, courtroom IT staff report that more than 50 percent of Courtroom technical issues would never occur if people simply tested their equipment in advance."
>
> Shannon Lex Bales,
> *The Trial Presentation Companion*, 20
> NITA (2018)

A. Six Prerequisites for an Effective Courtroom Presentation

Six prerequisites must be fulfilled before you can effectively display visuals in a courtroom. First, if the courtroom is not properly equipped, counsel will need to provide the required hardware, such as a computer, tablet, screen, projector, and cords. Second, counsel will need to adhere to the court's rules and procedures. Third, counsel will need backups in case of a technological failure. Fourth, the person who is going to operate the technology needs to test the equipment and practice using it. Fifth, the courtroom must be staged properly so the audience can see and hear what is being shown. Sixth, courtroom communication between the trial lawyer and operator of the equipment must produce a smooth presentation of the visual.

Atul Gawande, surgeon, public health researcher, and author of *The Checklist Manifesto: How to Get Things Right* (2011), stressed in his book that to prevent disasters when "conditions of complexity" exist, such as performing surgery or piloting an airplane, a checklist is a critical tool. Because trial presentations with technology entail "conditions of complexity," even an experienced professional can miss a step that could derail the presentation. This is why each chapter in this book after the introductory first chapter ends with a checklist. Also, much of what we offer in this chapter comes in the form of checklists.

1. The Hardware

a. The Necessary Hardware

The equipment you need to project a computer slideshow in your courtroom depends upon how current the technology is in the courtroom. If the courtroom lacks what you need, you will have to supply it. To do this, you will need the court's permission to use the technology.

Unless you are acquainted with the courtroom, you need to determine what equipment you will need. For example, as we discussed on page 20, for a federal court you can go online for full information regarding what technology exists in the courtroom and tutorials on how to operate the equipment. If the courtroom is fully equipped, such as the one on pages 26-30, then all you need to do is familiarize yourself with that technology.

If it is not a modern courtroom, you will need to become familiar with the layout. Where is the best place to put the projector? The screen or monitor? How long do the cords need to be to reach the wall or floor plugs?

You can use either a laptop or a tablet loaded with linear software, such as PowerPoint and/or nonlinear litigation software, such as TrialPad, TrialDirector, or Sanction. The visuals can be shown on a monitor or projected onto a screen, preferably a large one.

Your equipment must be up to the task. It must be up-to-date and properly maintained. Applications should be updated and tested. The computer should have enough storage space and be able to run the software. Nonlinear software, including Sanction, TrialDirector, must be run with Windows. You can use a Mac, but you will need to partition its hard drive and add Windows with Bootcamp (see pages 237-38).

The cost of the requisite hardware is a factor. However, shortchanging yourself by not purchasing or renting quality hardware can lead to a low or no quality presentation at trial. If the law firm infrequently goes to trial, the hardware can be rented, rather than bought. Another alternative is to buy some hardware and software, such as the computers and nonlinear software, and rent others, such as a monitor and projector.

b. Comprehensive Hardware Checklist

The following is a comprehensive checklist of the essential hardware for a trial or mediation presentation. The list comes with tips regarding the operation of the hardware.

1. **Laptop**. You want a quality laptop for your presentations because everything depends on it. You want enough storage on your hard drive to run your software, preferably a terabyte. Make sure that the computer is replaced before it exceeds its life span. Some laptops have a three- to five-year life span; others longer. If your trial laptop has taken a beating, it may need to be replaced sooner.

    Your laptop must be compatible with the software that you want to use. Nonlinear trial software, including Sanction, TrialDirector, and OnCue, will run only on Microsoft Windows. You can partition a Mac's hard drive and load Windows on it, but to do so eats storage. On the other hand, linear software, including PowerPoint, operates on an Apple computer.

    Prepare your laptop for trial. Change the display on your laptop and your screen saver to blank screens because you do not want to distract the jury with inappropriate pictures. Also, switch your default settings for putting the computer to sleep to "never." You do not want your computer going to sleep on you when you need it awake.

As an example of what the software may require, the following are the system specifications for TrialDirector 360:[1]

	Minimum Specification for TrialDirector 360	Recommended Specifications for TrialDirector 360
OS:	Windows 10 – 64bit	Windows 10 – 64bit
CPU:	Quad Core	Quad Core
Memory:	8GB	8GB
Disk space:	256GB	500GB
Graphics card:	1GB dedicated video memory	Nvidia or AMD – 6GB dedicated video memory

Minimum and recommended system specifications for Sanction 4.0[2] are as follows:

Category	Minimum	Recommended
Operating system	Windows® 7 Service Pack 1 for 32 bit processor	Windows 7 Service Pack 1 for 64 bit processor
Software	During the installation process, Sanction will install the following components if they are not already installed on your computer: • Microsoft® .NET® Framework version 4.5.1 (Web Installer) This component might require you to restart your computer. If you want to install this component on your own, prior to installing Sanction, you can download it from Microsoft.com. To learn more, visit the Microsoft .NET® Framework page at Microsoft.com. • Microsoft Expression® Encoder 4, Service Pack 2 If you want to install this component on your own, prior to installing Sanction, you can download it from Microsoft.com. To learn more, visit the Microsoft Expression Encoder 4 with Service Pack 2 (SP2) page at Microsoft.com.	
Media player	Windows® Media Player 12 For more information or to download, visit the Get Windows Media Player 12 page at Microsoft.com.	
Processor	2 GHz	2 GHz Intel Core 2 Duo or higher
Memory (RAM)	2 GB	4 GB
Disk space	250 MB for Sanction program files	1 GB or more
	☑ Additional disk space is required if, prior to installing Sanction, these components are not already installed on your computer: • Microsoft Expression Encoder 4 SP 2 (2GB) • Microsoft .NET Framework 4.5.1 (850 MB for x86 processor; 2 GB for x64 processor).	
Monitor	1024 x 768	1280 x 800 or higher

---

1. https://iprotech.com/software/trial-director-360/.
2. Sanction 4.0 User Manual, 221.

Also, the aspect ratio (the ratio of width to height of an image) of your computer presentation should be compatible with the equipment in the courtroom. For example, if your presentation has a 4:3 ratio (corresponds to a square), and you have created the presentation on your computer with a higher 16:9 ratio (roughly a rectangle or widescreen), you will squeeze a square into a rectangle, distorting the image. To create a presentation suitable for that courtroom, you would need to adjust the resolution (the width times the height measured in pixels displayed on your computer or monitor) in your computer's system display tool. A resolution of 1440×1080 equates to 4:3, and a resolution of 1920×1080 equates to 16:9.

When hooking up a laptop to a monitor/projector, it is critical that you remember that you should have the cords plugged in correctly and the display device (monitor and/or projector) turned on before you boot up the laptop.

2. **Projector**. You will either be projecting an image on a screen or showing it on a monitor. Or, you may have a screen for the jury and a monitor for the judge when the screen cannot be placed in a location where both the judge and jury can view the same screen or monitor.

Regarding specifications for a projector, we recommend that you have a projector with multiple inputs (HDMI, VGA). The projector should be high definition. Also, you want the projector to be bright enough that it will be easy to see what is projected on the screen in a well-lit courtroom. In a courtroom with bright ambient light, 5000 lumens ratings (lumens ratings indicate the brightness of a projector) or more works best. With this brightness you should not need to dim the lights. You also want to know what the throw distance is. Throw distance is the distance from the tip of the projector lens to the screen in order to fill the screen and show images clearly. Also, the projector should have a zoom lens that will enable you to zoom in and out and not have to move the projector.

Your projector can be either a DLP (Digital Light Processing) or an LCD (Liquid Crystal Display) projector. Less maintenance is required for a DLP than an LCD projector. However, a downside of a DLP projector is that it is not well-suited for zoom lenses, but they work well for monitors. On the other hand, LCD projectors (like the one pictured below) are compatible with zoom lenses, making them good for large screens.

If you intend to utilize a monitor rather than projecting images on a screen, you will need a high-definition one with a sizable screen.

3. **Projection screen**. Three types of projection screens are: the fast-fold screen that is large and can be up to 20 feet wide; the pull-up screen that is manually pulled up from a container; and the old-style tripod screen. An 80-inch tripod screen is pictured next.

   The bigger the screen the better would seem to be the guiding principle because it will provide the jury with larger images on the screen. However, the screen must be able to be placed where the jury can see it, and because of the courtroom's configuration a large screen may not fit into a place where the jurors can view it. Also, you will need to be able to place the projector in the right location to project onto the screen. Therefore, you will need to know the size of the screen the courtroom will accommodate and pick your screen accordingly.

4. **Monitor**. A monitor may be preferable to a projector and screen if the courtroom does not allow you to configure and position the projector and screen where you would like. You will want a monitor with a large screen for the jury's easy viewing. As we recommended for a projector, we also suggest that you have a monitor with multiple inputs (HDMI, VGA). The aspect ratio (ratio of width to height) for the monitor should be 16:9, which is a rectangle, for a wide-screen monitor.

5. **Carts/stands**. You will need a cart(s) for transporting equipment to and from the courtroom and to support the equipment. An AV Cart is pictured next.

If counsel is the technician, then counsel will have the laptop on the counsel table. On the other hand, if another person is serving as the technician, that person may be at counsel table or at another place in the courtroom. If the technician is going to be sitting somewhere other than at counsel table, you may need a portable computer table.

6. **Extra-long extension cords and a power strip**. Run your cords so that they are as much out of the way of where people will walk as possible. To the extent possible lay the cords along the periphery of the courtroom. You do not want people tripping over them. The power strip should have a fail-safe backup capability for the projector. Also, we suggest battery-powered power strips because you might lose power.

7. **Gaffer's tape**. You will need to secure the power cords so that no one trips over them. Use industry-standard gaffer's tape because it has strong adhesive properties, and it neither damages the surface of whatever it is adhered to nor leaves a residue.

8. **Portable mouse and wireless keyboard**. You can use a simple Gyration wireless mouse.[3] You can use any wireless keyboard with a laptop (via Bluetooth).

---

3. https://www.gyration.com/.

9. **Remote control.** For linear presentations, such as a PowerPoint presentation for opening statement or closing argument, use a remote control, also referred to as a "clicker." A remote allows you to walk around courtroom away from the computer. When you insert the remote's receiver into your computer's USB port, it gives the remote a Bluetooth connection to your computer allowing you to be at a distance from your computer and click through your slideshow.

    The Logitech R800 2.4 GHZ Wireless Professional Presenter (shown next) works well. A remote will allow you to advance the slideshow or go back. The remote has a button that allows you to make the screen go black when you want the audience to focus only on you. Also, some remotes have a laser pointer. Always, in advance of your presentation, test the remote to see how far you can move away from your computer before you loose the connection. Finally, you must have spare batteries in case those in your remote lose power.

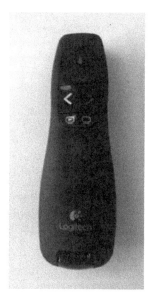

    A step up from Logitech R800 2.4 GHZ Wireless Professional Presenter is the Logitech Spotlight (shown in the following picture). Once you have loaded the software for the Spotlight on your computer, it allows you to do several tasks, including: go forward or back in your slideshow; black out the screen; magnify words or images on the screen with a spotlight; change volume on your computer with a gesture; and play videos.

10. **Laser pointers**. When you wish to have the audience look at a particular part of the visual on the screen, you can utilize a laser pointer. As was mentioned before, your remote may have a laser pointer built into it. The laser pointer will put a red or green dot on the screen, and you can just point at what you want the audience to look at or circle the targeted area with the dot. Test the pointer on the screen before you make your presentation to make sure that it will work. Some laser pointers do not work well with certain flat screen technology

    You will want two laser pointers: a green one for counsel and a red one for the witness, whom you have instructed to use the laser with caution, never pointing it at a person.

11. **Audio speakers**. Several choices are available, but make sure to select ones that are powerful enough to be heard throughout the courtroom. Test your speakers to make sure they work in your courtroom.

12. **Document camera**. You will need a document display camera, such as an ELMO, DOAR, or WolfVision. The document camera has value as both a way to display visuals and a backup if something goes wrong with your computer presentation.

13. **HDMI wireless adapter**. There are a few options for HDMI wireless adapters, including Google and Microsoft.[4] An adapter plugs into the HDMI port of any monitor or projector and allows you to send what you want from your phone, tablet, or computer.

---

4. https://www.microsoft.com/surface/en-us/accessories/wireless-display-adapter.

14. **VGA (Video Graphs Adaptor) or HDMI (High Definition Media Interface) switcher and splitter**. A splitter allows you to plug multiple monitors into the same laptop feed when you want to use multiple devices. Other devices, such as a document camera or a backup laptop, also can be plugged into the switcher. A switcher allows you to switch from one source to another.

    When opposing parties share equipment and cost, the switcher enables the parties to switch back and forth. The switcher can also provide backup when connected to two computers. If one computer fails, the presentation can continue by switching to the other computer.

    Switchers can be either equipped with VGA, HDMI, or both types of inputs. VGA is considered old-school. VGA is an analog standard and consists of a three-row 15 pin DE connector. HDMI is a digital standard, and it is best used to transmit video from a device, such as a computer, to a monitor or screen, producing a sharper image.

15. **Adapter**. If your computer is a Mac, you will need an adapter (pictured next) to connect to the VGA cord that connects to the projector.

    While Microsoft Surface Pro devices use a Type-C connector (dongle), many laptops use HDMI connectors; iPads use a Lightning connector or Type-C connector depending on the product.

    If you use multiple devices plugged into the USB connections of your laptop for power or wireless connectivity, you may need to purchase a powered WolfVision hub. These expand your laptop's USB capacity.

16. **Scaler**. A scaler is a device that can scale down high-resolution HDMI signals to low-resolution VGA signals. It can also upscale low-resolution standard screen VGA signals to high-resolution HDMI resolution. With

a scaler, the courtroom system can work with both high-definition wide-screen signals as well as low-resolution standard screen signals.

17. **MiFi device.** When the courtroom is without Wi-Fi and you intend to go wireless, you will need a MiFi device. This device taps into 3G or 4G mobile phone networks and uses this connection to create a mini wireless hotspot. This will allow you to utilize your tablet or computer wirelessly.

18. **HDMI female to female coupler/extender.** You may need to connect the court's cord to your cord. Keep in your tech bag.

19. **Privacy screen.** Consider a privacy screen for your laptop.

20. **Comfortable chair.** Last but not least, the technician must have a comfortable chair.

c. *Operating the Equipment Checklist*

The following is a step-by-step checklist of how to operate the equipment:

1. Plug your cord (usually HDMI) into your laptop.
2. Plug the other end of your cord into your monitor or projector.
3. Boot up the laptop. The laptop should display on the monitor. If it does not, first try the action/video button on the monitor because this changes between different input sources. If that does not work, try the channel button.
4. If that does not work, hit the Windows button + P buttons to enter the projection menu.

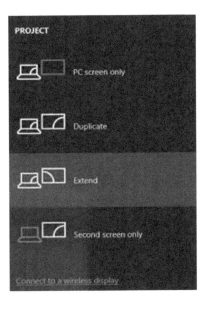

5. If that doesn't work, right-click anywhere on the desktop, select Properties > Settings > Advanced > Monitor. A menu allows you to select extend or duplicate view, depending on your preference.

If these steps fail, check your connections and re-boot the computer. If that doesn't work, use the slides that you printed out from PowerPoint in advance for your backup on the document camera.

Some older projectors only broadcast in 1024 x 768. Consequently, if you connect a newer laptop to an older projector and your laptop is set to a higher resolution than 1024 x 768, nothing may be projected. If you change your laptop settings to 1024 x 768, it should fix this issue.

2.   Court Rules and Procedures

Once you know the judge assigned to your trial and you know the technology you need to bring into the courtroom, you need to determine whether the judge will allow you to do so. While one judge may embrace the use of technology and indeed encourage the parties to use it, another judge will reject a request to utilize technology in whole (even denying the party the use of a document camera) or in part.

The judge who rejects technology may have had unfortunate experiences involving technological glitches. Some judges may be concerned that one party would have an advantage because it will be able to utilize the technology when the other side does not have the same opportunity because, for example, they cannot afford it. Sharing the cost and the equipment between the parties is one solution that may alleviate the judge's concern. Yet another reason some judges are soured on technology is the mistreatment of the judge's courtroom, such as damaging counsel table or not cleaning up. It is incumbent upon those who operate technology in a courtroom to do so efficiently, without technological glitches, and to leave the courtroom in a pristine condition.

In addition to gaining permission to use technology, the judge will likely have views about where the projector and screen or monitor should be placed in the courtroom for proper viewing by the judge, counsel, and the jury.

The court may have standing rules and procedures regarding technology and electronic exhibits. If you are not familiar with the court's rules and procedures, check the judge's website because commonly they will be posted there. Also, check with court personnel to determine whether there are other procedures for technology that should be followed.

An example of a court's requirements for use of technology in a modern courtroom are those stated on the website for the United States District Court for the Western District of Washington. The website states:

The court has equipment integrated into each courtroom for attorney use. During a proceeding, the judge's courtroom deputy is the primary contact for courtroom technology. Please be aware that any requested changes may need to be reviewed and approved by the judge prior to any changes being made. Contact the courtroom deputy with any change requests.

Knowing how to use the courtroom's equipment is the attorney's responsibility. Training is available....[5]

If a court lacks current technology, it may have rules that encourage but do not require the parties to present their exhibits in electronic form. For example, the Santa Clara California Superior Court has Guidelines and Protocols for Complex Civil Litigation that state in part:

XIV. TRIAL EXHIBITS

1. Introduction

a. The electronic representations of such exhibits may be presented to the Jury/Court as substitutes for the exhibits themselves. Counsel should keep in mind that one of the purposes of the complex project is to enhance the orderly presentation of evidence to the fact finder, and to maintain the record for potential post trial proceedings.

b. Exhibits may be in either electronic or physical form. Physical exhibits are not required to be presented in a digitized format. However, at the conclusion of trial the court may order that a photo be substituted and stored electronically in lieu of the physical evidence.

c. Parties must exchange exhibits excluding documents for bona fide impeachment at the Pre-Trial Meet and Confer. Each counsel must provide the Court with an EXHIBIT LIST describing each exhibit, indicating whether the exhibit is to be admitted into evidence by stipulation.[6]

The court may enter a Trial Management Order laying out its requirements regarding exhibits and technology. The following sections from a TMO for the District Court of Teton County, Wyoming Ninth Judicial District dictate how visual exhibits will be published, how the equipment will be tested, and who will be held responsible if things go wrong:

---

5. https://www.wawd.uscourts.gov/attorneys/trial-support/courtroom-technology.

6. Santa Clara California Superior Court Guidelines for Complex Civil Litigation, revised March 29, 2018; see Appendix 15.1 on the companion website, http://www.fastcase.com/visual litigation, for the complete set of Guidelines.

4. EXHIBITS...

c. To the extent a party wishes to publish an exhibit to the jury, counsel shall be prepared to publish such exhibit to the jury members simultaneously, to the extent feasible, e.g. publishing a photograph or document or other exhibit capable of being shown to the jury simultaneously, either by overhead projection, or by providing a photocopy to each juror individually. The Court will avoid having the jury split their attention on an exhibit being passed around the jury box while testimony is being offered. Likewise, the Court will avoid, to the extent feasible, halting the presentation of testimony when such an exhibit is being passed around the jury box for individual inspection.

5. TECHNOLOGY. Any presentation by a party involving the use of courtroom technology shall be tested, and the court reporter consulted for assistance, no less than three (3) days prior to trial. The party using such technology is advised that any risk of failure associated with the use of courtroom technology is borne by the party seeking to use the same.[7]

Courtesy counts. The trial lawyers are always courteous to the judge, but sometimes fail to be courteous to other important people in the courtroom: the lower bench made up of the clerk, bailiff, and court reporter. If counsel is discourteous while the judge is in chambers, the judge may likely learn of the behavior from these court personnel. Consult with and work with the member of the court's staff in charge of the court's technology. When installing the equipment, be courteous to the court's staff and listen if they have thoughts about what you are doing. It will pay off in a return of courtesy and perhaps a helping hand.

Besides complying with the court's rules and procedures, you should consult with and obtain permission from courthouse security to bring the equipment into the building. When you intend to bring the equipment into the courthouse at night or on the weekend, special arrangements may need to be made with security.

3. Backup and the Document Camera

A document camera, also known as a visual presenter, is not just valuable as a backup in case of a computer failure, it is a splendid piece of equipment that you can use to display your visuals. It provides a good change of pace from testimony on the stand or a computer presentation. Some of the brands of document cameras are: Elmo, Epson, and WolfVision.

---

7. Trial Management Order, District Court of Teton County, Wyoming Ninth Judicial District; see Appendix 15.2 in the companion website, http://www.fastcase.com/visuallitigation, for the complete order.

a. Backup

Whoever is going to operate the hardware must have a backup in case a glitch occurs, such as a power failure, a burned-out bulb, or a computer crash. In addition to the computer or tablet that you will be relying on to make the presentation, you should have another source for the software program, which could be another computer with the software on it. If your computerized presentation fails, you need another way to show your visuals. This is where the document camera can be a game-saver. All you need are paper printouts of your visuals. Just place the visual on the document camera, and it is projected on the screen.

b. Document Camera

A document camera, such as the one pictured below, does not require much expertise to operate. You merely place the exhibit on the base under the camera, and the image will be shown on the screen. With the controls, you can zoom in on the object no matter how small, and it will be magnified on the screen. Then, you or a witness can annotate the visual, such as a letter-sized diagram, by marking directly on the exhibit with a pen.

With a document camera you are not restricted to two-dimensional exhibits such as photographs and documents. It can also be used to magnify three-dimensional objects, such as a watch, on the screen.

When you want to use a document camera in trial, prepare yourself by learning the features of the document camera. You should practice with the controls. It may autofocus, but, if not, you should practice with the focusing control. Those controls normally will allow you to zoom in and out on the exhibit. You can also freeze the image on the screen, which allows you to remove the exhibit from below the camera and the image will remain on the screen.

Prepare your witness for the experience of working with the document camera by explaining what you intend to do at trial with the document camera. In trial, lay a foundation for the exhibit and then offer it into evidence. Once it has been admitted, you ask the judge for permission to publish it on the document camera. When the judge grants the request, you can place the exhibit on the base of the document camera. Next, you can have the witness remain on the witness stand and describe for the jury what is being shown on the screen. Alternatively, you can ask the judge for permission to have the witness step down and go to the document camera. When the court allows the witness to go to the document camera, you can have the witness explain what is being shown by pointing at and/or marking the exhibit. Once the witness has finished discussing the exhibit, don't forget to tell the witness that she can resume her seat in the witness chair.

4.   Preparation and Testing

The person who is going to operate the equipment must practice using it. To ignore this axiom is to flirt with a mishap. Once the equipment is in place, it needs to be tested; this includes not just before trial but also retesting it before trial commences on each day of trial when it is to be utilized. If something goes awry with the technology, even if the consulting technician has done the entire preparation and is operating the equipment, there is no question who will be seen as responsible—the trial lawyer.

It is critical for the person operating the hardware, whether it is you, your legal assistant, or a communications' expert, to have a backup in case a computer crashes or another glitch occurs.

5.   Staging the Courtroom

Be aware of the physical makeup of your courtroom when setting up your equipment. It is a good idea to draw a diagram of the courtroom either by hand or (better) with software such as PowerPoint. The diagram should show the courtroom layout, including tables, the bench, and lower bench, witness stand, jury box, spectator area, plugs, and any equipment that is already in the courtroom. With the diagram, you can plan where you would like to set up your equipment. Also, you can use the diagram to prepare your witnesses for trial.

If the technician is not the trial lawyer, it is critical that the technician be in a place where the technician has an unobstructed, clear view of the monitor's screen or the screen onto which the images are projected. Ideally, the technician would be seated at counsel table because that will facilitate communication between the lawyer and the technician.

Here is an example of how a courtroom can be arranged in order for a 100-inch screen that 99 percent of the people in the courtroom could see with a projector and a 40-inch flat screen monitor that the rest of the courtroom (the witness) could see. The key to this setup was that the flat screen allowed the witness always to be looking at the jury.

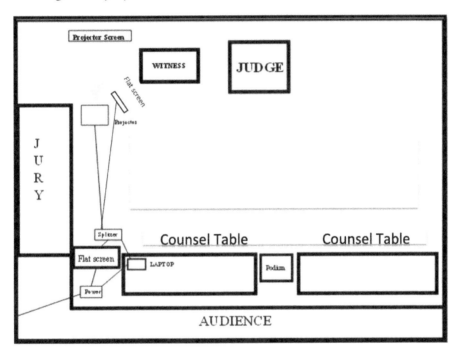

The following photograph shows yet another courtroom configuration. In this one the monitor is on the wall behind the witness's chair and monitors are situated around the room to provide viewing by counsel and the court.

6. Courtroom Communication

As we previously discussed, clear communication between the trial lawyer and the person who is the technician operating the equipment (co-counsel, associate, paralegal, or a communication expert) is an indispensable component of a smooth courtroom presentation. As the trial lawyer, you want to have the visual appear promptly when you ask your technician to display it. How you identify the item you want to display is important. An item could be described as "that June 3rd email," or by exhibit number. You need to have an understanding with your technician regarding how you will identify items because if you do not, the technician may have to ask for other information that will identify the item, and that will disrupt the flow of the presentation.

The best designation for a visual is the exhibit number because that is what the courtroom players—judge, clerk, and jurors—all know and can relate to. Also, linking the description of the item to the exhibit number will not only communicate what you want called up on the screen to your technician but also those courtroom players. For instance, you could say, "Please call up Exhibit 44, the June 3rd email."

In addition to how you identify the item you want displayed, it is also important that you and your technician have a clear way of communicating about what you wish done with the item. Your technician must understand not only how to annotate but also the terminology you will use in directing the technician to annotate a visual. For example, if you want to annotate a document that is being displayed, you could ask your technician to "Call out the second paragraph of Exhibit 44, the June 3rd email." Terminology that can be used to describe how to annotate a visual are covered on page 246.

For clear communication and a presentation free of glitches, you should have one, and only one, lawyer communicating with the technician during the presentation. As with all in-trial communications, a team member should not interrupt the lawyer who is performing. For example, if another team member, other than the director, asks that the technician call up an item or take it down, that can result in muddying the presentation and/or throwing the presenter off course. This one-lawyer approach should be discussed with all trial team members during pretrial preparation. The team member who wants to communicate can either pass a note or speak to counsel when counsel asks whether something else needs to be done.

If a lay or expert witness will be interacting with the presentation in any way, that witness should be thoroughly prepared to work with it. Steps for preparing a witness who will work with a visual are discussed at pages 83-84. Preferably, if you are going to be questioning the witness and another person will be acting as your technician, you should prepare your witness with the technician present and operating the equipment just as it will be done in trial.

B. Whose Hardware?

If the courtroom or pretrial venue does not have the necessary hardware, whose hardware will be used for the presentations? Yours? The other side's? Shared? For your best presentation, ideally you would operate your own equipment. You are familiar with your equipment, and you know how to operate it. If something goes wrong with your hardware, such as a projector malfunctioning, you know the best way to bring your hardware back into operation.

Do you own the equipment or rent it? The upside of owning the equipment is that you become closely acquainted with it, know how to set it up, operate it, and fix it if something goes wrong. The downside is that the equipment can be expensive, and you will need to store it and transport it. While renting hardware can be the less expensive alternative, you will not be as intimately familiar with the hardware as you would be if you owned it, and the equipment may not be available when you need it.

Sharing equipment and technical assistance with the opposing side is appropriate cooperation between the parties and favored by the bench. If the plan is to rent from a vendor, it should one that is aligned with neither side because conflict can erupt if something goes wrong with the unaffiliated party's presentation. A preventative measure is to employ an impartial vendor, and the vendor can bill each side separately.

Checklist—Hardware and Effective Courtroom Presentations

The following is a checklist of necessary hardware:

- ❏ A laptop that:
  - ✓ Has enough storage and is up to date;
  - ✓ Has a blank screen saver; and
  - ✓ Meets the specifications needed to run the software.
- ❏ A projector that:
  - ✓ Has multiple inputs;
  - ✓ Is high definition; and
  - ✓ Is bright enough to be used without dimming the courtroom lights.
- ❏ A large projection screen.
- ❏ A monitor to use in conjunction with the projected image or alone.
- ❏ Carts/stands for transporting and supporting the equipment.
- ❏ A comfortable chair for the technician.
- ❏ A large projection screen.
- ❏ Extra-long extension cords and a power strip.
- ❏ Gaffer's tape.
- ❏ Portable wired mouse and wireless keyboard.
- ❏ Remote control.
- ❏ Laser pointers.
- ❏ Audio speakers.
- ❏ Document camera.
- ❏ HDMI wireless adapter.
- ❏ VGA or HDMI switcher and splitter.
- ❏ Adapter for Mac.
- ❏ Scaler.
- ❏ MiFi device.
- ❏ HDMI female to female coupler/extender.
- ❏ Privacy screen for laptop.
- ❏ A comfortable chair.

Operating the Equipment

1. Plug your cord into your laptop;
2. Plug the other end of the cord into the monitor or projector; and
3. Boot up the laptop.

Court Rules and Procedures

❏ Determine whether the judge will permit you to bring your equipment into the courtroom;

❏ Determine where the judge would like the equipment placed in the courtroom;

❏ Determine what if any court rules or procedures the court has regarding technology and electronic exhibits; and

❏ Consult with and obtain permission from courthouse security.

Backup and Document Camera

❏ Have a backup in case of a glitch with the computer presentation—that backup can include:
   ✓ A backup computer; and/or
   ✓ A document camera

Preparation and Testing

❏ Technician practices with the equipment and
❏ A backup is in place.

Staging the Courtroom

❏ Know the courtroom layout;
❏ The technician must have an unobstructed view of the monitor or the screen; and
❏ Stage the screen and/or monitor so the judge and jury can clearly see the images.

Courtroom Communication

❏ Have a uniform way in which electronic visuals will be identified, shown, and annotated;

❏ Have only one lawyer communicating with the technician during the presentation; and

❏ During pretrial preparation, have the witness who will interact with the electronic visual practice what will occur in court during the trial.

Chapter 16

Assignments for Experiences

A. Experiential Learning
B. Case Synopses and Case Files
C. Teacher's Manual, Actors' Guide, CLE Schedule of Instruction, and Syllabus
D. Case Synopses
   1. Civil Case Synopsis
   2. Criminal Case Synopsis
E. Experiential Learning Assignments
   Assignment 1: Introduction to Visual Litigation and Technology
   Assignment 2: Addressing the Jury and Ethical and Legal Issues
   Assignment 3: Linear Software
   Assignment 4: Hardware and Effective Courtroom Presentations
   Assignment 5: Opening Statement
   Assignment 6: Direct Examination, Cross-Examination, and Nonlinear
      Software
   Assignment 7: Prosecutor in the Criminal Case: Direct Examination of Lake
   Assignment 8: Prosecutor and Defense Attorney in the Criminal Case: Direct
      Examination and Cross-Examination of Baldwin
   Assignment 9: Defense Attorney and Prosecutor in the Criminal Case: Direct
      Examination and Cross-Examination of Carroll
   Assignment 10: Plaintiff's Counsel in the Civil Case: Direct Examination of
      Lee
   Assignment 11: Alternative Dispute Resolution Visual
   Assignment 12: Professional Technicians and Visual Designers
   Assignment 13: Closing Argument

"I hear and I forget. I see and I remember. I do and I understand."

Confucius

A. Experiential Learning

This chapter offers you the opportunity to work with litigation visuals and today's technology. By completing these assignments, you can learn how to make presentations in both pretrial alternative dispute resolution settings and trial. Your instructor may select as many of the assignments as are appropriate for your situation. For instance, many of the assignments may be utilized in a pretrial or trial advocacy course that allots a significant number of class sessions to visual litigation. Or, selected assignments may serve as the curriculum for a continuing legal education seminar or a law school course dedicated exclusively to litigation visuals and technology.

B. Case Synopses and Case Files

This chapter provides you with synopses of *Dinh v. Ride The Ducks Int'l*, which is an actual civil case, and *State v. Carroll*, which is a modified hypothetical case of felony assault in the first degree. Your instructor can select one or both cases to serve as the fact patterns for you to use in performing the assignments.

Participants are provided with case files for both the civil *Dinh v. Ride The Ducks Int'l* case and the criminal *State v. Russell Carroll* case. The civil and criminal case files are posted on http://www.fastcase.com/visuallitigation. The case files contain all the information needed for the assignments, including witness statements, photographs, jury instructions, a complaint and answer for the civil case, and information for the criminal case.

C. Teacher's Manual, Actors' Guide, CLE Schedule of Instruction, and Syllabus

Your instructor's teacher's manual contains teaching notes. It also includes supplementary materials for the course, such as a schedule of instruction for a continuing legal education seminar, and a syllabus for law school classes. Your instructor also receives a guide that provides other court documents as well as role-playing instructions for witnesses. Your instructor may have you rely on either the law stated in Chapter 8, "Evidentiary Predicates," or your state's law.

D. Case Synopses

1. Civil Case Synopsis

Dinh v. Ride The Ducks International

Ride The Ducks of Seattle (RTDS) is a tourist attraction. Tourists climb aboard an amphibian landing craft developed during World War II. The tour starts at Seattle's waterfront and moves to Lake Union where it enters the water and travels around the lake before returning to the road and heading downtown. Along the route, the captain (driver) entertains the passengers with banter and a description of the city's sites.

On September 24, 2015, one of the amphibians, Duck #6 from the RTDS fleet was filled with tourists when it started across the Aurora bridge. While crossing the bridge its front axle failed, and the Duck drifted into the oncoming lane. It collided with a charter bus carrying international students from North Seattle College.

Upon impact, passengers in Duck #6 flew out the open windows of the vehicle. Students on the bus were tossed around. The crash resulted in five international students dying and sixty people injured.

Forty plaintiffs sued Ride The Ducks International (RTDI), which is based in Branson, Missouri, and RTDS (a licensee of RTDI) for negligence in manufacturing and maintaining Duck #6. The plaintiffs also sued the City of Seattle and the State of Washington for negligently failing to erect a barrier between the north and south lanes on the Aurora bridge on the theory that head-on collisions had occurred in the past on the bridge and that a barrier would have prevented Duck #6 from colliding with the bus.

In 2003 and 2004, before the Ride The Ducks business was sold to new owners of RTDI, fractures were found in the axle housings of the Ducks. Without consulting with an engineer or mechanic, the then-owner cobbled together a solution to the problem with material scavenged from a junk yard. On July 2013, more than two years prior to the Ride The Ducks disaster on the Aurora bridge, the left wheel fell off a Duck that was being driven in Branson, Missouri. Shortly after that, another Duck, which was being driven in Branson, had an axle defect that caused the wheels to cant. RTDI did not employ an engineer to fix the axle problem. Rather, RTDI did its own repairs.

Although RTDI was a manufacturer of the Ducks, it did not register as a manufacturer. Manufacturers, under federal regulations, are required to report vehicle defects, but RTDI did not report that the axles were failing.

RTDI did do something: it issued a service bulletin with a diagram showing how to fix the axle. The bulletin stated that the fix should be done "as soon as practical" and before 2014. RTDI would repair defects for its franchisees but was not required to do so for licensees. Because RTDS was a licensee, RTDI merely sent RTDS a service bulletin. RTDS did not make the fix the bulletin recommended. RTDS asserts that it was inundated with RTDI service bulletins, some of which were trivial.

On September 20, 2015, four days before the Ride The Ducks disaster on the bridge, the driver of Duck #6 pulled the Duck over while crossing the Aurora bridge because she felt something unusual and heard an unusual sound. The driver contacted the mechanics and told them something was wrong. The mechanics, who were overworked and understaffed, did not remove the rubber boot that covered the axle. The mechanics had not been provided with the service bulletin.

Simon Lee was driving behind Duck #6 as it crossed the Aurora bridge. He saw the wheel on the Duck give way and the vehicle go out of control, leaning to the left and careening into the oncoming bus. A vehicle behind Lee's ran into Lee's vehicle. After the crash, Lee got out of his car and helped the injured people.

Phuong Dinh, the lead plaintiff, was riding in the charter bus that was hit by Duck #6. She was 18 years old. As a result of the crash, she suffered a broken arm and leg. Her health care would last for months and cost hundreds of thousands of dollars. She resided in a long-term care facility.

Note that in the civil case file, Entry 1 is the initial complaint filed in the case, which was later amended to add multiple plaintiffs, and Entry 2 is an answer to the first amended complaint that was filed in the Ride The Ducks case.

2. Criminal Case Synopsis

State v. Carroll

Russell Carroll, age 45, is charged with assault in the first degree with a deadly weapon, a firearm. Mr. Carroll is the Lakeside High School's basketball coach. He is six feet, six inches tall and weighs 240 pounds.

Alleged victim Beatrice Baldwin is in her early thirties and an English literature teacher at Lakeside High School. Carroll and Baldwin visited together while at work and eventually developed a relationship. The relationship became intimate, and on three occasions she stayed overnight at Carroll's house on Madison Avenue. Their relationship ended in January of last year.

On April 11 of last year, Baldwin was at McGilvra's Bar and Restaurant eating dinner by herself. Carroll came into McGilvra's at 9:30 p.m., saw that Baldwin was sitting alone, walked over, and sat at her table. After a few minutes, Pete Lake, the manager who was serving as the bartender that night, heard a loud quarrel break out between Baldwin and a tall man whose back was to him. Baldwin paid her bill and left McGilvra's. Lake observed the tall man follow her out the door.

According to Baldwin, when Carroll caught up with her in the parking lot located behind McGilvra's, Carroll grabbed her by the left arm and told her that she was going with him. Carroll dragged her toward his silver SUV. Baldwin called for help, but no one responded. When they arrived at the car and Carroll opened the passenger door, Baldwin was still struggling to free herself. Then, according to Baldwin, Carroll pulled up his shirt and patted a pistol tucked in his belt, saying, "You know what this is. You're gonna die bitch. Get in."

He pulled the gun out of his pants, pointed it at Baldwin, and told her to get in the car.

Frightened for her life, Baldwin called "Help" and tried to punch Carroll in the face with her right hand. At that moment, Carroll loosened his grip on Baldwin's arm, and she broke free, falling to the ground.

Just then, a car entered the parking lot, and the driver honked. Carroll ran to the driver's side of his own car, got in, and drove out of the parking lot. Tyler Carson, who was planning to have a libation at McGilvra's, was the driver of the car who honked his horn when he saw Baldwin swing her arm at the man and then fall to the ground. He saw Carroll's car start up and leave the lot. And he noted that the car license's first letter was B; the other letters and numbers on the license did not register with Carson.

Carson got out of his car and went to Baldwin. Baldwin told Carson what had happened. Carson immediately called 911, reporting what he knew and describing the car and license.

Investigating Detective Jimmy Peterson interviewed Baldwin, Carson, and Lake. Carson was unable to identify the defendant in a photo montage as the person he had seen in the parking lot because the suspect was turned away from him. Lake, likewise, was unable to identify the defendant from the photo montage because, as the manager Pete Lake indicated, the couple was in the restaurant side of McGilvra's away from the bar, and he did not get a good look at the man's face as he left the bar. Both men said the suspect was well over six feet tall.

Peterson drove to defendant Carroll's residence where he saw a silver SUV parked in front. The license on the vehicle read BIT4043. A records check showed that the defendant was the owner of the SUV.

Peterson arrested Carroll and advised him of his rights. Carroll made no statements to Peterson. Peterson obtained a search warrant for Carroll's residence and vehicle. During a search of the vehicle, Peterson found a Glock 23 Smith & Wesson .40 caliber pistol on the car's floorboard in front of the driver's seat. He took photographs of both the vehicle and the handgun on the floor of the SUV in front of the driver's seat where he recovered it.

Peterson again contacted Lake, the manager of McGilvra's, and learned that the restaurant maintained a surveillance camera trained on its parking lot. Lake provided Peterson with the surveillance video that showed Carroll pulling Baldwin toward his vehicle and opening the car door. Because his back was to the camera, it was not possible to see whether Carroll pulled up his shirt to reveal a gun. The video also showed Baldwin swinging her fist at Carroll and then falling to the ground.

The county prosecutor charged Carroll with first-degree assault. Carroll is out on bail awaiting trial. When interviewed by the media, Carroll called the allegations "patent lies."

The defense intends to offer an email from Baldwin to Carroll that was dated January 15 of last year. The email indicates it was sent from bea99@comcast.net, which is Baldwin's email address, and it states, "Russell—It's over between us. You'll regret it if you ever come near me again. BB."

E. Experiential Learning Assignments

Assignment 1: Introduction to Visual Litigation and Technology

This assignment introduces you to the purposes served by litigation visuals and today's technology.

Preparation

Read: Chapters 1 (Introduction to Book and Online Supplement), 2 (Overview Visuals and Today's Technology), and 9 (Creating Demonstrative and Video Evidence) in *Visual Litigation: Visual Communication Strategies and Today's Technology (Visual Litigation)*, and Irfanview, Audacity, and Camtasia outlines on our class website.

Outside of class: Download and install Audacity and Camtasia (free demo is fine). You can find them online at http://audacity.sourceforge.net/ and https://www.techsmith.com, respectively.

You must do this **in advance of class** as sometimes it takes over 24 hours to obtain your demo license—Mac and Windows versions available).

Assignment for Class

In class: Be prepared to discuss the substance of Chapter 2 in *Visual Litigation*, including software that can be utilized in preparing a computer slideshow presentation. Also, in class, you will work with Camtasia.

Assignment 2: Addressing the Jury and Ethical and Legal Issues

This assignment covers opening statement and closing argument as well as legal and ethical boundaries that cannot be crossed when visuals and technology are used in a courtroom. This assignment is designed to prepare you to make trial presentations of visuals free of any legal or ethical issues.

Preparation

Read: Chapters 3 (Opening Statement Visuals), 4 (Closing Argument Visuals), and 10 (Ethical and Legal Issues) in *Visual Litigation*.

Assignment for Class

In class: Be prepared to discuss opening statement and closing argument visuals as well as the ethical and legal boundaries for what can be shown to a jury.

Assignment 3: Linear Software

This assignment explores today's linear software—PowerPoint.

Preparation

Read: Chapters 13 (Linear Software) in *Visual Litigation*.
Outside of Class: **Prior to class** have PowerPoint installed on your computer.

Assignment for Class

In class: Be prepared to discuss linear software—PowerPoint. Also, come ready to prepare a linear slideshow.

Assignment 4: Hardware and Effective Courtroom Presentations

This assignment covers the essential hardware needed for a high-tech courtroom presentation and the prerequisites for an effective courtroom presentation.

Preparation

Read: Chapter 15 (Hardware and Effective Courtroom Presentations) in *Visual Litigation*.

Assignment for Class

In class: Be prepared to discuss both how to make an effective courtroom presentation and the essential hardware you will need for that presentation.

Assignment 5: Opening Statement

It is time for your opening statement. You know that this is important because it is your opportunity to communicate your case narrative to the jurors. To have the greatest impact you want to visually deliver your case story. You will tell the case story with linear software, such as PowerPoint or Keynote.

Preparation

Read: Chapter 3 (Opening Statement Visuals).

Outside of Class: Prepare an opening statement that is accompanied by a computer slideshow using linear software. Rehearse your opening statement with the technology that you will utilize in presenting your opening. File your computer slideshow on our class website.

Assignment for Class

In class: As indicated by your instructor, assume the role of either plaintiffs' counsel or defense counsel in the civil case or the role of the prosecutor or defense counsel in the criminal case. Bring your presentation on a flash drive. Be prepared to present opening statement.

Assignment 6: Direct Examination, Cross-Examination, and Nonlinear Software

This assignment covers how to employ electronic and conventional visuals in direct examination and cross-examination. Further, it covers the use of nonlinear software, such as Sanction, TrialDirector, and ExhibitView. Specifically, you will learn how to lay a foundation for exhibits, and how to use Sanction to retrieve electronic visuals, and display and annotate them during direct and cross-examinations.

Preparation

Read: Chapters 5 (Direct Examination Visuals), 6 (Cross-Examination Visuals), and 12 (Nonlinear Software) in *Visual Litigation*.

Outside of Class: **Prior to class** install the free demo of Sanction software on your computer. Installation of Sanction is not required.

Assignment for Class

In class: Be prepared to discuss the use of electronic and conventional visuals during direct and cross-examination and how to use nonlinear software to effectively display electronic visuals. Also, be prepared to have a hands-on experience with nonlinear software.

Assignment 7: Prosecutor in the Criminal Case: Direct Examination of Lake

Lake, the manager of McGilvra's, was acting as the bartender on the night that Baldwin was allegedly assaulted in the restaurant's parking lot. The prosecutor will call Lake as a witness. Lake's direct examination will concentrate on portions of the witness's testimony that can be told with visuals.

Preparation

Read: (1) Criminal Case File Entries 6-9 and (2) Chapters 5 (Direct Examination Visuals) and 8 (Evidentiary Predicates) in *Visual Litigation*.

Outside of Class: Prepare your witness Lake to testify in advance of class and practice with the electronic visuals and the technology. Bring to class not only the electronic visuals on a hard drive but also hard copies of exhibits, such as photographs, that you intend to introduce into evidence.

Assignment for Class

In class: Assume the role of the prosecutor and conduct the direct examination of Lake, concentrating on the events inside McGilvra's Bar and Restaurant on the night that Carroll allegedly assaulted Baldwin in the parking lot behind McGilvra's. As directed by your instructor, introduce one or more of the following items into evidence and display it to the jury:

a.   Photographs of McGilvra's Restaurant and Bar;

b.   Photographs of McGilvra's parking lot;

c.   A diagram of the interior of McGilvra's Restaurant and Bar; and

d.   The surveillance video of the parking lot at the time of the alleged assault. For this last assignment, bring to class an envelop containing a USB flash drive with PL initialed on it, which will serve as the exhibit containing the surveillance video.

Assignment 8: Prosecutor and Defense Attorney in the Criminal Case: Direct Examination and Cross-Examination of Baldwin

Baldwin allegedly is the victim of a first-degree assault with a deadly weapon committed by defendant Carroll, and the prosecutor intends to call her as a witness during the state's case in chief. She is the prosecution's most important witness, and the prosecutor will employ visuals to communicate her story to the jury.

Following the direct examination, Carroll's defense attorney will cross-examine Baldwin with the aid of a visuals, including the email that the defense asserts she sent to the defendant.

Preparation

Read: (1) Criminal Case File Entries 4, 7-13, and 16-17 and (2) Chapters 5 (Direct Examination Visuals), 6 (Cross-Examination Visuals), and 8 (Evidentiary Predicates) in *Visual Litigation*.

Outside of Class: The prosecutor prepares the state's witness Baldwin to testify and practices with the trial visuals and technology. Bring to class not only the electronic visuals on a hard drive but also hard copies of exhibits, such as photographs, that you intend to introduce into evidence. If the prosecutor intends to do a courtroom demonstration involving Baldwin and another person portraying the defendant, rehearse the demonstration prior to class.

Assignment for Class

In class: The prosecutor conducts the direct examination of Baldwin, focusing on the events inside McGilvra's Bar and Restaurant and in the parking lot behind McGilvra's. As directed by your instructor, the prosecutor will introduce one or more of the following items into evidence and display the visual(s) to the jury:

    a.   Photographs of McGilvra's Restaurant and Bar;

    b.   Photographs of McGilvra's parking lot;

    c.   Photographs of Carroll's car;

    d.   Photograph of the handgun recovered from Carroll's car;

    e.   A courtroom demonstration of how the defendant assaulted Baldwin and pulled up his shirt to reveal the gun in his belt; and

    f.   Any other exhibit your instructor indicates that you should introduce into evidence.

Defense counsel, you will cross-examine Baldwin. As directed by your instructor, you will introduce one or more of the items (listed above) into evidence and display the visual(s) to the jury. In addition, defense counsel will cross-examine Baldwin about the email dated January 15 of last year that she allegedly sent to the defendant.

Assignment 9: Defense Attorney and Prosecutor in the Criminal Case: Direct Examination and Cross-Examination of Carroll

Defense counsel intends to call the defendant Carroll to testify. He will deny having touched Baldwin. He will further testify that he never pointed his revolver at her. Defense counsel will use visuals to communicate the defendant's story to the jury.

Following the direct examination, the prosecutor will cross-examine the defendant with the aid of visuals.

Preparation

Read: (1) Criminal Case File Entries 7-17 and (2) Chapters 5 (Direct Examination Visuals), 6 (Cross-Examination Visuals), and 8 (Evidentiary Predicates) in *Visual Litigation.*

Outside of Class: Prepare the defendant to testify in advance of class and practice with the electronic visuals and the technology. Bring to class not only the electronic visuals on a hard drive but also bring hard copies of exhibits, such as photographs, that you intend to introduce into evidence. If you are planning to do a courtroom demonstration involving Carroll and another person portraying Baldwin, rehearse the demonstration.

Assignment for Class

In class: In class, assume the role of defense counsel and conduct the direct examination of Baldwin, focusing on the events inside McGilvra's Bar and Restaurant and in the parking lot behind McGilvra's. As directed by your instructor, introduce one or more of the following items into evidence and display it to the jury:

a. A printout of the email dated January 15 of last year, which is addressed to the defendant and sent from bea9@comcast.net;

b. Photographs of McGilvra's Restaurant and Bar;

c. Photographs of McGilvra's parking lot;

d. Photographs of Russell Carroll's car;

e. The handgun recovered from Russell Carroll's car;

f. A courtroom demonstration of how Baldwin attempted to strike him; and

g. Any other exhibit your instructor indicates that you should introduce into evidence.

Prosecutor, you will cross-examine defendant Carroll. As directed by your instructor, you will introduce one or more of the items (listed above) into evidence and display the visual(s) to the jury.

Assignment 10: Plaintiff's Counsel in the Civil Case: Direct Examination of Lee

Simon Lee was driving on the Aurora bridge behind Duck #6 when its wheel gave way and it crossed into oncoming traffic and crashed into the charter bus carrying international students from North Seattle College.

Read: (1) Civil Case File Entries 3-4, 16-23, and 49 and (2) Chapters 5 (Direct Examination Visuals) and 8 (Evidentiary Predicates) in *Visual Litigation.*

Outside of Class: Prepare your witness Lee to testify and practice with the electronic visuals and the technology. Bring to class not only the electronic visuals on a flash drive but also bring hard copies of exhibits, such as photographs, that you intend to introduce into evidence.

In class: In class, assume the role of plaintiffs' counsel and conduct the direct examination of Lee. As directed by your instructor, introduce one or more of the following items into evidence and display it to the jury:

a. Photograph of a Duck;

b. Photographs of the Aurora bridge;

c. Photographs of aftermath of the collision;

   d. Aerial photograph of the scene of the collision; and

   e. Any other exhibit your instructor indicates that you should introduce into evidence.

Assignment 11: Alternative Dispute Resolution Visual

Your client, Phoong Dinh, is a plaintiff in the Ride The Ducks case and has agreed to mediation. A mediator has been selected. You want to create a visual or visuals that will persuade Ride The Ducks International and Ride The Ducks Seattle to settle and will convince the mediator of the strength of your case. It is time to create a litigation visual.

Preparation

Read: (1) Civil Case File Entries 29-35 and 50 and (2) Chapters 7 (Alternative Dispute Resolution Visuals) and 9 (Creating Demonstrative Evidence) in *Visual Litigation*.

Outside of Class: **In advance of class**, download SmartDraw. Note that SmartDraw permits you to try the software for seven days. Therefore, you will need to plan your schedule in such a way that you can complete this assignment within the seven days. Create a litigation visual or visuals for mediation. File your computer slideshow on our class website.

Assignment for Class

In class: Bring your litigation visual(s) on a flash drive. Be prepared to display your litigation visual and discuss how it will enhance your case.

Assignment 12: Professional Technicians and Visual Designers

You want to familiarize yourself with what you can gain by employing professional technicians and professional visual designers.

Preparation

Read: Chapter 10 (Professional Technicians and Visual Designers) in *Visual Litigation*.

Outside of Class: Visit websites for professional visual designers and technicians. Take notes regarding what they have to offer and prepare to discuss what you have learned with the class.

Assignment for Class

In class: Be prepared to talk about one professional visual design vendor whose website you visited. Be ready to explain what the vendor has to offer.

Assignment 13: Closing Argument

This is the finale of the course and the case. Both sides have rested, and it is time for your closing argument. As you did with opening statement, you want to make your closing dynamic with the use of persuasive visuals. You will utilize linear software, such as PowerPoint or Keynote, to present your computer slideshow.

Preparation

Read: Chapter 4 (Closing Argument Visuals) in *Visual Litigation*.

Outside of Class: Prepare your closing argument to include a computer slideshow using linear software. While you can, of course, include the visuals contained in the case file, go beyond those and create argument visuals that will persuade the jury. Rehearse your closing argument with the technology that you will utilize in presenting it. File your computer slideshow on our class website.

Assignment for Class

In class: As indicated by your instructor, assume the role of either plaintiffs' counsel or defense counsel in the civil case or the role of the prosecutor or defense counsel in the criminal case. Bring your presentation on a flash drive. Be prepared to present your closing argument with the aid of visuals shown with linear software.

Visual Credits

We gratefully acknowledge and give credit to those who granted us permission to include their visuals in this book.* The visuals and sources are as follows:

Chapter 2

9-11: Joseph O'Toole, Sound Jury Consulting. **12**: Joseph O'Toole, Sound Jury Consulting (top); High Impact Visual Litigation Strategies (bottom). **27-30**: United States District Court, Western Washington Division, Seattle, Washington.

Chapter 3

37: Joseph O'Toole, Sound Jury Consulting. **42**: Michael Jackson case—Getty Images (Stringer). **45**: TimeMap. **46**: Joseph O'Toole, Sound Jury Consulting. **47**: SKE Forensic Consultants Inc. **49**: New Jersey State Police (top); Google Earth (bottom). **50**: Google Maps. **51-52**: Karen Koehler, Ride The Ducks case.

Chapter 4

57, 59, 63, and **64**: Joseph O'Toole, Sound Jury Consulting. **66**: *State v. Lord*, 822 P.2d 177 (Wash. 1992). **69-74**: Joseph O'Toole, Sound Jury Consulting. **75**: *Murder on a Sunday Morning* documentary courtesy of Direct Cinema Limited.

Chapter 5

84: O.J. Simpson—Getty Images (Celano, contributor). **86**: Paul Manafort case—courtesy of Department of Justice. **95**: High Impact Visual Litigation Strategies. **96**: *The Staircase* documentary (Netflix 2004)—Dr. Faris Bandak

---

* If an image in the book is not listed here, it is because it is the work product of the author and/or in the public domain.

and Shutterstock Inc. (top). **97-98**: High Impact Visual Litigation Strategies. **99-100**: FARO 3D Laser Scanner. **101**: Colton Legal Media.

Chapter 6

113: Joseph O'Toole, Sound Jury Consulting.

Chapter 7

127-30: Karen Koehler, Ride The Ducks case. **131-33**: Joseph O'Toole, Sound Jury Consulting. **139**: Colton Legal Media. **140**: High Impact Visual Litigation Strategies (bottom).

Chapter 9

187-201: SmartDraw. **203-04**: Camtasia.

Chapter 10

214: *State v. Walker*, 341 P.3d 976 (Wash. 2015).

Chapter 11

228: Joseph O'Toole, Sound Jury Consulting. **229**: High Impact. **230**: Medi-Visuals (top); SKE Forensic Consultants, Inc. (bottom); **231**: Courtroom Visuals (bottom). **232**: Prolumina Litigation Communication.

Chapter 12

239-48; 250-51; 253-55: Sanction. **257-66**: ExhibitView.

Chapter 13

290-92; 296-300: Joseph O'Toole, Sound Jury Consulting.

Chapter 14

297-304: TrialPad.

Chapter 15

313-14: Epson. **316**: Uline cart. **316**: Logitech Spotlight. **323**: United States District Court, Western Washington Division, Seattle, Washington.

Chapter 16

333: Karen Koehler, Ride The Ducks case.

Index